The Illustrated Encyclopedia of
SCIENCE

NEW YORK

Academic Advisors:
Professor Ian MacDonald M.D., D.Sc., F.L., Biol.,
Professor of Applied Physiology,
Guy's Hospital Medical School, London.

Editors:
Michael Bisacre
Richard Carlisle
Deborah Robertson
John Ruck

© Marshall Cavendish Limited 1978—84

First published in the USA
1984 by Exeter Books

Distributed by Bookthrift
Exeter is a trademark of Simon & Schuster, Inc.
Bookthrift is a registered trademark of
Simon & Schuster, Inc.
New York, New York

ALL RIGHTS RESERVED

Printed and bound in Italy by New Interlitho SpA.

ISBN 0-671-07036-3

This volume is not to be sold in Australia
or New Zealand

Contents

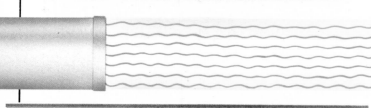

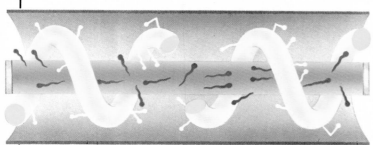

Matter
and
Energy

Atoms and Molecules

Everyone nowadays has at least a vague idea of the atomic theory of matter. The theory gives a picture of all matter as being composed of basic building blocks, the 92 different sorts of naturally-occurring atoms corresponding to the 92 different naturally-occurring chemical elements. In addition, there are over a dozen man-made elements.

At the centre of each atom is a tiny *nucleus*, very heavy and positively charged, which is made up of particles called *protons* and *neutrons*. The nucleus is surrounded by a cloud of much smaller particles, the negatively charged *electrons*.

The 92 natural elements have from one to 92 protons in the nucleus and these protons carry its positive electric charge. But while the number of electrons surrounding the nucleus corresponds to the number of protons, the number of neutrons can vary. These particles carry zero electric charge (although of approximately the same mass as a proton). The protons attract the electrons because they have opposite electric charges, as unlike charges attract each other whereas like charges repel each other. Overall, each atom is electrically neutral, as the positive charges in the nucleus are balanced by the negative charges of the electrons.

The difference between an atom of one element and an atom of another lies simply in the numbers of protons, neutrons and electrons they each contain. For example, an atom of helium has two protons, two neutrons and two electrons, while a carbon atom has six protons, six neutrons and six electrons. The particles are exactly the same in each case, it is only the numbers that are different.

Atoms can combine together to form *molecules*, such as the two-atom gas molecules of hydrogen (H_2) and oxygen (O_2) and the three-atom molecule of water (H_2O). Molecules may be much bigger than this however, and some which occur in living or organic substances contain thousands of atoms.

An atomic theory of matter had been conceived by early Greek philosophers, notably Democritus (about 420BC) and Epicurus (about 300BC). This atomic theory was not accepted by many other important philosophers, however, and Aristotle (384-322BC) rejected Democritus' theory in favour of the view that all matter was composed of different combinations of the 'four elements'—earth, water, air and fire.

This concept displaced the atomic theories and formed the basis of alchemy, the study of matter that dominated science up until the seventeenth century. Alchemy was widely practised in Arabia, China and Renaissance Europe, and two of its main objectives were to find a way of turning a base metal, such as lead, into gold and to find a 'elixir of life'.

Alchemy was supported by religious leaders of the time, whereas atomic theories with their implied atheism were suppressed by Jewish and Christian teachers. Many earlier texts survived, however, including the *De rerum natura*

Drawn & Etched by J. Stephenson.

Mary Evans

Above: An atomic model of a crystal of common salt, sodium chloride. The shape and the physical properties of a crystal are determined by the forces which bind the atoms together, forces which include ionic and covalent bonds, the metallic bond and the van der Waal's forces. The ionic bond is the electrical attraction between charged atoms and the covalent bond involves pairs of atoms sharing electrons. The metallic bond occurs in crystals of metals, where the positive metal ions are neutralized by a cloud of electrons which move freely throughout the lattice. This arrangement gives metals their characteristic physical properties, including their ability to conduct electricity. Van der Waal's forces are weak bonds caused by momentary disturbances in the electron clouds within the lattice.

Above: John Dalton, the English philosopher who devised the first scientific theory of the atomic structure of matter. He was born at Eaglesfield, Cumberland, in September 1766, and by the age of 12 he was teaching at his local school. He had a lifelong interest in meteorology, and kept a daily record of the local weather from his early childhood to his death in July 1844. This interest in the weather led him to study the atmosphere and subsequently the nature of gases and their properties. Through his experiments with gases, he arrived at the conclusions which formed the basis of his atomic theory. When he died over 40,000 people filed past his coffin.

Below: A molecule of nucleic acid, a heavy, complex organic acid which combines with a protein to form a nucleoprotein, an important part of the nucleus of a living cell. The helical bands represent chains of a compound called a nucleotide, and carry four other compounds, adenine (A), thymine (T), cytosine (C) and guanine (G). Bonding between T and A and between C and G holds the chains together.

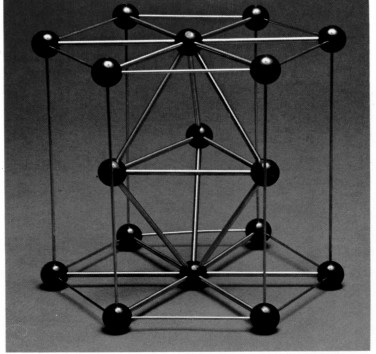

Right: There are a large number of crystal shapes, which arise from the way in which the atoms are grouped together. This hexagonal shape is a model of a zinc crystal.

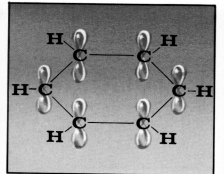

Tear shaped electron orbits of carbon atoms

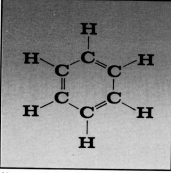

Alternate single and double bonds between carbon atoms

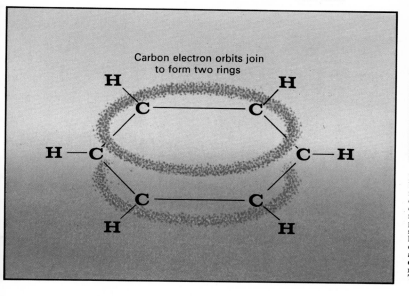

Carbon electron orbits join to form two rings

Messer. Griesheim

Left: The structure of benzene (C_6H_6) was a mystery for over a century, because its chemical properties were not consistent with its presumed structure pf single bonds linking the hydrogen atoms to the carbon atoms, and alternate single and double bonds linking the ring or carbon atoms. The explanation was that some of the shared electrons travel in tear-drop shaped orbitals at right angles to the carbon atoms and, because these atoms are so close together, these orbitals overlap to form ring-shaped orbitals above and below the carbon ring. Benzene is used in making aspirin, aniline dyes, and some types of plastic.

Above: This sheet of clear plastic was charged up by bombarding it with electrons. When it was discharged at one edge, the departing electrons created this pattern in it.

Below: This cutting torch uses a stream of plasma (ionized gas) carrying a current of about 250 Amps.

('On the Nature of Things') written in the first century BC by the Roman poet Lucretius. In the first half of this six-volume poem, Lucretius described and defended the theories of Epicurus, and it was used as a source of reference by several seventeenth and eighteenth century philosophers.

At the beginning of the nineteenth century, John Dalton (1766-1844) produced the first atomic theory to be backed up by experimental evidence. Following on from the work of A. L. Lavoisier and J. L. Proust, Dalton investigated the way that elements forming chemical com-pounds combine in definite proportions by weight. He was then able to work out the relative weights of the atoms of various elements, including hydrogen, oxygen, nitrogen and sulphur.

For example, he calculated that when hydrogen and oxygen combine to form water they do so in the ratio, by weight, of one part hydrogen to seven parts of oxygen (it is actually eight parts of oxygen, Dalton's analysis was slightly incorrect). From this he deduced that an oxygen atom was seven times heavier than a hydrogen atom, because he assumed that a water molecule contained only one atom of each. In fact, a water molecule contains two hydrogen atoms and one oxygen atom, and oxygen is about sixteen times heavier than hydrogen.

Despite these errors, however, the theory formed the basis for a serious scientific study of the atomic structure of elements, and during the nineteenth century scientists were able to identify about 90 (out of 92 naturally-occurring) different sorts of atom.

Inside the atom

Investigations of the structure of atoms themselves began in the late nineteenth century. The crucial experiments involved investigation of the nature of the 'matter' taking part in electrical discharges in sealed tubes not unlike fluorescent lighting tubes.

Before 1890, rays streaming from the negative electrode or *cathode* of such tubes had been observed and were named *cathode rays*. The physicist J. J. Thomson (1856-1940) showed that the rays, when subjected to magnetic or electrostatic fields behaved exactly as negatively charged particles would be expected to.

These electrons, as the cathode rays were renamed, were assumed to be constituents of atoms. However, because it was difficult to separately measure either their electric charge or their mass, no-one knew how they fitted into the atom or how important they were.

Thomson proposed a model of the atom, the 'plum pudding atom', consisting of a not very massive sphere of positive charge in which thousands of plum-like electrons rotated in rings. This model needed a very large number of electrons in the atom because it was thought that they accounted for most of the atom's mass.

New experiments soon made Thomson's model unrealistic. When positively charged *alpha particles* (each comprising two protons and two neutrons) were directed on to thin films of atoms, a significant number bounced backwards. This could not have happened if Thomson's model had been correct; the positively charged 'pudding' would not have been able to repel the particles because it

Paul Brierley

3

was too light. Additionally its positive charge would have been neutralized by the electrons and so would not have repelled the positively charged particles.

Ernest Rutherford (1871-1937) proposed a different model which explained the backward scattering, and this model has been the basis of our understanding ever since. If the positive charge in the atom is heavy and concentrated, not light and diffused as in the Thomson model, then the experimental results can be explained. Rutherford's atom consists of a small $(10^{-13}$cm) heavy nucleus with a positive charge, surrounded by a diffuse cloud $(10^{-8}$cm) of light electrons.

It is tempting to visualize Rutherford's atom as a miniature solar system, with the nucleus as the sun and the electrons as the planets. In place of gravity, the attraction between the oppositely charged nucleus and electrons would hold the atoms together. But, according to the old laws of electromagnetism, even this picture would have been impossible. If the electrons revolved around the nucleus they would radiate electromagnetic waves, lose energy and spiral into the centre, attracted to the nucleus by its positive charge. According to the old laws, the atom could not be stable.

An excellent, though temporary, solution to the problem was provided by Niels Bohr (1885-1962). Instead of radiating continuously and spiralling in to the centre the electron, according to Bohr, could travel only on certain discrete closed orbits. The electron would radiate but it would do so suddenly, and at the same time jump between one orbit and another of lower energy (as if the Earth suddenly jumped into Venus' orbit).

Cavendish Laboratories

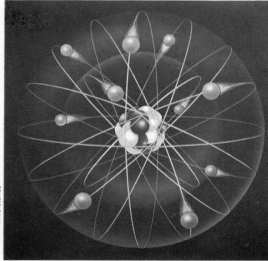

Above: Sir Ernest Rutherford, Lord Rutherford of Nelson (right), the founder of nuclear physics. He was born near Nelson, New Zealand, in 1871 and went to Cambridge University in 1895 to work with J. J. Thomson. He investigated radio-active decay, which led him to the discovery of alpha and beta radiation.

During his experiments with alpha rays he came to the conclusion that the atom had a heavy central nucleus surrounded by electrons. In 1918, at Manchester University, he discovered the proton when he 'split' nitrogen atoms by bombarding their nuclei with alpha particles. Rutherford died in October 1937.

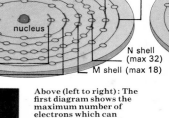

ELECTRON SHELL

O shell (max 23)
P shell (max 10)
nucleus
K shell (max 2)
L shell (max 8)
M shell (max 18)
N shell (max 32)

Above (left to right): The first diagram shows the maximum number of electrons which can occupy electron shells K to P. The second diagram shows hydrogen, which has a single electron which occupies one of the available energy states in the K shell, and the third shows helium, whose two electrons fill its K shell.

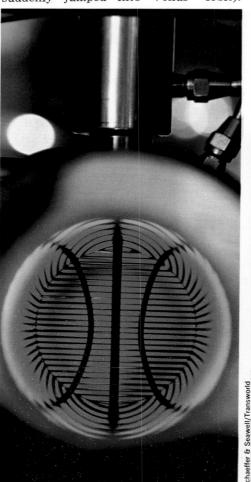

Schaeffer & Seawell/Transworld

Left: Prospecting for uranium using an instrument called a spectrometer, which detects any radiation from the rock which would indicate the presence of uranium ore. Uranium atoms emit alpha particles and thus gradually decay into 'daughter' elements, which in turn decay until they eventually become lead.

Far left: The ripple patterns in the light given off by an electrical discharge depend on the atomic structure of the electrodes between which the discharge occurs. The study of these patterns has helped scientists understand more about the structure of atoms and molecules.

UKAE

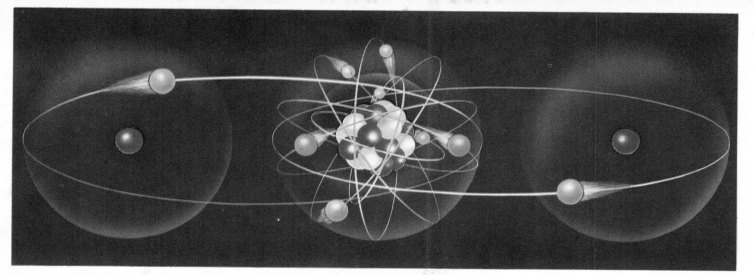

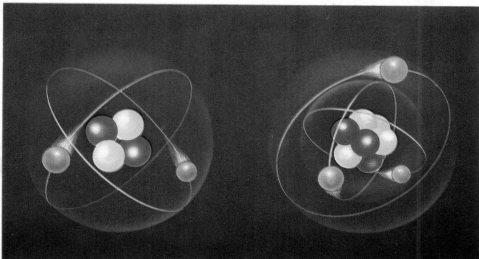

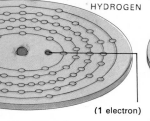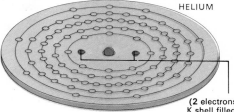

HYDROGEN

HELIUM

(1 electron)

(2 electrons, K shell filled)

Left: The chemical properties of an atom depend on the number of electrons and unfilled energy states in its outermost shell. Helium has its outermost shell filled by its two electrons and so, having no spare electron or energy state which it can share with other atoms, it cannot react or combine with them.

Finally, there was an orbit of minimum energy (like Mercury's orbit), from which the electron would not radiate. Once the electron reached this *ground state* it was stable.

Within a dozen years, the physical results of Bohr's model had been refined and justified by a new physical theory, *quantum mechanics*. Through this, nature was viewed in quite a different way. In the new theory, a particle's position and velocity could not simultaneously be measured with absolute precision (*Heisenberg's uncertainty principle*) and the concept of force, as it had been known, disappeared.

Our present understanding of electron structure in atoms is based on the system of discrete energy levels (like Bohr's orbits) that quantum mechanics allows, together with a new principle discovered in 1924 by Wolfgang Pauli (1900-1958): the *exclusion principle*.

The exclusion principle forbids more than one electron being in any possible 'state' of an atom or molecule. The states are sub-divisions of the energy levels, which surround the nucleus like a series of concentric shells and are known as the K, L, M, N, O, P and Q shells respectively, the K shell being the innermost. In

naturally-occurring elements, the maximum numbers of states, and thus electrons, which can exist in these shells are 2, 8, 18, 32, 23, 10 and 2 respectively.

If it were not for the exclusion principle all electrons would fall to the lowest state, the level of minimum energy. The chemical properties of atoms are determined by the electrons in the outermost (highest) energy levels.

Molecular bonds

The way in which chemical behaviour, that is, the formation and properties of molecules, is determined by the electrons in the atom's highest energy levels, can be described in terms of different sorts of molecular bond.

The *ionic bond* occurs when one atom in a two-atom molecule has only one or two electrons in its outermost level, and the other atom has room for one or two more in its outermost level or *electron shell*. The electrons pass from the first atom to the second, so the first atom becomes positively charged because it has lost electrons and the second atom becomes negatively charged because it has gained electrons. These *ions*, as the charged atoms are now called, attract each other with their opposite charges,

forming a stable molecule. One example is salt where sodium atoms lose their highest electrons to chloride atoms.

The other simple sort of bond is the *covalent bond*. This occurs when similar atoms form molecules, such as the gas molecules hydrogen (H_2), oxygen (O_2) and nitrogen (N_2). The electrons are shared between the two atoms, being clustered between the two positively charged nuclei and attracting them both.

Isotopes

The amount of positive charge on a nucleus is determined by the number of protons within it. The number of protons in the nucleus is the *atomic number* of the atom, and this is also the number of electrons the atom possesses.

The mass of the nucleus is determined by the number of protons plus the number of neutrons. The mass of a proton is about the same as the mass of a neutron and over 1,800 times the mass of an electron.

The atomic weight of an element should be just the number of protons and neutrons together, but some elements were found to have atomic weights which are not whole numbers. This was an unsolved problem for more than a century until it was realized that although atoms of a given element had a fixed number of protons, the number of neutrons was variable. The different forms were called *isotopes*, and the elements found in nature are mixtures of different isotopes.

The discovery of isotopes ushered in the nuclear age, an age of the study and application of nuclear forces. It was found that nuclei heavier than uranium could be built up and that nuclei could be broken apart. Nuclear bombs have been made, but the question of why the nucleus does not fly apart on its own, as it might be expected to due to the positively-charged protons repelling each other, has not yet been really answered.

But the questions the Victorians asked, 'Are atoms real? Can they be seen?' have been answered. Photographs of atoms taken by electron microscopes and field emission microscopes, in which streams of electrons take the place of the visible light used in optical microscopes, are as real as the pictures on a television set.

Elementary Particles

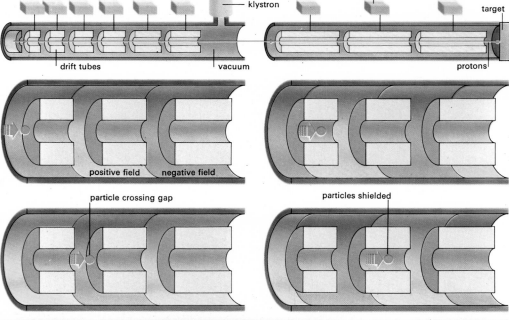

All matter, living or dead, is composed of atoms, which were originally thought to be solid and indivisible. Towards the end of the nineteenth century, however, scientists began to realize that the atoms themselves were made up of even smaller particles. The physicist J. J. Thomson established that electrons were constituents of atoms, then in 1911 Ernest Rutherford proposed the theory that the atom had a central nucleus around which the electrons were grouped.

The idea of the nucleus led to the science of nuclear physics, the study of the nucleus and its components. Rutherford suggested the existence of the proton in 1914 and in 1932 the neutron was discovered by James Chadwick. Particle physics, the study of matter at its deepest, most fundamental level, is an extension of nuclear physics and developed from it almost by accident.

In 1934 the Japanese physicist Hideki Yukawa suggested that the force keeping the protons and neutrons together in the nucleus was due to a new particle, which came to be called a *meson*.

A systematic search for new particles began and about 30 were discovered during the next two decades, including one with the properties Yukawa had predicted. But the hope that the new particles would provide a detailed explanation of the structure of the nucleus was not completely realized. Emphasis shifted to the problem that seemed more basic, namely, the ways in which the new particles interacted with each other. Experiments designed to investigate this question revealed an embarrassing number of new particles and particle-like phenomena.

Gravity and electromagnetism
Following the discovery of the electron it was possible to think of atoms as being made up of electrically charged particles between which two types of force acted. One force was electromagnetism, due to the electric charges of the particles, and the other was gravity, although its effects were only slight.

The presence of gravitational forces on this scale was in accordance with Sir Isaac Newton's universal law of gravitation. This states that between any two objects in the universe, even such small objects as particles, there is an attractive force proportional to the masses of the objects and inversely proportional to the square of the distance between them.

In this idealization, the particles created smooth, continuous electromagnetic and gravitational *fields* or areas of influence around them. If a particle moved, the fields would change and the forces on other particles would consequently be altered.

Quantum theory
Einstein upset this simple picture of particles and fields. He found a circumstance in which it was more sensible to regard light, one of the forms of electromagnetic radiation, as being composed of a stream of particles rather than being a

Picturepoint

Rutherford Laboratory

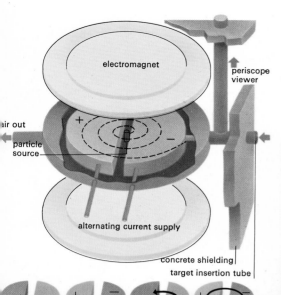

electromagnet

periscope viewer

air out

particle source

alternating current supply

concrete shielding
target insertion tube

Left: A cyclotron has a pair of hollow, D-shaped units mounted in a vacuum chamber between the poles of a powerful electromagnet. These units are alternately charged positive and negative, so a particle put into the centre will spiral outwards and accelerate until it reaches the outer edge and hits the target.

Below: The Van de Graaff generator produces a very high voltage by accumulating an enormous amount of electrostatic charge and this voltage can be used in a laboratory to accelerate particles. This picture shows the top of the six million volt generator at the nuclear laboratories at Aldermaston in England.

Above left: In a linear accelerator, particles such as protons are accelerated along a tube by high frequency alternating electric fields supplied by a device called a klystron. A proton is accelerated when there is a negative field ahead of it. As the field is alternating —constantly changing from negative to positive and back—the protons have to be shielded from the positive field so that they are not decelerated by it. They travel through a series of 'drift tubes' which provide this shielding. The timing of the field and the lengths of the tubes are arranged so that the field is negative when the protons cross the gaps between the tubes, and positive when they are within the tubes and shielded by them. When the protons hit the nuclei of the target atoms they break them up into particles.

Left: The interior of a linear accelerator.

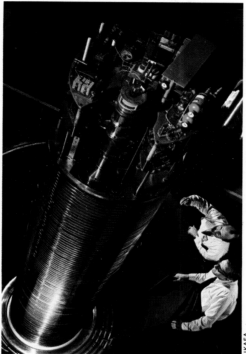

UKAEA

particles from linear accelerator

vacuum tube

electromagnet

injector

switching station

magnets   accelerating units

to target

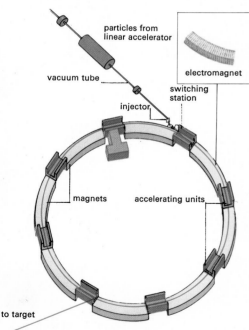

Left: A 7 GeV proton synchrotron.

Above: A synchrotron is fed with accelerated particles from a linear accelerator and as they travel round the machine they are further accelerated each time they pass one of the accelerating units. When they reach a high enough velocity they are diverted out of the synchrotron to the target. The energy a particle possesses depends on the accelerating voltage. Particle energies are thus expressed in terms of 'electron volts'. For example, the tube of a television is a simple form of accelerator, accelerating electrons with a voltage of about 10,000 V. Thus each electron hits the screen with an energy of 10,000 electron volts or 10keV. Accelerators commonly operate at MeV (mega, or million, electron volt) and GeV (giga, or 1,000 million, electron volt) energy levels.

smooth, continuous field of energy.

The circumstance in question was known as the *photoelectric effect*. It had been discovered that, under certain conditions, light shining on a metal surface caused electrons to be emitted from it. The effect would occur only if the light was towards the blue end of the spectrum. A red light, even if it were intense or left on for a long time, would not cause the emission.

Einstein's explanation was that light was composed of particles called *photons*. The energy of a photon was proportional to the frequency of the light, and so was higher for blue light than for red light because blue light has a higher frequency. The emission of an electron from the metal surface was due to it being struck by a photon. A blue photon had sufficient energy to do this, but a red one did not.

The explanation of the photoelectric effect in terms of discrete bundles or *quanta* of energy carried by photons was in fact the second time such an idea had been used. Five years before, in 1900, Max Planck (1858-1947) had introduced the idea of discrete quanta of energy in his discussion of the spectrum of energy emitted by objects heated to incandescence.

Planck and Einstein forced physicists to accept that the electromagnetic field sometimes behaved like an assembly of particles (the photons) and sometimes like a continuous wave.

Quantum mechanics

In the 1920s, Prince Louis de Broglie suggested that the wave and particle aspects of light had to be considered together, not separately, since the energy of the particle depends on the frequency of the wave. In addition, he proposed that other particles besides the photon could also behave like waves. If this were so, electrons would be expected to exhibit characteristic interference patterns such as occur when two stones are dropped into a pond and the spreading ripples overlap. Three years later precisely such an effect was found.

The next step was taken by Werner Heisenberg, Wolfgang Pauli and Max Born, who developed a form of *quantum mechanics* which gave a complete understanding of the structure of stable atoms. Quantum mechanics predicted stable energy states for electrons in the presence of a positively charged nucleus. With the help of Pauli's exclusion principle, Bohr's theory of the atom was given a firm basis.

Paul Dirac applied the new quantum mechanics to the electromagnetic field and showed how it could be regarded as an assembly of photons. The resolution of the wave-particle paradox was that the intensity of the wave could be regarded as the density of particles in it. In certain situations the density would be so high that the grainy nature of the wave could be overlooked. In other situations, with low density, the fact that there was a wave at all might be neglected.

Almost all physics was explained by quantum mechanics. The structure of the atom and the formation of molecules could be understood, and electromagnetic radiation (such as light, radio waves and X-rays) was emitted and absorbed in accordance with Dirac's theory. All physics and chemistry, for example the formation of crystals and magnets and the action of solvents and adhesives, could be described in terms of particular effects of electromagnetic radiation.

In the stage of understanding reached by 1930, the original two long-range forces ruled all nature: gravity for very large masses on an astronomical scale (its effects being so weak at atomic levels that it could be ignored) and electromagnetism operating everywhere else. By analogy with the concept of the photon as the quantum (or particle) of electromagnetic radiation, many people suppose that the gravitational field is also composed of particles, which are called *gravitons*. As yet, however, there is no experimental evidence for them.

Strong and weak forces

After the discovery of the neutron, and the realization that the nucleus consisted of a collection of positively charged protons and uncharged neutrons, it became clear that a third basic force must exist in nature. This force was necessary to overcome the repulsive forces between the positively charged protons that would tend to push them apart. In addition, this *strong* or *hadronic force* would have to be very attractive and very short range to explain the small size of the nucleus (10^{-13} cm) as opposed to the overall size of the atom (about 10^{-8} cm), and to explain the fact that the nuclei, shielded by the electron clouds, seem to have no effect on one another.

Yukawa suggested that this strong force was transmitted by mesons, the mesons carrying the strong force in the way that photons carry electromagnetism.

There is one further force in nature, the so-called *weak force*. It is not thought responsible for creating any 'bound

7

Right and below: A storage ring collects bursts of particles from an accelerator and builds them up into two intense beams of particles travelling in opposite directions around the ring. The beams are then fired at each other so that very high energy collisions occur between the particles, and new particles are created by the break-up or combination of the original particles. This diagram and the picture on the right show the rings at the European Centre for Nuclear Research (CERN) near Geneva. Protons from a linear accelerator are further accelerated in a synchrotron then directed into the rings.

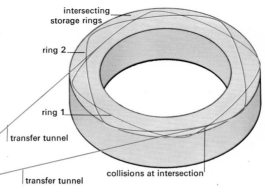

intersecting storage rings
ring 2
ring 1
transfer tunnel
collisions at intersection
transfer tunnel

Paul Brierley

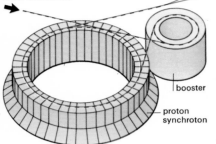

linear accelerator
booster
proton synchroton

Below and right: One of the devices used to detect and identify particles produced by accelerators is the bubble chamber. The chamber contains liquid hydrogen which is kept under pressure by a piston. The particles are fired into the chamber, the pressure is momentarily released and the particles leave a trail of bubbles in the liquid as they pass. The chamber is surrounded by powerful electromagnets; the size and charge of a particle can be found from the curve and the direction of the path it takes under the influence of the magnetic field. The particles' tracks are recorded by cameras.

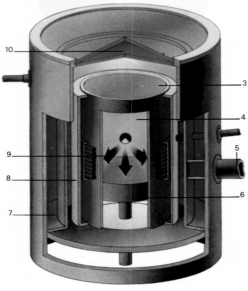

CERN

1 Camera
2 Lights
3 Bubble chamber window
4 Liquid hydrogen
5 Pipe to vacuum pump
6 Piston
7 Radiation shield
8 Liquid hydrogen chamber cooling tank
9 Beam of particles
10 Radiation shield window

Right: An aerial view of the CERN complex near Geneva. There are two laboratories, CERN I and CERN II, employing a total of about 3,650 staff. A super proton synchrotron, about 5 km (3 miles) in diameter, is being constructed for CERN II, capable of a peak energy of 400 GeV. CERN's 1975 budget was 247 million US dollars.

CERN

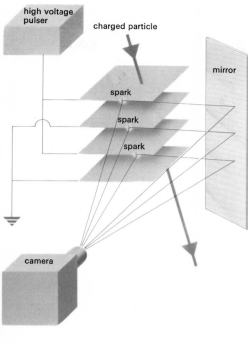

high voltage pulser

charged particle

mirror

spark

spark

spark

camera

CERN

states' like the solar system, the atom or the nucleus, as gravity, electromagnetism and the strong force do. It is, however, thought to be responsible for the decay of many particles, in particular for the decay of a free neutron into a proton, an electron and a neutrino (a particle with no charge). The weak force is held responsible for all interactions involving neutrinos. A neutrino has so little mass, and such a weak interaction with matter, that only rarely will it disturb it as it passes through.

It is believed that the weak force may be transmitted by a particle called the *intermediate vector boson*, W, which was predicted by Yukawa in 1938.

Antiparticles

Conservation of energy is one of the principles of physics which, it is assumed, is never violated. Energy may change its form—it may reside in the mass of a particle at rest, and then become partly rest mass and partly the kinetic energy of the particle's decay products—but it is never created or destroyed. Energy is thus conserved absolutely.

Another quantity which is conserved absolutely is net electric charge, Q. This is slightly more subtle than energy conservation, because electric charge can in fact be created or destroyed, but only in pairs of opposite charges. For example, pairing a negative electron with a positive electron produces a zero electric charge, and it is the net charge which never changes.

The positive electron or *positron* is the *antiparticle* of the ordinary negatively charged electron. It has the same mass as an electron, only it is oppositely charged. The electron pairs gave rise to the idea of antiparticles generally and so, when sufficiently powerful particle accelerators became available in the 1950s, there was great interest in whether an antiproton could be created. This was much more difficult than creating the electron pairs because the rest mass energy required is nearly 2,000 times greater.

Particle accelerators are machines which accelerate particles to enormous velocities. These particles then bombard target atoms to break up their nuclei and create new particles. The antiproton was found and it then became possible to conceive of an 'antiworld' made up of antiatoms—antiprotons surrounded by positrons. Such a world meeting ours would annihilate both in a great flash of light.

The existence of the antiproton brought into the open another absolutely conserved quantity, *baryonic charge* B. Like the electric charge, it is conserved net. It allows creation or destruction of proton-antiproton or neutron-antineutron pairs, but forbids their creation in single particles. The baryonic charge of electrons and mesons is zero, and it can be said that protons do not decay into positrons because the baryonic charge would not be conserved. If it were not for the conservation of baryonic charge, atoms would disintegrate into light and a flux of neutrinos.

Isomultiplets and strangeness

The discovery of the mesons and higher mass particles with baryonic charge +1 disclosed two further patterns or symmetries. Every particle had a place in a group called a *charge multiplet* or *iso-*

Above and above right: In the spark chamber particle detector, a stack of aluminium foil sheets, separated from each other by a gap of about a centimetre, is enclosed in a chamber containing an inert gas such as argon. A high voltage is applied to the plates and any charged particle passing through leaves a track of ionized gas in its wake. The ionized gas is electrically conductive and allows a spark to jump from one plate to the next along the route taken by the particle. The sparks are observed by a film or television camera. The photograph above shows the two mirrors of a spark chamber used at CERN in studying leptons—which include electrons, muons and neutrinos.

CERN

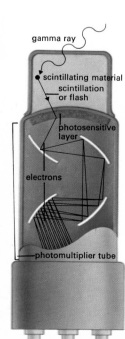

gamma ray

scintillating material

scintillation or flash

photosensitive layer

electrons

photomultiplier tube

Above and left: The rate at which particles are being produced in an experiment can be measured by a scintillation counter. Some materials, such as certain types of plastic, give off a flash of light when a high-energy charged particle passes through them. The top of the counter, on the right in the photograph, contains a block of one of these scintillating materials. When a particle passes through it, the flash of light is picked up by the photomultiplier tube, a device which converts it into an electrical pulse. This pulse is relayed to a computer which counts and times the pulses. The accuracy is within a thousandth of a millionth of a second.

Right: At a banquet in Paris for the Soviet leader Nikita Kruschev in 1960, all the food was checked with a geiger counter in case it had been poisoned with a radioactive substance. Any charged particle passing through the detector causes an electrical discharge which is indicated by a click in the phones.

Keystone

9

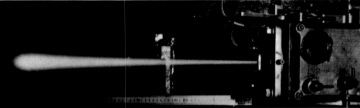

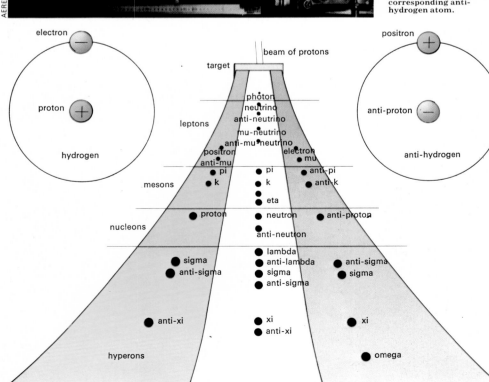

Right: The blue glow of Cerenkov radiation in a pool of water containing used fuel rods from a nuclear reactor. This radiation is caused by particles travelling faster through the water than light can. As the particles travel through the water they make its atoms give off this characteristic blue glow.

CERN

Above: A bubble chamber photograph showing the spray of mesons given off when a 20 GeV proton beam hit the stationary protons of the hydrogen atoms in the chamber.

Below: A beam of deuterons, each comprising one proton and one neutron, emerging from a cyclotron.

UKAEA

AERE

Below: Some of the known particles shown in an imaginary accelerator beam. The lightest particles are at the top; those on the left are positively charged, those in the centre neutral and those on the right are negatively charged. Also shown are a hydrogen atom and its corresponding anti-hydrogen atom.

electron

proton

hydrogen

positron

anti-proton

anti-hydrogen

beam of protons

target

leptons — photon, neutrino, anti-neutrino, mu-neutrino, anti-mu-neutrino, positron, electron, anti-mu, mu

mesons — pi, pi, anti-pi, k, k, anti-k, eta

nucleons — proton, neutron, anti-proton, anti-neutron

hyperons — lambda, anti-lambda, sigma, anti-sigma, sigma, anti-sigma, sigma, anti-sigma, anti-xi, xi, anti-xi, xi, xi, omega

multiplet, each group consisting of particles having approximately the same mass but differing electric charges. For example, the proton and neutron form a multiplet. Their masses are nearly the same, but their electric charges are different, being one and zero respectively. Another example are the *pi mesons* or *pions*, the mesons predicted by Yukawa; their masses are the same but they can have either a positive, negative or zero charge.

The other pattern that was discovered was the operation of yet another kind of charge conservation, but this one was peculiar. The accelerators, by banging protons together, created many more particles. Some of these had a baryonic charge of +1 but were more massive than pions, and these higher mass particles were never produced singly. This suggested that a new sort of charge, which was termed *strangeness*, S, was being conserved. It would be zero for pions and nucleons (protons and neutrons), but possibly different for the heavier particles.

Quarks

The structure of the many particles that have now been detected is not yet fully understood. One theory is the *quark* model, which is able to account for the multiplets and for the strangeness of the observed particles in terms of just three basic particles and their antiparticles, the quarks and the antiquarks. The quarks have been allocated various values of electric and baryonic charge and strangeness, so that known particles can be explained in terms of combinations of quarks, or quarks and antiquarks.

The original quark model does not explain everything, however, and since it originated in 1963 by Murray Gell-Mann and George Zweig it has been greatly modified. One modification requires 12 kinds of quark. In addition to the three 'flavours' of quark, *up*, *down* and *sideways*, there is a fourth flavour, the *charmed* quark. As well as the four flavours of quark they come in three 'colours', red, yellow and blue. The various flavours and colours of the quarks depend on their mass, electric charge, strangeness and whether or not they possess the additional property known as 'charm'.

The quarks are considered to be truly elementary particles, that is, they are basic and indivisible. They are thought to be the constituents of the *hadrons*, the particles such as protons and neutrons which interact by means of the strong force. The other elementary particles are the *leptons*, a group which are not affected by the strong force. These are the electron and the *muon*, which interact through the electromagnetic force, and the electron neutrino and the *muon neutrino* which interact through the weak force. In addition to the four leptons there are also four corresponding anti-leptons.

Despite the fact that hundreds of particles have now been discovered, the answers to the original questions about the nature of energy and forces, and just what exactly the smallest constituents of matter are, have not yet been fully answered. The new, immensely powerful accelerators now coming into use may provide some of the answers; but there is still a great deal that remains beyond our understanding.

Electricity and Magnetism

Below: Michael Faraday was born in September 1791, and after a very basic education he was apprenticed to a London bookbinder. While working there he read an article on electricity in a copy of the *Encyclopaedia Britannica* and this interested him so much that he decided to take up the study of science. In 1812 he went to work for Sir Humphry Davy at the Royal Institution, and this was the beginning of his scientific career. In 1823 he discovered methods of liquifying gases; in 1825 he discovered benzene. His most important work, however, was his study of the relationship between electricity and magnetism.

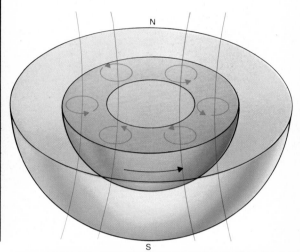

Electricity and magnetism are phenomena which arise from the nature and behaviour of the electrically charged particles—the *protons* and *electrons*—which together with the uncharged *neutrons* are the principal constituents of atoms. The exact nature of an electric charge is still unknown, but it can be measured, and its effects can be predicted and put to use, being the basis of all electrical and electronic equipment.

The charge carried by a proton is called a *positive* (or +ve) charge, and that carried by the electron is called a *negative* (or —ve) charge. A pair of similar charges, two positive ones for example, will repel each other, but two unlike charges, one positive and one negative, will attract each other.

The region around a charged particle in which these forces of attraction and repulsion operate is called an *electric field*. The strength of the force a particle can exert, and thus the intensity of its electric field, decreases as the inverse of the square of the distance from it. This means that if the distance from the particle is doubled, the strength of the force will be quartered, and if the distance is trebled the force will be reduced to one ninth.

Objects normally have no net electric charge as they contain as many electrons as they do protons, and so their positive and negative charges are balanced. If, however, electrons are taken from an object, it will have a net positive charge. Conversely, if it is given extra electrons it will have a net negative charge.

These effects can be created by rubbing a substance which has an affinity for electrons with one which is willing to give some up. For example, when dry hair is combed with a plastic comb the hair becomes positively charged and the comb

Ferrofluidio Corp.

Below: The induction coil is a device for producing high voltage pulses. There is a soft iron core, around which is wound a primary coil and a secondary coil. Interrupting the electrical current in the primary coil creates a very high voltage in the secondary which has many more turns of wire wound on it.

Right: The disc dynamo built by Faraday in 1831. The copper disc is rotated with its edge between the poles of the magnet, so that it cuts through the lines of flux. This causes electric currents to be set up within the disc—and the electricity is collected by copper brushes which rub against the disc.

Above: The magnetic field of a bar magnet can be represented by lines of force which form closed loops around it, leaving the magnet at one pole and joining it again at the other. If a magnet is placed under a piece of paper, and iron filings spread on top, the filings will group together along the lines of force.

Below: The Earth's magnetic field may be caused by electric currents, circulating horizontally, within the liquid rock between the core and the crust. These currents may be produced by friction within the planet due to its rotation and they produce a magnetic field at right angles to their plane of rotation.

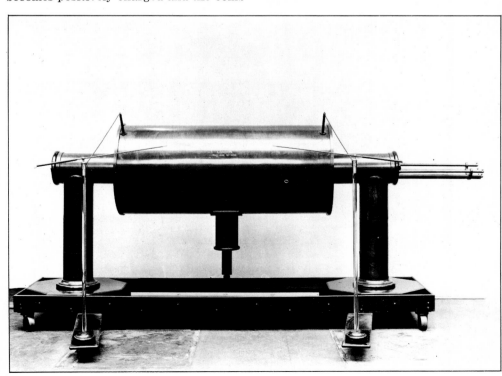

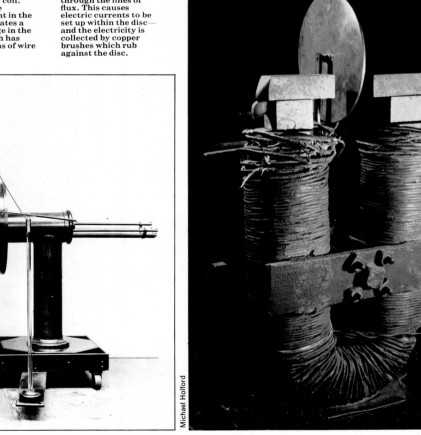

Michael Holford

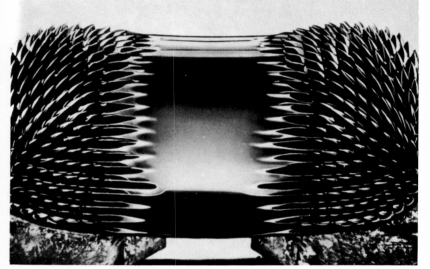

Above and left: These two pictures show the spikes formed on the surface of magnetic fluids (also called ferrofluids) when subjected to a vertical magnetic field. Ferrofluids contain particles of ferrite, a ceramic material made from an iron oxide and small quantities of other metal oxides. The particles are coated with a type of plastic so that they can slide over each other with virtually no friction, and the fluid is made by suspending the particles in water. Because the particles are so small, they do not settle at the bottom of the water and the resulting fluid still has almost the same consistency as water. Despite appearances the spikes are fluid.

negative. If the comb is then held near the hair, strands of hair will be attracted towards it because of their opposite electric charge.

This type of attraction is called *electrostatic* attraction because, apart from the initial transfer of electrons during the combing, it is due to stationary or *static* charges.

If the difference in charge between two objects is great enough a *static discharge*, in the form of a spark, may occur as the surplus electrons on the negatively charged object jump across to make up the deficiency on the positively charged object. A spectacular example of this is the lightning flash which occurs between highly charged thunderclouds and the ground.

Electric current
An ordinary electric current is the flow of electrons around a circuit, created when one end of the circuit is made more positive or negative than the other. A good example of a simple circuit is that of an electric torch.

Chemical reactions inside the battery continually create a surplus of electrons at one terminal and a deficiency at the other. When the circuit is completed by switching the torch on, the electrons in the circuit, that is in the connections to the lamp and in the lamp filament, move towards the terminal that is deficient in electrons, drawn to it by its net positive charge. As the electrons move towards the terminal, electrons from the other terminal move into the circuit to take their place.

The result is a steady flow of electrons around the circuit from one terminal to

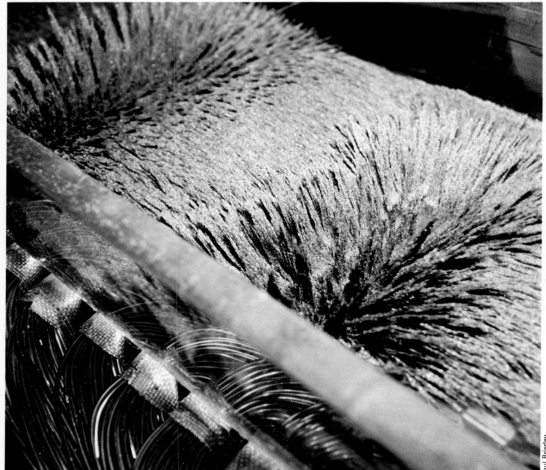

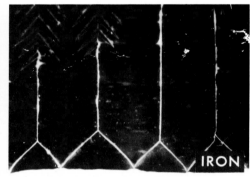

IRON

IRON

Left: Iron filings spread on top of the windings of a linear electric motor show the nature of its magnetic field. The motor is constructed so that its magnetic field travels along it, and so any metallic object placed on top will be carried along by the moving field while also supported by it.

Top and above: These two pictures show how crystals of iron behave when they are magnetized. The upper picture shows a sample which is not very highly magnetized, and the lower one shows the internal strains created when the magnetization is increased. This causes the crystals to deform as the atoms re-align.

Paul Brierley

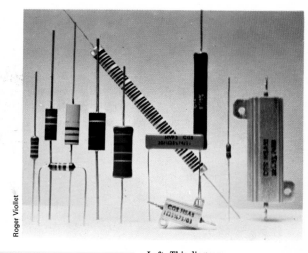

Left: A Leyden jar, one of the first devices built for storing electric charges. The glass jar has a metal lining and a metal covering. When a high voltage is applied across these two metal sections, one becomes positively charged and the other negative. This picture shows the stored charge being discharged.

Right: Some of the wide range of resistors used in electronic circuits. The resistance of these devices is utilized to reduce the current flowing in a particular part of a circuit, or to reduce the voltage level at a given point in a circuit. The commonest types are made of carbon powder mixed with clay and resin.

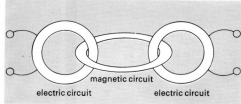

magnetic circuit

electric circuit   electric circuit

Left: This diagram illustrates the way in which the electric and magnetic circuits of a transformer are interlinked. The current in the primary electric circuit, on the left, sets up a magnetic circuit, centre, which then causes a current to flow in the secondary electric circuit on the right.

Right: In an electro-magnetic machine, the forces involved act at right angles to each other. In a motor, for example, the current in the rotor will set up a magnetic field at right angles to its direction of flow, and the turning force on the rotor will be at right angles to both the current and the magnetic field.

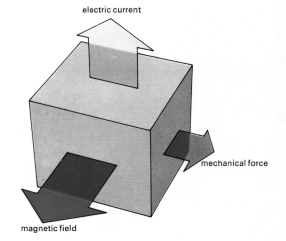

electric current

mechanical force

magnetic field

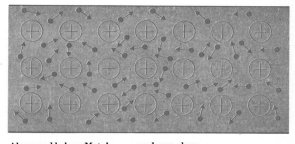

Above and below: Metals are good conductors of electricity because of the way in which electrons are free to move around within their crystalline structures. When no voltage is applied to them they move around at random, as shown above. However, applying voltage makes them drift towards the positively charged end, as in the diagram below. This electron drift is what constitutes an electric current in solid conducting materials.

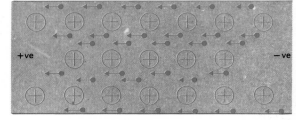

+ve   −ve

the other, kept going by the chemical reactions within the battery. Until it was realized that electric current was a flow of electrons from a negatively charged area to a positively (or less negatively) charged area, it was assumed that current flowed from positive to negative.

Ohm's law

The amount of current flowing through a circuit depends on two factors: the voltage applied to the circuit and the opposition to current flow within the circuit.

The voltage is a measure of the difference between the levels of charge at each end of the circuit. This difference, known as the *potential difference*, provides the *electromotive force* (emf) which drives the current around the circuit, just as pressure drives water through a system of pipes.

In a *direct current* (dc) circuit, where the current flows smoothly in one direction only, the opposition or *resistance* to current flow is caused by collisions between the electrons and the atoms of the material through which they are passing. These collisions interfere with the electron flow and so reduce the rate at which they can pass through the material.

Metals are good conductors of electricity because they have a low resistance. This is because their atoms are arranged in crystal structures, and the outer electrons of the atoms are free to move within the crystal lattices.

At the other end of the scale, insulating materials (which have a very high resistance) have their electrons tightly bound within their molecules, and so it takes a great deal of voltage to make them

move through the material.

The relationship between voltage, current and resistance is expressed by *Ohm's Law*, formulated by the German physicist Georg Ohm (1789-1854). This states that the resistance (R) of a circuit is the ratio of the voltage (V) to the current (I), that is, $R = V/I$. It can also be expressed as voltage = current x resistance, or $V = IR$.

Magnetism

When a charged particle such as an electron is stationary it is surrounded by its own electric field. When it moves, however, an additional field, a *magnetic field*, is set up. This occurs whenever an electric current flows, but it also happens within an atom because the electrons *spin* while moving in their orbits. In the atoms of most substances the magnetic fields produced by the electrons cancel each other out, but in others there is a net magnetic field and the atom itself behaves like a tiny magnet.

In the materials known as *ferromagnetic materials*, of which iron is the best known example, the application of a magnetic field will pull the magnetic fields of the atoms into line. The fields are then acting in unison, and the material becomes a magnet. Pure or 'soft' iron will not retain its magnetism when the magnetizing force, produced for example by the electric current flowing in a coil of wire, is removed. The atoms will return to their random alignment, instead of remaining in the aligned state. Steel, however, is iron alloyed with carbon, and the resulting structure is such that the atoms remain aligned after the magnetizing force has been removed.

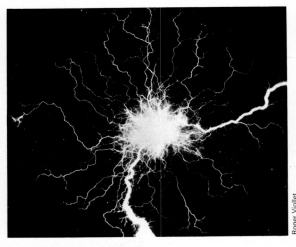

Roger Viollet

Above: A lightning flash is a very powerful discharge of static electricity. The thundercloud's charge is created by friction, caused by powerful air currents within it. This charge eventually becomes so great that a massive discharge occurs between the cloud and the ground or objects on it, such as trees.

Left: Iron filings show the pattern of the lines of force around a coil carrying a current.

Below: An electromagnet consists of a soft iron bar with a coil wrapped round it. When current flows in the coil, the bar acts like a permanent magnet because of the magnetic field passing through it.

Snark

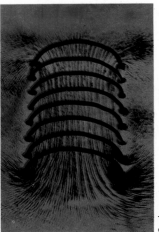

Reyrolle Parsons Ltd

current flowing in coil — to battery + magnetic field created by current in coil

iron core

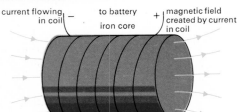

Below: This diagram represents the inseparable nature of electric and magnetic circuits. The designers of electromagnetic machines aim to make both of these as short as possible, with large cross-sectional areas, to minimize the losses of energy due to resistance and reluctance within the circuits.

electric (copper) circuit

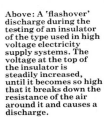

magnetic (iron) circuit

Above: A 'flashover' discharge during the testing of an insulator of the type used in high voltage electricity supply systems. The voltage at the top of the insulator is steadily increased, until it becomes so high that it breaks down the resistance of the air around it and causes a discharge.

Below: The ribbed glass insulators on a 400 kV transmission line. The insulators hold the lines, which are uninsulated themselves, away from the steel tower which is carrying them. The sections of line on either side of the tower are connected by lengths of line which bypass the insulators and the tower arms.

Paul Brierley

Just as there are two types of electric charge, positive and negative, a magnet has two *poles*, one at each end. These poles are called 'north' and 'south' respectively, and two similar poles will repel each other while two unlike poles will attract each other. However, an object cannot have just one pole, in the way that it can have either a positive or a negative charge. Poles always exist in pairs, one north and one south.

If a bar magnet, a small bar of magnetized steel, for example, is suspended by a piece of thread tied around its middle, it will turn so that its north pole points to the Earth's magnetic north. This is the way a compass needle works, and the reason why the magnetic poles are called 'north' and 'south'. The north or 'north seeking' pole always swings towards the north, and the south or 'south seeking' pole likewise always swings towards the south.

Electromagnetism

In 1831, Michael Faraday (1791-1867) made many important discoveries which demonstrated the relationship between electricity and magnetism. He found that a coil of wire carrying an electric current produced a magnetic field, and behaved like a bar magnet. Such an *electromagnet* could exert a force on a piece of un-magnetized ferromagnetic substance, on a permanent magnet, or even on a similar current-carrying coil. It would also exhibit polarity, having a north and a south pole, and it would obey the rules of attraction and repulsion between poles.

The magnetic field can be visualized as lines of force radiating from one pole of a magnet and looping round to enter it

14

Light and Sound

Much of our awareness of the world around us comes from information received by our eyes and ears. Our eyes respond to visible light, which is one of the many forms of *electromagnetic radiation* (other forms include radio waves and X-rays), and our ears respond to sound or *acoustic radiation*. Electromagnetic and acoustic radiation can both be thought of as travelling in waves. The waves on the sea are the most familiar examples of waves, but light and sound also reveal a wave-like nature when studied closely in the laboratory.

Sound

When we hear a sound it is because the air is vibrating, alternately pushing and pulling our eardrums and forcing them to vibrate. So to make a sound that can be heard by others we must obviously make the air vibrate somehow. This is not difficult; any object that vibrates, such as a drumskin or a vocal cord, pushes and pulls at the air which surrounds it. Every time it moves forward it presses against the air in front and when it recedes again the air has to rush back to fill the partial vacuum thus created. In other words the air in front of the vibrating object (which can be called a *sound source*) is subjected to an alternating pressure.

The air of course is composed of separate molecules, many millions of them in every cubic centimetre, and the molecules next to the source are unhappy at having to suffer the alternations in pressure, so they pass the strain on to their neighbours, who pass it on to their neighbours in turn. In this way the pressure alternations at the source are passed through the air. Every time the source vibrates another cycle of alternating pressure is passed along and the succession of these pressure cycles moving through the air constitutes a sound wave.

Such a wave moves through the air at a fixed speed—the velocity of sound, which in dry air at sea level is about 344 metres/sec (770 mph). Sound waves can travel through almost any gas, liquid or solid but they cannot travel through a vacuum, because in a vacuum there are no molecules to transmit the pressure to their neighbours. In liquids and solids sound waves move faster than in gases like air—about 1,400 metres/sec (3,130 mph) in water and 5,000 metres/sec (11,180 mph) in steel.

The number of vibrations made by the source in a second (the number of *cycles* per second) is known as its *frequency*, and since all the molecules affected by

Above: This device, in a Tokyo street, is indicating the sound level in the vicinity. The number it is displaying represents the local sound level in decibels. The formula for decibels is 10 x log E_N/E_R, where E_N is the sound energy present and E_R is the energy of the quietest sound the ear detects.

Right: Sound waves can be represented by graphs, with the vertical axis representing the intensity or amplitude of the sound, and the horizontal axis showing seconds. The frequency of the wave is the number of complete cycles per second. One cycle per second is known as 1 Hertz (1 Hz).

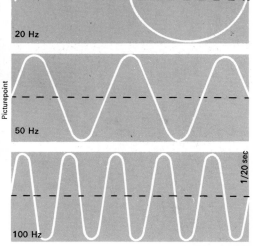

1 cycle

20 Hz

50 Hz

100 Hz

1/20 sec

Left: Ultrasonic waves are used to detect flaws in engineering materials. The test sample is scanned with pulses of very high frequency sound which normally travel right through it. If they meet a flaw in the material, however, they are reflected back again. The machine will detect these reflections and thus record the presence of the flaw.

Above: High levels of sound are dangerous to health, causing hearing defects and creating fatigue which can lead to accidents. This picture shows sound level monitoring apparatus analyzing the noise in a workshop.

Right: This tractor is being tested in an *anechoic chamber* which enables accurate measurement and analysis of its noise level to be made. The sound-absorbent, wedge-shaped blocks lining the entire inner surface of the chamber are designed to eliminate any echoes within it which would result in incorrect measurements.

Below: Echoes occur when sounds strike a hard surface and are eventually reflected back to their source.

ECHOES

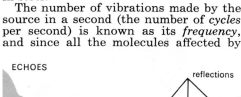

reflections

original sound

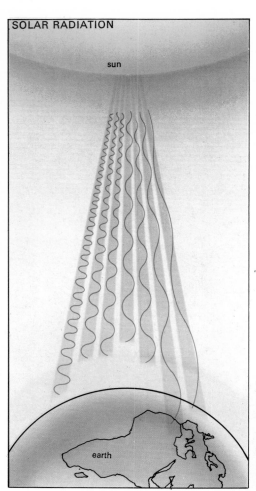

SOLAR RADIATION

sun

earth

THE ELECTROMAGNETIC SPECTRUM

ultra violet

infra red

x-rays

microwaves

visible

gamma rays

| EHF | SHF | UHF | VHF | HF | MF | LF | VLF |

radio waves

0.01 nm   0.1 nm   10 nm   100 nm   0.01 mm   0.1 mm   1 cm   10 cm   10 m   100 m   10 km   100 km

0.001 nm   1000 nm   1 m   1 km   1000

Far left: The sun sends a wide spectrum of electromagnetic radiation to the earth, much of which is absorbed by the atmosphere. The sun's radiation includes low frequency radio waves (on the right) and high frequency X-rays and gamma rays (on the left). Microwaves, infra-red rays, visible light and ultraviolet rays are in between.

Left: This enormous structure is a radio telescope, used by astronomers to detect the radio waves emitted by stars. The energy of the waves reaching the earth is extremely low, and the dish-shaped part of the radio telescope acts as a reflector, focussing the waves on to the actual aerial so that a stronger signal is obtained.

Right: Rainbows are the result of a phenomenon called *refraction*. When light passes from one medium, such as air, to another, such as water, its angle is altered slightly. The size of this change depends on the light's wavelength, red (long wavelength) light being affected less than blue (short wavelength) light. Sunlight passing through raindrops will, if the angle is correct, be split into its component colours by the raindrops in such a way as to form a rainbow.

Below: Photons (blue) striking a photoelectric material, dislodge electrons (red), creating an electric current.

the wave it produces vibrate at the same frequency we can talk of the frequency of the wave. Frequencies are measured in *Hertz* (symbol *Hz*), one Hertz being one complete cycle of vibrations (from maximum to minimum and back to maximum) per second.

The speed at which sound travels is independent of its frequency, and so the peaks of high frequency sound waves are closer together than those of low frequency waves. The distance between successive wave peaks is known as the *wavelength*, and the wavelength of any type of wave can be calculated by dividing its velocity by its frequency.

Speech and music are a mixture of frequencies from about 20 Hz to 20,000 Hz (20 kHz). The higher frequencies are heard as treble notes and the lower as bass. Frequencies below 20 Hz are felt rather than heard; a large part of the vibration caused by earthquakes is in fact due to low frequency sound waves moving in the Earth's crust. Sounds above 20 kHz cannot be detected by human ears, although they are audible to other animals such as dogs and bats.

Electromagnetic waves
Electromagnetic radiation can be thought of in two ways, either as continuous waves of energy or as streams of 'particles' or pulses of energy known as *photons*. Whether it is considered as waves or as particles depends on which particular properties of it are under discussion; in some cases its behaviour is best explained by its wave-like properties, and in others it is better to think of it as streams of photons.

16

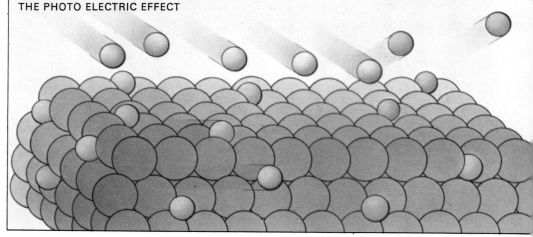

THE PHOTO ELECTRIC EFFECT

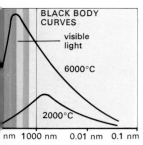

BLACK BODY CURVES

visible light

6000°C

2000°C

nm 1000 nm 0.01 nm 0.1 nm

Above: 'Black body curves' show the distribution of energy radiated at various frequencies by heated objects. These curves show how an object at 6,000°C radiates more energy, at higher frequencies, than one at 2,000°C.

Right: A microwave antenna. Microwaves, because of their high frequencies, can be made to carry more information than lower frequency radio waves.

Left: The whole electromagnetic spectrum, from gamma rays, through the visible region, to the longest radio waves.

LIGHT EMISSION FROM A HEATED ATOM

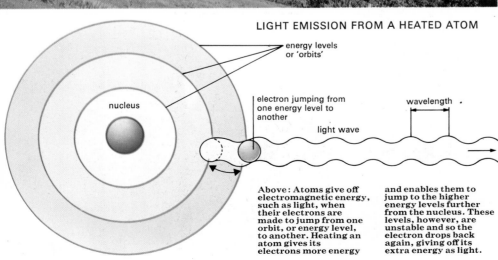

energy levels or 'orbits'

nucleus

electron jumping from one energy level to another

light wave

wavelength

Above: Atoms give off electromagnetic energy, such as light, when their electrons are made to jump from one orbit, or energy level, to another. Heating an atom gives its electrons more energy and enables them to jump to the higher energy levels further from the nucleus. These levels, however, are unstable and so the electron drops back again, giving off its extra energy as light.

The optical properties of light, for example, such as reflection and refraction, are related to its wavelength and so in these aspects light is best thought of as waves. The photoelectric effect, on the other hand, where light falling on to certain materials causes an electric current to flow in them, is best explained in terms of high-energy photons striking electrons in the material, freeing them from their atoms so that they can travel through the material as an electric current.

Unlike sound, which is propagated by the mechanical vibrations of the molecules of substances, electromagnetic radiation originates at a sub-atomic level and travels most easily in a vacuum where there are no atoms or molecules to impede its progress. An electromagnetic wave has two components, an electric field and an associated magnetic field that travels along with it.

Anything which produces either an alternating electric field or an alternating magnetic field is also a source of electromagnetic radiation. An alternating electric current flowing in a wire, for example, creates both an alternating electric field and an alternating magnetic field around it, and these two fields spread out together from the wire as an alternating electromagnetic field. This alternating field travels as a wave-like series of alternations in the strengths of the electric and magnetic fields, the 'peaks' of the waves being at points where the field strengths are greatest. As with sound, the frequency of the wave equals the frequency of the source, and the wavelength, that is the distance between two successive points on the wave where the fields are equal, is found by dividing the velocity by the frequency. The higher the frequency, the shorter the wavelength.

The velocity of electromagnetic waves in a vacuum, as calculated by James Clerk Maxwell who first suggested their existence in 1864, is an incredible 299,792·458 km/second (186,282 miles/sec, or 670,615,200 mph). This is the same as the measured velocity of light, a coincidence which persuaded physicists to accept the existence of electromagnetic waves long before their transmission was first demonstrated by Heinrich Hertz in 1887. It was also obvious that one of their forms is visible light itself.

Visible light, however, is only the most obvious form of electro-magnetic radiation, which can be observed also as radio waves, microwaves, infra-red and ultraviolet light, X-rays and gamma rays. All these differ from each other only in wavelength and frequency, and there is a certain amount of overlap between these different groups, the highest frequencies of one group being the same as the lowest of the next.

The longest wavelengths are those of radio waves, which range from over 1000 km down to about 10 cm, and these are the simplest to generate artificially. An alternating current of the right frequency is passed through a straight wire aerial, creating an alternating magnetic field around the aerial which radiates the waves into the air. An equally simple aerial can be used to detect radio waves, which induce a tiny alternating electric current in any wire which points at the same angle and direction as the transmitting aerial.

Shorter electromagnetic wavelengths, 17

unlike radio waves and microwaves, cannot be produced electronically. Infra-red radiation, which covers the wavelengths from 1 mm down to 1 micrometre (a millionth of a metre), is produced by the natural vibrations of atoms, particularly those in solids. Atoms are composed of electrically charged particles, and when these vibrate they create alternating electric and magnetic fields which project themselves away as infra-red rays. The hotter an object gets, the faster its atoms vibrate and the higher the frequency (hence the shorter the wavelength) of their radiation.

Since it is generally true that any emitter of waves will also absorb them, infrared waves readily give up their energy to the atoms of any solid they encounter. This raises the temperature of the absorbing solid, so that infra-red can also be considered as radiated heat.

If an object is heated above about 530°C (986°F), it begins to radiate appreciable amounts of radiation at wavelengths as short as 750 nanometres (1 nm is 1 thousand millionth of a metre), which human eyes can detect as red light. Visible light wavelengths range from this down to 390 nm for violet light. Anything heated above about 1,200°C (2,192°F) radiates a mixture of visible light wavelengths which appears white to our eyes. This is the physical meaning of the terms 'red hot' and 'white hot'.

Shorter still than visible light is ultraviolet light, a term used to describe electromagnetic radiation with wavelengths from 390 nm down to 1 nm. Ultraviolet waves can be produced, like infrared, by atomic vibrations, but the temperature must be about 5,000°C (9,032°F) before a significant amount is produced. The sun and other stars are at higher temperatures than this and consequently radiate a good deal of ultraviolet, but the bulk of their output is still in the visible range. However, ultraviolet and some visible light can also be produced at much lower temperatures by changes in the energy of electrons in atoms and molecules.

According to the *quantum theory*, electrons orbiting atomic nuclei can only have certain definite energy levels, and each time an electron changes from one energy level to another it emits a short burst of electromagnetic radiation called a photon. The frequency of the photon is directly proportional to the change in the electron's energy, and the possible energies of electrons are such that the emitted photons are visible or ultraviolet light. The higher the frequency of the photon, the more energy it possesses.

Black Body Radiation

The relationship between frequency and energy was first explained by the German physicist Max Planck (1858-1947) in 1900. The explanation was contained in Planck's quantum theory, which he formulated when studying the spectrum of radiation emitted by heated objects. Physicists had been unable to explain why, when an object was heated, it gave off much less high-frequency energy than they expected it to.

Planck's explanation was that the energy was emitted in discrete bundles or *quanta* (photons), and that a quantum of high frequency contained more energy than a low frequency one. Consequently the energy needed to enable an object to

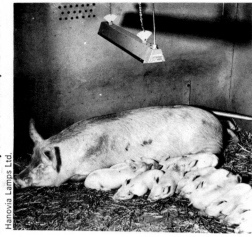

Hanovia Lamps Ltd.

Picturepoint

IMAGE INTENSIFIER

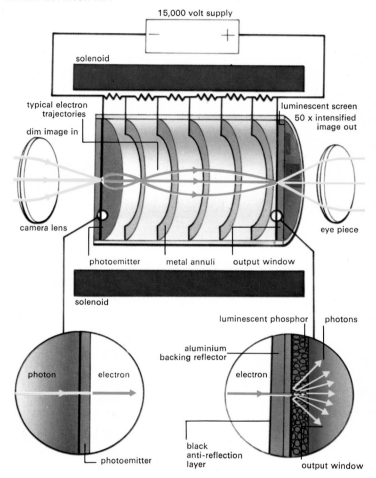

15,000 volt supply

solenoid

typical electron trajectories

dim image in

camera lens

photoemitter   metal annuli   output window

solenoid

luminescent screen 50 x intensified image out

eye piece

photon   electron

photoemitter

luminescent phosphor   photons

aluminium backing reflector

electron

black anti-reflection layer

output window

Above: Over 80% of the light emitted by an ultraviolet bactericidal lamp is 254 nm ultraviolet, which kills most kinds of germs.

Left: An image intensifier takes a dim image and focusses it onto a *photoemitter*. This emits electrons in proportion to the pattern of light of the image. These electrons are accelerated by the 15,000 volt supply, and focussed by the solenoid's magnetic field, and when they hit the luminescent screen they make it give off photons, creating a bright picture of the original scene.

Below left: An image intensifier gun sight and (below) Stonehenge viewed at night through an intensifier.

RCA

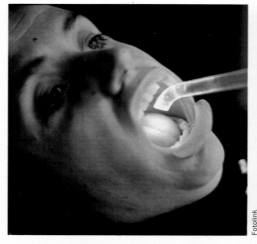

Far left: A litter of young pigs and their mother being kept warm by an infra-red heater. Infra-red radiation raises the temperature of any solid object on which it falls, but passes through air without heating it. Infra-red heaters such as this one provide ample warmth for the objects they are intended to heat, but do not waste energy by heating up the air around them.

Left: Banknotes can be 'marked' with Anthracene, which does not show up under ordinary light, but when lit with ultraviolet light it absorbs it and re-emits it as visible light. This effect is called *fluorescence*.

Fotolink

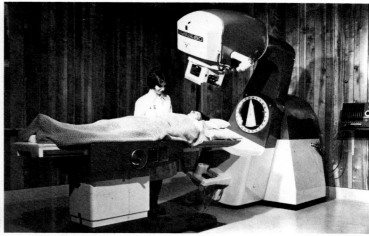

UKAEA

Hanovia Lamps Ltd.

Rolls Royce

Above left: Ultraviolet light is the component of sunlight which causes sunburn. Its effects on skin tissue can be used medically: this picture shows a powerful ultraviolet lamp being used to seal a patient's gum tissue after a tooth has been extracted. The light also kills any germs present.

Above: Gamma rays can be used to destroy the cells of tumor tissue. This machine uses radioactive cobalt as a gamma ray source.

Left: Gamma ray and X-ray photography are used to study the internal structure of machinery. Here, a jet engine is being studied with X-rays.

form and emit high frequencies was greater than that needed for the formation of low frequencies. In the case of a heated object, the higher its temperature the more energy was available for the emission of radiation. Thus a relatively moderate amount of heat was required to make the object give off low frequencies (in other words to make it red hot), but a great deal more heat was needed to make it give off higher frequencies (to make it white hot). This is why a piece of metal can be made to glow red at about 530°C, but must be heated to around 1,200°C or more to make it glow white.

The energy levels at different frequencies, radiated by an object heated to a given temperature, can be predicted by using data based on the behaviour of the theoretical 'black body'. This theoretical body, being perfectly black, absorbs all the energy from all frequencies of radiation falling on it, but it radiates this energy at different frequencies. The amount of energy it emits at a given frequency depends on its temperature.

X-rays and gamma rays

X-rays have extremely short wavelengths, from 10 nm down to 0.001 nm. The longer X-rays are called 'soft' and the shorter 'hard'. Some soft X-rays are produced by electron energy changes in atoms, but they are usually generated by firing high speed electrons at a metal target. The sudden deceleration of a charged electron when it hits the target causes a very rapid change in the electric field surrounding it, which leads to the emission of radiation in the form of an X-ray photon.

Gamma rays, shortest of all electromagnetic radiation, are emitted as a result of energy changes in the elementary particles which comprise an atomic nucleus. They can be generated, somewhat haphazardly, in the core of a nuclear reactor, but are produced naturally in any radioactive process such as the disintegration of radium. Some gamma rays have wavelengths in the hard X-ray range—others are as short as 0.0001 nm (one billion billionth of a metre).

THE DOPPLER EFFECT

wave front

direction of plane

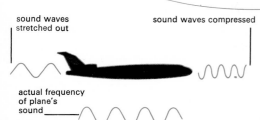

sound waves stretched out

sound waves compressed

actual frequency of plane's sound

Left: The pitch of the sound of an object travelling towards an observer sounds higher than it really is because it 'compresses' the sound waves in front of it. The sound appears lower when the object is travelling away, because the sound waves are 'stretched out'. This is called the *Doppler effect*, and

at extremely high speeds it has a similar effect on the frequency of light coming from an object. The light from an approaching object appears bluer than it is, as its frequency is higher, and conversely that from a receding object appears redder. The effect was discovered by C. Doppler in 1842.

The Foundations of Chemistry

We take the world around us very much for granted. But do we know what the wallpaper, the paint, the furniture, the transistor radio and the man-made fibres in our clothes are made of? Even if we were given the basic ingredients we would still need to know how to change them into the final product.

Chemistry is largely concerned with finding out more about substances, including their components and structure, their properties and how they can be made. The chemist's job is to analyse and synthesize things. In the past 30 years this has led to a vast range of new products: plastics, man-made fibres, dye-stuffs, fertilizers, medicines, synthetic rubbers, refrigerants, detergents, fire-fighting chemicals and rocket fuels, the list is endless. Chemistry has also gone hand in hand with physics; for example, in the development of the semiconductors used in transistors and integrated circuits.

The building blocks

All these achievements depended on a knowledge of the basic chemical *elements* or building blocks of matter. For about 1,600 years it had been left to the alchemists to try to untangle these secrets. Misguided by Aristotle's philosophic theory that all matter was composed of 'four elements'—earth, air, fire and water—and dedicated to the pursuit of turning base metals into gold and finding the 'elixir of life', they actually halted the progress of science.

However, in 1661 Robert Boyle correctly defined an element as 'a substance which cannot be split into anything simpler by a chemical change'. The search for elements began and within 100 years Antoine Lavoisier, the brilliant French chemist, had listed 27 of them. Today all 92

Derby Museum

Above: White phosphorus was unwittingly discovered by a German alchemist, Hennig Brand, in 1669, while looking for the elixir of life. He filled a retort with urine and heated it. The glowing residue was the element phosphorus. It was not until 100 years later that the search for elements began seriously.

ELEMENTS SHOWN IN THE PERIODIC TABLE

Ar	Argon	H	Hydrogen
Ac	Actinium	Ha	Hahnium
Ag	Silver	He	Hellium
Al	Aluminium	Hf	Hafnium
Am	Americium	Hg	Mecury
As	Arsenic	Ho	Holmium
At	Astatine	I	Iodine
Au	Gold	In	Indium
B	Boron	Ir	Iridium
Ba	Barium	K	Potassium
Be	Beryllium	Kr	Krypton
Bi	Bismuth	La	Lanthanum
Bk	Berkelium	Li	Lithium
Br	Bromine	Lu	Lutetium
C	Carbon	Lr	Lawerencium
Ca	Calcium	Md	Mendelevium
Cd	Cadmium	Mg	Magnesium
Ce	Cerium	Mn	Manganese
Cf	Californium	Mo	Molybdenum
Cl	Chlorine	N	Nitrogen
Cm	Curium	Na	Sodium
Co	Cobalt	Nb	Niobium
Cr	Chromium	Nd	Neodymium
Cs	Caesium	Ne	Neon
Cu	Copper	Ni	Nickel
Dy	Dysprosium	No	Nobelium
Er	Erbium	Np	Neptunium
Es	Einsteinium		
Eu	Europium		
F	Fluorine		
Fe	Iron		
Fm	Fermium		
Fr	Francium		
Ga	Gallium		
Gd	Gadolinium		
Ge	Germanium		

O	Oxygen	Ta	Tantalum
Os	Osmium	Tb	Terbium
P	Phosphorus	Tc	Technetium
Pa	Protactinium	Te	Tellurium
Pb	Lead	Th	Thorium
Pd	Palladium	Ti	Titanium
Pm	Promethium	Tl	Thallium
Po	Polonium	Tm	Thulium
Pr	Praseodymium	U	Uranium
Pt	Platinum	Ung	Unnilguadium
Pu	Plutonium	Unb	Unnilbentium
Ra	Radium	Unh	Unnilhexium
Rb	Rubidium	V	Vanadium
Re	Rhenium	W	Tungsten
Rf	Rutherfordium	Xe	Xenon
Rh	Rhodium	Y	Yttrium
Rn	Radon	Yb	Ytterbium
Ru	Ruthenium	Zn	Zinc
S	Sulphur	Zr	Zirconium
Sb	Antimony		
Sc	Scandium		
Se	Selenium		
Si	Silicon		
Sm	Samarium		
Sn	Tin		
Sr	Strontium		

1st period
2nd period
3rd period
4th period
5th period
6th period
7th period

3	4	5
Li	Be	B

11	12	13
Na	Mg	Al

19	20	21	22	23	24	25	26
K	Ca	Sc	Ti	V	Cr	Mn	Fe

37	38	39	40	41	42	43	44
Rb	Sr	Y	Zr	Cb	Mo	Tc	Ru

55	56	57	58	59	60	61	62	63	64	65	66	67	68	69
Cs	Ba	La	Ce	Pr	Nd	Pm	Sm	Eu	Gd	Tb	Dy	Ho	Er	Tm

87	88	89	90	91	92	93	94	95	96	97	98	99	100	101	1
Fr	Ra	Ac	Th	Pa	U	Np	Pu	Am	Cm	Bk	Ct	Es	Fm	Md	

Left: In 1940 scientists found they could make synthetic elements by bombarding uranium with atomic nuclei. Shown here is plutonium, atomic number 94. It is being handled by remotely-controlled tongs. A radioactive metal of the actinide group, it was used in some of the first atomic bombs instead of uranium.

Below: Many compounds in our world occur as mixtures which can be separated in various ways; by filtering, by gravity differences and by distillation. Air can be separated into its gases by liquefying and distilling it. Here salt is being extracted from sea water simply by letting the water evaporate off in the sun.

naturally-occurring elements, of which about 70 are metals, have been identified. In addition, about 14 artificial ones have been made during nuclear reactions, but being radioactive they are often short-lived.

If a massive chemical analysis of the Earth's crust was possible, the abundance of elements would be approximately 50 per cent oxygen, 26 per cent silicon, 7 per cent aluminium, 4 per cent iron, 3 per cent calcium, 2.5 per cent sodium, 2.5 per cent potassium, 2 per cent magnesium and all the other elements together 3 per cent.

Relatively few elements are found 'free' in nature; most occur chemically combined with one or more other elements, forming *compounds*. There are, however, rules governing which elements combine and the proportions in which they com-

bine. A compound is a pure substance with its own properties, often widely different to its constituent elements. For example, when sodium, a soft, highly reactive metal, is burned in chlorine, a poisonous choking gas, a harmless compound is produced, sodium chloride or household salt.

There is a further complication; in the world around us most compounds and any 'free' elements exist as *mixtures*, which are held together by physical rather than chemical means. The air, sea water, soil, rocks and crude oil are all mixtures of this kind. The separation of mixtures is important to many industries, for example, in oil refining, in the desalination of sea water, in the extraction of metals from mixed ores, and in brewing.

Atoms and the Periodic Table

Each element is, in fact, made up of millions of tiny particles known as *atoms*. The structure of these atoms helps to explain the chemical and physical properties of the various elements and how they form compounds.

At the heart of the atom is a cluster of positively charged protons and uncharged neutrons, which together form the nucleus. Surrounding the nucleus is a cloud of negatively charged electrons. These electrons are so light in comparison to the nucleus that an atom of hydrogen could be compared to a pea orbited by a speck of dust. In reality electrons are very important as they alone are responsible for chemical changes, but only the outermost ones are involved in these changes.

The electrons have to go into particular energy levels or concentric 'shells' around the nucleus and there is a maximum number of electrons which can exist in each shell. There are never more than eight electrons in the outermost shell. Those with the full complement of eight are chemically very stable. They are the rare or 'inert' gases; neon, argon, krypton, xenon and radon.

In all atoms the number of protons in the nucleus equals the number of elec-

rare (inert) gases

electropositive metals

non metals

transition metals

hydrogen

rare earths and actinides

elements with both metallic and non-metallic properties

Left: A modern Periodic Table. Above the symbol for each element is its atomic number, equal to protons in the nucleus. In each period all elements have the same number of electron shells. Broad classes exist, but sometimes they include smaller families having the same number of electrons in their outermost shell.

8	9	10
O	F	Ne

16	17	18
S	Cl	Ar

29	30	31	32	33	34	35	36
Cu	Zn	Ga	Ge	As	Se	Br	Kr

47	48	49	50	51	52	53	54
Ag	Cd	In	Sn	Sb	Te	I	Xe

72	73	74	75	76	77	78	79	80	81	82	83	84	85	86
Hf	Ta	W	Re	Os	Ir	Pt	Au	Hg	Tl	Pb	Bi	Po	At	Rn

104	105	106
Rf	Ha	

Above: In a solid the atoms stack in an orderly fashion, giving rise to beautiful crystalline forms. This applies equally to atoms of the same kind (as found in elements like iron, copper, sulphur and iodine), or different kinds, as in this compound, a natural mineral form of calcium carbonate, called calcite.

trons, making them electrically neutral. For example, the second lightest element is the gas helium which has two protons and two neutrons surrounded by two orbital electrons which fill the K shell. This makes helium as stable as the inert gases, which is why it is much safer to use helium in balloons than highly inflammable hydrogen. On the other hand, lithium, the lightest solid element, has three protons, four neutrons (the number of neutrons does not have to equal the number of protons) and three electrons. It is highly reactive because the third electron has to go into the second shell where it is loosely bound and easily lost to another atom.

Each element is assigned an *atomic number* based on the number of protons in the nucleus. It is also given an *atomic weight*, which is equal to the total number of protons and neutrons in the nucleus. (The electrons are so light they can be ignored.) Naturally this does not say how many grammes an atom weighs, but is useful for comparing the relative weights of elements.

Apart from the atomic numbers of elements, some system of classification other than metal or non-metal was sought. The first successful attempt to place the elements in some order was made by a Russian chemist, Dmitri Mendeleyev, in 1868. He noticed that when elements were listed in order of increasing atomic weight there was a definite periodic repetition of those with similar properties. He placed the elements in rows and columns and, as only about 60 elements were then known, left spaces and predicted the properties of the 'missing' elements. Today, this *Periodic Table* is complete and slightly more complex.

Elements may be grouped together on the basis of having the same number of electrons in their outermost shell. For example, all the halogens—fluorine, chlorine, bromine, iodine, and the unstable radioactive member, astatine—have seven electrons in their outermost shell. Elements can also be arranged in horizontal rows or periods. All the elements in a period have the same number of electron-shells, but they themselves may differ widely chemically because they have different numbers of electrons in the outermost shell. For example, in the third period we find the highly reactive soft alkali metal sodium, plus aluminium, sulphur, the reactive gas chlorine and the inert gas argon.

In broader terms elements may be classified as being rare gases, electropositive metals, non-metals, transition metals, the rare earth elements and the actinides or radioactive elements—uranium, thorium, plutonium and so on. The transition metals are interesting as they have two unfilled electron shells—normally elements only have the outermost shell unfilled—and this gives them the ability to form a wider range of compounds. Iron, chromium, and copper are transition metals.

Symbols are widely used in chemistry. The Swedish chemist Berzelius first suggested our short-hand way of writing down elements and their compounds. The symbol for an element is usually an abbreviation of its present or original name: P for phosphorus, Zn for zinc, but Fe for iron from the Latin *ferrum*, and Na for sodium from the Latin *natrium*. The subscript numbers in a molecule or compound represent the numbers of atoms of each element present.

A molecule of water, whose symbol is H_2O, has two hydrogen atoms and one oxygen atom. Sulphuric acid, H_2SO_4, has two hydrogen atoms, one sulphur atom and four oxygen atoms. This universal chemical shorthand comes in very useful when describing chemical reactions. For example, when dilute sulphuric acid is poured on to a small piece of zinc, hydrogen gas bubbles off and the zinc dissolves, forming zinc sulphate, or, as in this equation:

$$Zn + H_2SO_4 = ZnSO_4 + H_2 \uparrow$$

The arrow pointing up indicates a gas, while one pointing down would indicate a precipitate (or insoluble solid) forming in a solution, rather than the new compound remaining in solution.

Esso

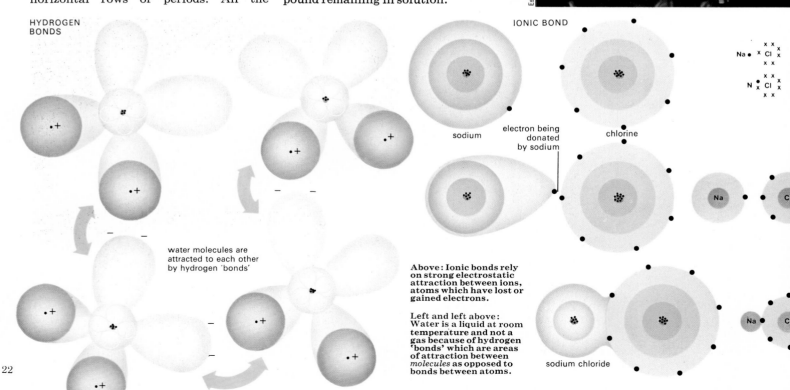

HYDROGEN BONDS

water molecules are attracted to each other by hydrogen 'bonds'

IONIC BOND

Na · ⨯ Cl ⨯⨯⨯
N ⨯ Cl ⨯⨯⨯

sodium

electron being donated by sodium

chlorine

Na · Cl

Above: Ionic bonds rely on strong electrostatic attraction between ions, atoms which have lost or gained electrons.

Left and left above: Water is a liquid at room temperature and not a gas because of hydrogen 'bonds' which are areas of attraction between *molecules* as opposed to bonds between atoms.

Na · Cl

sodium chloride

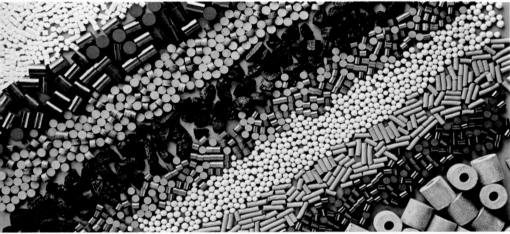

Valency and bonds

When elements form compounds the *valency* or combining power of one element with another is determined by the number of atoms of hydrogen that will combine with one atom of the element. For example, oxygen has a valency of two because two atoms of hydrogen combine with it to form water. But the full story of combining or bonding is more complex than this. Atoms tend to be able to combine by forming the stable inert gas configuration of eight electrons, and there are two ways of doing this.

In an *ionic* or electrovalent bond, such as that formed by sodium chloride, the sodium atom readily loses its single outer electron. This leaves it with a proton in the nucleus which is now unneutralized as it no longer has a negatively charged electron to balance its own positive charge, and the sodium atom then becomes a special type of atom—a positive *ion*, or *cation*. Chlorine, however, has seven outermost electrons and willingly accepts another to achieve the stable eight electron state, becoming a negative ion, or *anion*. The sodium ion, Na^+, and the chloride ion, Cl^-, are held together by a strong electrostatic attraction. Ionic compounds are usually solids, the ions being packed together in a stable pattern called a crystal lattice.

Apart from losing and gaining electrons, bonds may be formed by sharing electrons between atoms. These are known as *covalent* bonds. For example, in the gas methane, CH_4, the carbon atom has four electrons in its outermost shell and each hydrogen atom has one electron. By mutual sharing of electrons each hydrogen atom can have the stable two electron state, while the carbon ends up with a stable eight electron state. Sometimes more than one electron pair is shared between atoms, forming a 'double' bond or sometimes a 'triple' bond, as in acetylene. Both these bonds are less stable than a single bond. Covalent bonding is widespread in carbon compounds found in plants and animals. Some elements are also covalent bonded: oxygen, O_2; nitrogen, N_2; and chlorine, Cl_2. Only covalent compounds or elements form these discrete particles of two or more atoms known as *molecules*.

All chemical bonds have two things in common; they arise from a stable arrangement of electrons around the atoms involved, and they result in more stable 'low energy' compounds being formed. This means that energy is required to break the bonds, but when they are being formed it is released, often as heat. For example, a tiny piece of sodium dropped on to water vigorously reacts with it to give the compound sodium hydroxide, and much heat is produced in the process of forming bonds.

Chemical reactions often only occur at high temperatures; copper reacts with oxygen to give black copper oxide only if they are heated together. However, extra heat is produced as the result of bond formation between the copper and the oxygen. Thus, to recover pure copper from its oxide, that much energy would need to be absorbed before the bonds could be broken. It is this release of energy during chemical bonding that provides the heat when fossil fuels are burned. Indeed, knowledge of such chemical changes can provide chemists with the key to the search for new materials.

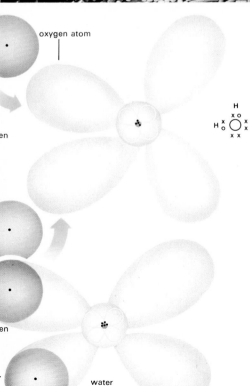

oxygen atom

en

en

water

Left and below: Covalent bonds link atoms in molecules by sharing electrons, to give strange shapes where orbitals overlap. In water the two hydrogen nuclei are held at a 105° angle, keeping one side of the molecule positive and the other negative, which is useful for hydrogen bonding. Below, the gas methane.

Above: A selection of catalysts used in the oil and chemical industries. Chemical reactions are often difficult to get started or very slow, so to speed things up catalysts are used. They do not chemically change themselves. The black coal-like lumps are iron oxide, used for making ammonia from hydrogen and nitrogen.

COVALENT BONDS

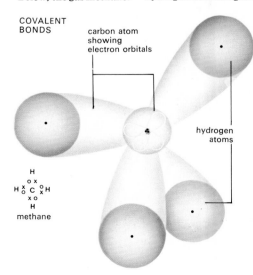

carbon atom showing electron orbitals

hydrogen atoms

methane

23

Elements
of Nature

The usefulness of the various naturally-occurring chemical elements varies almost as much as their chemical and physical properties. Some, such as the gases oxygen and nitrogen, are essential to living creatures, while others, such as astatine, have little or no practical importance. This article deals with the nature and properties of some of the most important elements and the ways in which they are used.

Oxygen and nitrogen

Oxygen (O) and nitrogen (N) are the two main constituents of the earth's atmosphere. Pure dry air contains, by volume, approximately 21 per cent oxygen and 78 per cent nitrogen, the remainder being a mixture of other gases, including hydrogen and inert gases such as argon and helium.

In addition to the vast amount of oxygen within the atmosphere, it is also the most abundant element within the crust of the earth, where it occurs in combination with other elements such as iron, silicon and aluminium. Water, which covers over 70 per cent of the earth's surface, is made up of oxygen in combination with hydrogen.

Oxygen is an *electronegative* element, accepting electrons from other elements (which, in giving electrons away, are thus *electropositive*) when it combines with them to form compounds. Pure oxygen can be obtained in small amounts by heating certain of these compounds, such as potassium chlorate and manganese dioxide, but on a commercial scale it is extracted from air.

Oxygen and water are both essential to living creatures, but oxygen also has many industrial uses. One of the most important is in cutting and welding metals, where it is burned together with acetylene gas to produce a very hot flame which melts the metals. It is also used in making iron and steel, where it is used to help burn away impurities in the molten metal. Liquid oxygen is used in rocket engines, where it is burned with a second fuel, such as kerosene, to produce the powerful stream of exhaust gases which drive the rocket.

Nitrogen, the principal constituent of air, occurs in combined form as Chile saltpetre (sodium nitrate, $NaNO_3$) and, in addition, it is a constituent element of proteins and so is a part of all living organisms.

Nitrogen is a very stable, non-reactive gas at normal temperatures, but at high temperatures the bonds holding the atoms within the nitrogen molecules break up, and the freed nitrogen atoms become very reactive. In a pure form it can be obtained either by heating suitable nitrogen-containing compounds or by extracting it from air.

Nitrogen is prepared industrially by the fractional distillation of liquefied air. The boiling point of liquid oxygen is 90 °K (−183 °C) and that of liquid nitrogen is 78 °K (−195 °C), so the two gases can easily be separated by controlling the temperature of the liquid air so that the nitrogen 'boils off' leaving the oxygen behind. One of the most important uses of nitrogen compounds is in the manufacture of fertilizers, while others are used in making explosives. Liquid nitrogen is widely used as a coolant.

Silicon

After oxygen, silicon (Si) is the next most abundant element in the earth's crust. It occurs mainly as *silica* (SiO_2), which is the main constituent of sand, and as metallic silicates such as $K_2Al_2Si_6O_{16}$, a compound of potassium, aluminium, silicon and oxygen which is one of the group of rocks known as *feldspars*. Silicon is also found in *kaolinite* ($Al_2O_3.2SiO_2.2H_2O$), which is one of the main ingredients of china clay.

Silica occurs in either crystalline or *amorphous* (noncrystalline) forms. A good example of crystalline silica is quartz, while the precious stone opal is composed of amorphous silica.

Silica is the main ingredient of glass and silicon itself is used in many important synthetic materials such as synthetic rubbers. These *silicone rubbers* are more resistant to chemical attack than other rubbers. The enormous range of silicon-based products includes oils, greases, waxes and polishes, and solid resins such as those used for electrical insulating materials.

Sand, which is mostly silica, is used in large quantities for making concrete and mortar. *Kieselguhr* or *diatomaceous earth* is a type of silica formed in the earth from the skeletons of tiny organisms called diatoms. It is used in making fireproof cements and clays, as a filtering medium,

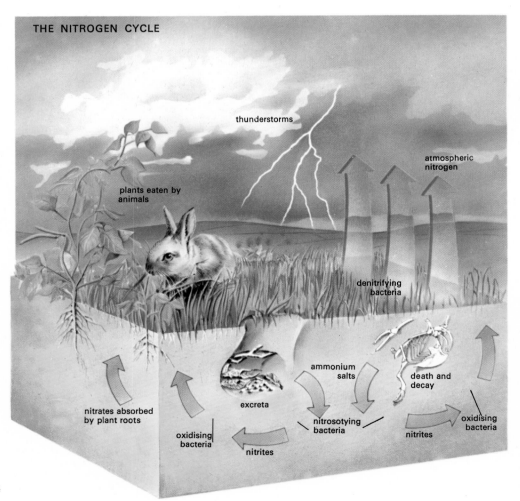

THE NITROGEN CYCLE

thunderstorms

atmospheric nitrogen

plants eaten by animals

denitrifying bacteria

ammonium salts

death and decay

excreta

nitrates absorbed by plant roots

oxidising bacteria

nitrites

nitrosotying bacteria

nitrites

oxidising bacteria

Paul Brierley

Left: The *nitrogen cycle*, the natural circulation of nitrogen compounds between plants, animals, the soil and the air. Nitrogen from the atmosphere is converted into various nitrogen compounds within the soil by the action of bacteria living in the roots of plants such as peas and beans. In addition, some nitrogen compounds are formed during thunderstorms. Nitrogen compounds in the soil are absorbed by plants, and then by animals which eat the plants, being returned to the soil in excreta or by the decay of dead animals and plants within the soil. Some nitrogen is returned to the atmosphere by the action of denitrifying bacteria.

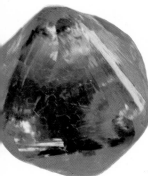

Left: Diamond, one of the allotropes of carbon, is the hardest substance found in nature. Carbon will only crystallize into diamond at very high temperatures and pressures. Synthetic diamonds are now produced in large numbers, using apparatus capable of producing over 90,000 times atmospheric pressure at over 2,000°C (3,630°F), developed in 1953.

Below: The hardness of a diamond is due to the way in which the atoms are arranged within the crystal structure.

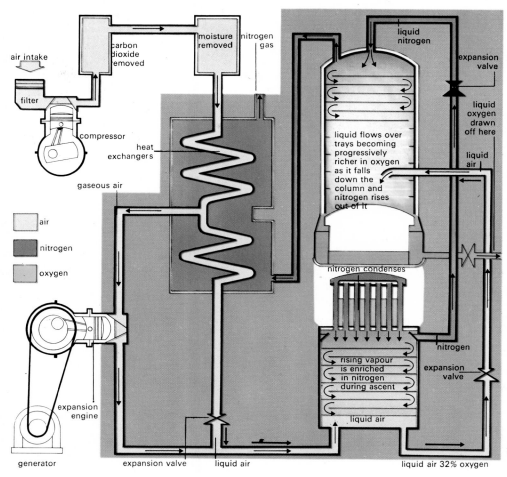

air intake

carbon dioxide removed

moisture removed

nitrogen gas

liquid nitrogen

expansion valve

liquid oxygen drawn off here

filter

compressor

heat exchangers

gaseous air

liquid flows over trays becoming progressively richer in oxygen as it falls down the column and nitrogen rises out of it

liquid air

air

nitrogen

oxygen

expansion engine

nitrogen condenses

nitrogen

rising vapour is enriched in nitrogen during ascent

expansion valve

liquid air

generator

expansion valve

liquid air

liquid air 32% oxygen

Right: Graphite, the second main form of carbon, has its atoms bonded together in layers. These layers can slide easily over each other, and this gives graphite its soft, slippery nature.

Left: A synthetic crystal of quartz, a form of silica (silicon dioxide, SiO_2). Silica occurs widely in nature, one of the commonest forms being sand.

Below: The rate of chemical decomposition of radio active compounds is reduced at low temperatures, and so they are stored in liquid nitrogen. This keeps them at below 78°K (−195°C), which is the boiling point of liquid nitrogen.

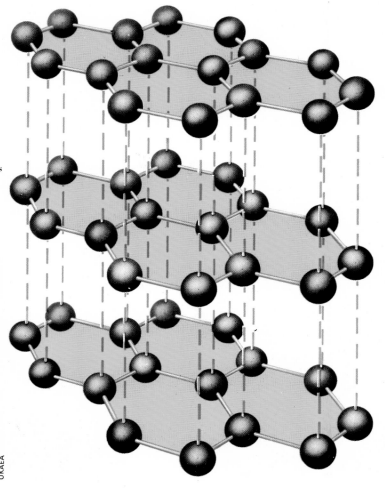

UKAEA

Above: Oxygen and nitrogen are obtained by the distillation of liquid air. Air is compressed and passed through absorbent materials which take away the carbon dioxide and moisture, then it is cooled in the heat exchangers. Next it is expanded so that its temperature drops further and it liquefies. Some of this expansion takes place in an expansion engine, which drives a generator to provide some electricity for the plant. In the distillation column the nitrogen boils out of the liquid first, as it has a lower boiling point than oxygen. The remaining liquid is almost pure oxygen.

and in the manufacture of explosives. Dynamite, for example, is made by absorbing nitroglycerine into a keiselguhr base.

Carbon

Compared with the great amounts of oxygen and silicon within the earth's crust, the amount of carbon (C) within it is very small—it comprises only about 0.3 per cent of the crust. This relatively small quantity, however, belies its extreme importance to living creatures. The molecules that form the basis of life, such as RNA and DNA, are based on carbon, and animals obtain their energy by the oxidation of the *carbohydrates* (compounds of carbon, hydrogen and oxygen) contained in the food they eat.

Carbon is also important to industry, being the basis of fossil fuels such as coal, and occurring in combination with hydrogen to form the *hydrocarbon* fuels such as oil and natural gas.

There are two naturally-occurring forms of crystalline carbon, both of which are pure carbon despite the great differences between them. These two forms or *allotropes* of carbon are diamond, a clear, very hard crystal, and graphite, a soft, smooth, black substance.

25

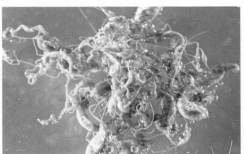

James Blake

Left: These three pictures show three of the allotropes of sulphur. The main allotropes are *rhombic* sulphur, which is in the form of octahedral crystals, and *monoclinic* sulphur, shown here in the top picture, which has needle-like crystals. The centre picture shows *plastic* sulphur, obtained by melting sulphur and pouring it into cold water where it cools into an amorphous (non-crystalline) form. The bottom picture is of an amorphous form known as 'flowers of sulphur'.

Below: Coloured firework flames are produced by the addition of various compounds to the basic gunpowder mixture. Brilliant white flame is produced by potassium, sulphur, arsenic or antimony compounds or by magnesium powder. Red flames are produced by strontium and lithium salts, green by barium salts, yellow by sodium salts, and blue by copper salts. Lithium, sodium and potassium belong to a group of elements called the *alkali metals*.

The differences between diamond and graphite are due to the way in which the carbon atoms arrange themselves within the crystal structures. In diamond, the atoms are arranged in a tetrahedral pattern in which the bonding between the atoms is very strong in every direction. The atoms in graphite, however, are arranged in sheets or layers, each layer being a network of hexagonal patterns of atoms. The bonding within these flat layers is strong, but the forces holding the layers together are weak and so the layers can easily slide over each other.

The structure of diamond accounts for its hardness and transparency, and also for the fact that it will not conduct electricity—its electrons are held tightly within it. On the other hand the ability of graphite layers to slide over each other gives this form of carbon its characteristic softness and also makes it a good lubricant. It is a good conductor of electricity and has many applications in the electrical industry. Another very common use of graphite is for the 'lead' of pencils.

Carbon and its compounds are so important that a whole branch of chemistry is devoted to the study and uses of these substances. This is known as *organic chemistry*, its name deriving from the role that carbon plays in the structure and life of plants and animals.

Sulphur

Sulphur (S), a hard, yellow substance, has been known for over 3,000 years. It was widely used by the Mediterranean civilizations in various medicines and the sulphur dioxide (SO_2) fumes given off by burning sulphur have been used for

Left: Incendiary bombs often use a material called *thermite*, which is a mixture of magnesium, iron oxide and aluminium powders that reaches a temperature of 2,500°C (4,500°F) when it ignites. Napalm, an incendiary oil, contains petrol, polystyrene and white phosphorus.

Below: Sodium, one of the alkali metals, is so intensely reactive with air or water that it must be stored under paraffin oil. If it is exposed to air it rapidly oxidizes to sodium oxide, and if it comes into contact with water it reacts violently to produce sodium hydroxide and hydrogen gas.

Right: The violent reaction created when a piece of sodium metal is placed on a wet surface. The hydrogen gas given off is ignited by the heat produced during the reaction. When this reactive metal is combined with the poisonous gas chlorine, the result is harmless common salt.

centuries for bleaching cloth.

Deposits of pure sulphur occur in many areas, including the southern USA and Sicily. It also occurs in combined states such as the sulphides of zinc (ZnS), lead (PbS) and iron (FeS_2), and sulphates such as *gypsum* ($CaSO_4.2H_2O$, hydrated calcium sulphate). Sulphur may also be present in crude oil.

The principal industrial use of sulphur is for making sulphuric acid (H_2SO_4), which is used in the manufacture of fertilizers, paints, detergents, plastics, synthetic fibres and dyes. Sulphur is also used in making rubber during the *vulcanization* process which makes the rubber stronger and more durable, and many drugs, such as the antibiotics penicillin and sulphonamides, contain sulphur compounds.

The halogens

The name 'halogen' comes from the Greek words meaning 'salt producer', as these elements will readily combine with other elements to form salts. The original members of this group were chlorine (Cl), bromine (Br) and iodine (I), which occur as salts in sea water, and later on the elements fluorine (F) and astatine (At) were added to the list. Fluorine and chlorine are gases at room temperature, bromine is a liquid and iodine and astatine are solids.

The chief characteristic of the halogens is the fact that they each have a valency of 1, their outer electron shells being one electron short of the number needed to give them the stable eight electron configuration.

Their compounds are known as the halides, and those formed with the more electropositive metals are held together by ionic bonding. Halides formed with non-metallic elements and the less electropositive metals have covalent bonding.

The halogens are highly electronegative, having a great affinity for electrons and readily forming negative ions. This is what makes the halogens so reactive. Their high electronegativity also makes them powerful oxidizing agents; it is this

property which makes chlorine, for example, effective as a bleach and as a disinfectant.

The most common chlorine compound is ordinary salt, sodium chloride (NaCl), and other chlorine compounds are used in plastics (polyvinyl chloride, pvc), weedkillers, insecticides and drycleaning fluids. The bromine compound silver bromide is one of the light-sensitive compounds used in photographic film, and ethylene bromide is added to petrol to prevent lead (from the anti-knocking additive tetraethyl lead) from building up within the engine.

Iodine is widely used as an antiseptic and within the human body small quantities of iodine are essential for the proper functioning of the thyroid gland. Fluorine is the most active chemical element and one of its best-known uses is in the production of compounds used to make teeth more resistant to decay. Other fluorine compounds are used as refrigerants, aerosol propellants, firefighting chemicals and anaesthetics. Non-stick pan coatings are made of the fluorine-based plastic called *polytetrafluoroethylene* (PTFE). Astatine is the least important of the halogens and also in fact one of the least important of all elements, as its most stable isotope is very short-lived, having a half-life of only 8.3 hours.

Alkaline earth metals

The alkaline earth metals are a group of very reactive metals, namely beryllium (Be), magnesium (Mg), calcium (Ca), strontium (Sr), barium (Ba) and radium (Ra). The most important are calcium, which makes up about 4 per cent of the

earth's crust, and magnesium, which accounts for about 2 per cent of the crust. Being so reactive, none of the alkaline metals occurs in an uncombined state.

The chief sources of calcium are calcium carbonate ($CaCO_3$), which occurs in many forms such as limestone, marble and calcite; gypsum and fluorspar (CaF_2). Natural chalk is a form of calcium carbonate, but the manufactured chalk used for writing on blackboards is calcium sulphate ($CaSO_4$). Calcium is an important constituent of bones and teeth, but the metal itself is not widely used in industry in its uncombined form. Calcium compounds, however, have many applications, a good example being limestone, which is used in cement making. Limestone is also used in steelmaking, where it acts as a flux which absorbs impurities from the molten metal.

Two important ores of magnesium are *dolomite* ($MgCO_3.CaCO_3$), a combination of magnesium and calcium carbonates, and *carnallite* ($KCl.MgCl_2.6H_2O$), potassium magnesium chloride, which is also an important source of potassium salts. *Chlorophyll*, the green colouring material in leaves, is a mixture of two substances known as chlorophyll-a and chlorophyll-b. These are complex compounds of carbon, hydrogen, oxygen, nitrogen and magnesium, their respective chemical formulae being $C_{55}H_{72}O_5N_4Mg$ and $C_{55}H_{70}O_6N_4Mg$. Magnesium also occurs in sea water, constituting about 0.5 per cent of it by weight.

Magnesium compounds are used in medicines, and the very light but strong magnesium alloys have many applications in the engineering industries.

27

Organic Chemistry

Organic chemistry is the branch of chemistry that deals with almost all the compounds that contain carbon. The exceptions, such as the carbon oxides and sulphides and the carbonates of metals, are considered to be chemically more similar to *inorganic* (non-carbon) compounds.

Organic chemicals are so named because those discovered first occurred in living organisms, and it was thought that they were the result of the action of some mysterious 'vital force' produced within living cells. This assumption gave rise to the belief that organic compounds could not be produced synthetically, as the necessary vital force would not be present.

The division of chemistry into organic and inorganic branches was the result of the work of the Swedish chemist Jons Jacob Berzelius (1779-1848). He believed in the vital force theory, which persisted throughout the first half of the nineteenth century. The first opposition to this theory had come in 1828 when Friedrich Wöhler (1800-1882) synthesized an organic compound known as urea ($H_2N.CO.NH_2$) from ammonium cyanate ($NH_4.CNO$), but the final blow to the theory did not come until 1860, when Pierre Berthelot (1827-1907) published a detailed treatise on the synthesis of organic compounds.

In the early days of organic chemistry the organic compounds were divided into two main groups, the *aliphatics* (from the Greek word *aleiphar*, meaning 'fat'), which were related to fatty substances, and the *aromatics*, which were related to the aromatic oils and spices (from the Greek word *aroma*, meaning 'spice'). These two main groups are today further divided into several smaller groups.

Aromatic compounds are derived from the benzene ring structure of six carbon atoms, whereas most aliphatics have straight or branched chains. *Alicyclic* compounds are aliphatics which are based on rings instead of chains.

Aliphatic compounds

The aliphatic group includes the aliphatic hydrocarbons called *alkanes*, *alkenes* and *alkynes*, which are made up of carbon and hydrogen, and the compounds of carbon, hydrogen and oxygen known as *alcohols*, *aldehydes*, *ketones*, *carboxylic acids* and *carbohydrates*. It also includes more complex substances containing additional elements such as nitrogen, sulphur and phosphorus, such as the amino acids and proteins which are fundamental constituents of living matter.

The alkanes, also known as the paraffin hydrocarbons, have the general formula C_nH_{2n+2}, where n represents a whole number. Thus the gases methane and ethane have the formulae CH_4 and C_2H_6 respectively. One of the most important sources of paraffin hydrocarbons is crude oil, which is a complex mixture of many different hydrocarbons.

Among the range of hydrocarbons yielded by fractional distillation of oil are the light gaseous ones such as methane and propane (C_3H_8); light liquids such as petrols (with from five to ten carbon

Above and above right: A fifteenth-century distillery and a modern whisky distillery. The first step in the production of spirits is the fermentation of a fruit or cereal base, during which yeasts convert sugars into alcohol. The weak alcohol solution thus obtained is then heated in a still so that the alcohol boils away, leaving the water behind. The alcohol condenses at the top of the still and runs down the outlet pipe.

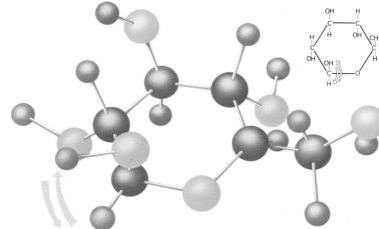

Right: A model of a molecule of the type of glucose called β-D-glucose. The carbon atoms are shown in black, the oxygen in red, and the hydrogen in blue. Glucose is a *monosaccharide*.

Above: A laboratory test to determine the viscosity or thickness of a motor oil. The most widely used lubricating oils are mineral oils, derived from crude oil, but in certain applications vegetable oils such as castor and palm oils are often used, either on their own or added to mineral oils.

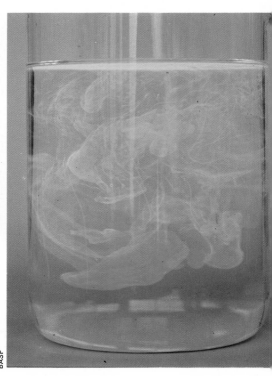

Right: The bright green dye uranin, first discovered in 1871, is an aromatic compound often used in cosmetics and for colouring bath salt tablets. A closely related dye called Eosin FA is used for making red ink, and it is also used to give a pink tint to the salt used for clearing ice from roads.

atoms per molecule); paraffin oils (kerosenes) with 10 to 16 carbon atoms; gas oils (C_{14} to C_{20}) and lubricating oils (C_{20} to C_{70}).

An important difference between the alkanes, alkenes and alkynes is the number of hydrogen atoms each contains in comparison with the number of carbon atoms in it. The alkanes are *saturated* hydrocarbons, that is, the carbon atoms are combined with the maximum possible numbers of hydrogen atoms (ie 'saturated' with them) and are joined to each other by single bonds. Alkenes, on the other hand, are *unsaturated;* the carbon atoms are not combined with the maximum number of hydrogen atoms and are joined by double bonds. The alkenes have a general formula C_nH_{2n} and include butylene (C_4H_8) ethylene (C_2H_4) and propylene (C_3H_6). The most important alkene is ethylene, which is used in the making of ethylene glycol (antifreeze) and the plastics polystyrene, pvc and polythene.

The alkynes are highly unsaturated, with relatively few hydrogen atoms per carbon atom and triple bonding between the carbon atoms. The alkynes have a general formula C_nH_{2n-2}, the most important alkyne being the gas acetylene (C_2H_2). Acetylene is highly reactive and one of its chief uses is in oxy-acetylene welding and cutting equipment.

Alcohols, another important group of aliphatic compounds, are formed by joining a *hydroxyl group* (consisting of one oxygen atom and one hydrogen atom) to an *alkyl radical.* Alkyl radicals are derived from the alkanes; they are essentially alkanes with one of the hydrogen atoms removed and thus have a general formula C_nH_{2n+1} (the alkanes being C_nH_{2n+2}). The names of the radicals are formed by changing the -ane of the alkane to -yl, for example methane's radical is methyl, and that of ethane is ethyl. The names of the alcohols are obtained by changing the final -e of the alkanes to -ol; thus we have methanol (methyl alcohol, CH_3OH), ethanol (ethyl alcohol, C_2H_5OH) and propanol (propyl alcohol, C_3H_7OH).

Ethanol is the alcohol found in alcoholic drinks and it is mixed with methanol, pryidine (C_5H_5N), petrol and a violet dye to make methylated spirits.

The oxidation of alcohols produces two further groups of compounds, the aldehydes and the ketones, which are both closely related. Further oxidation of aldehydes or ketones produces carboxylic acids. The general formula for aldehydes is $C_nH_{2n}O$, which is the same as for ketones. Despite this, however, the atoms of aldehydes are arranged differently within their respective molecules. Both contain a *carbonyl group*, comprising a carbon atom and an oxygen atom, but in aldehydes the carbonyl group is attached to a hydrogen atom and to an alkyl, while in the ketones it is attached to two similar alkyl groups or to two different alkyls.

The simplest aldehyde, and one of the most useful, is formaldehyde, $H.CHO$. When dissolved in water it forms formalin, which is used to preserve biological specimens. Formaldehyde is also an important germicide and an ingredient of several types of plastic. Other aldehydes are chloral, CCl_3CHO, used in making DDT, and benzaldehyde, C_6H_5CHO. which is used as a solvent and is the main constituent of oil of bitter almonds.

The best known ketone produced by the oxidation of alcohol is probably the solvent acetone, CH_3COCH_3. Methyl ethyl ketone, $CH_3COC_2H_5$, and methyl isobutyl ketone, $(CH_3)_2CHCH_2COCH_3$, are also used as solvents.

Carbohydrates

One of the most important groups of aliphatic organic compounds is that known as the *carbohydrates*, which includes such substances as sugars, starches and plant fibres. Their name is derived from the original idea that they were simply *hydrates* of carbon, that is, carbon atoms combined with water and having the general formula $C_x(H_2O)_y$. This idea was later found to be an oversimplification, as the molecules consist of chains of carbon atoms with the oxygen and hydrogen atoms arranged around them.

Carbohydrates, in common with most organic compounds, will form *isomers*. When compounds are composed of molecules containing large numbers of atoms, it is possible for these atoms to arrange themselves in many different ways within the molecules. This means that two or more compounds, with different properties, can have the same molecular formula; these compounds are known as isomers.

For example, the carbohydrate glucose, $C_6H_{12}O_6$, is one of 16 possible compounds with that formula, although only three occur naturally. Glucose is a *monosaccharide*, which is the simplest form of carbohydrate. *Disaccharides* are formed when two monosaccharides combine,

Above: The aromatic compound Rhodamine Base B Extra is a colourless powder, but when it comes into contact with the weak hydrochloric acid in perspiration it becomes Rhodamine FB, which is red. It can therefore be used as a thief detector, as it will dye the skin of anyone handling objects coated with it.

Below: Plastics are composed of heavy organic molecules known as polymers, networks or long chains of atoms built up by joining together smaller, simpler molecules known as monomers. The chemical process of forming a polymer from its component monomers is known as polymerization.

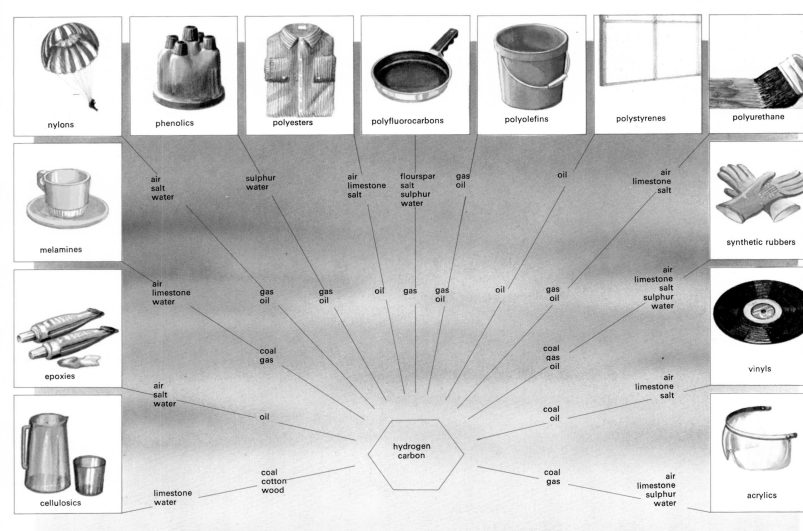

nylons

phenolics

polyesters

polyfluorocarbons

polyolefins

polystyrenes

polyurethane

melamines

epoxies

cellulosics

synthetic rubbers

vinyls

acrylics

air
salt
water

sulphur
water

air
limestone
salt

flourspar
salt
sulphur
water

gas
oil

oil

air
limestone
salt

air
limestone
water

gas
oil

gas
oil

oil

gas

gas
oil

oil

gas
oil

air
limestone
salt
sulphur
water

coal
gas

coal
gas
oil

air
salt
water

oil

coal
oil

air
limestone
salt

hydrogen
carbon

coal
cotton
wood

coal
gas

air
limestone
sulphur
water

limestone
water

sulphur

cotton

wood

water

coal

limestone

oil

gas

flourspar

salt

Yardley

Yardley

losing one water molecule between them. *Polysaccharides* are compounds with very large molecules formed by the combination of several monosaccharides.

One common carbohydrate is cellulose, a polysaccharide, which is the main constituent of plant cell walls and thus of plant products such as cotton and wood. It is also used in making plastics such as celluloid and Cellophane.

Starches are also polysaccharides; they are important constituents of many foods, including potatoes, vegetables and cereals. Sugars include glucose and the disaccharides sucrose (cane, beet and maple sugars) and lactose (milk sugar). Glucose and another monosaccharide, fructose (fruit sugar) are constituents of invert syrup and honey.

Aromatic compounds
The second main group of organic compounds are the aromatics, substances which are very important to many industries such as the plastics, drugs, and dye industries. The aromatic compounds are based on the compound benzene, C_6H_6, which can be thought of as having its carbon atoms arranged in a hexagon with alternate single and double bonds between them. There is a hydrogen atom bonded to each of the carbon atoms of this *benzene ring*, and the aromatic compounds are formed by replacing one or more of these hydrogen atoms with atoms of other elements. The main sources of benzene and its derivatives are coal tar and petroleum.

Chemically benzene is not very reactive, nor does it easily form addition products in the way that ethylene does, but suitable industrial processes have been developed and benzene has become the starting compound for a great range of important organic substances.

One of these processes is *halogenation*, which involves substituting the hydrogen atoms of the benzene for atoms of a halogen, such as chlorine or bromine. When chlorine is used, the compound chlorobenzene, C_6H_5Cl, is formed. This is a useful industrial solvent, and it is also

used in drug manufacture.

Alkylation of the benzene ring involves attaching an alkyl radical, for example $-CH_3$ or $-C_2H_5$, to the ring in place of a hydrogen atom. The radical is called the *side chain*, the attachment being formed by one of the carbon atoms of the side chain. The compounds obtained by alkylation are good starting points for the formation of more complex molecules.

Toluene, $C_6H_5CH_3$, is the simplest alkylation compound and it is used as a solvent for gums, resins and plastics. It is also used in the manufacture of the high explosive TNT, which is trinitrotoluene $C_6H_2.CH_3.(NO_2)_3$.

Xylene, $C_6H_4(CH_3)_2$, is synthesized from toluene. It is a solvent of rubber and plastics and it is also used in making synthetic fabrics such as Terylene.

Nitration involves substituting hydrogen atoms of the benzene ring by a corresponding number of *nitro-* ($-NO_2$) *groups*. One of the most important nitration products is nitrobenzene, $C_6H_5NO_2$, which can then be reacted with hydrogen to make aniline, $C_6H_5NH_2$. Aniline is an important chemical in the manufacture of such things as plastics, dyes and drugs.

Carboxylic acids
Carboxylic acids may be formed from either aliphatic or aromatic substances. Their chief characteristic is that they contain *carboxyl* (COOH) *groups*, which are made up from a carbonyl (CO) and a hydroxyl (OH) group. The simplest carboxylic acid is formic acid, HCOOH, which is found in ants and is also what gives stinging nettles their sting. Other aliphatic carboxylic acids are acetic acid, CH_3COOH, the main ingredient of vinegar, and the *fatty acids* such as palmitic acid, $C_{15}H_{31}COOH$, and stearic acid, $C_{17}H_{35}COOH$, which occur in natural oils such as tallow and palm oil.

Among the aromatic carboxylic acids, benzoic acid, C_6H_5COOH, is used in dyes, medicines and as a food preservative, and various derivatives of para-aminobenzoic acid are used as local anaesthetics, for example Novocaine.

31

Harnessing Power

The sun radiates energy at a rate of
380 million million million megawatts.
The energy output from this solar
furnace at Alburquerque, New Mexico
– one of the largest in the world –
is 5 megawatts.

Hydraulics

One of the simplest methods of transmitting power is by using a liquid under pressure, and any device operated by this means is a form of hydraulic mechanism. The theory of hydraulics is based on two principles. The first is that liquids are virtually incompressible even when subjected to very high pressures and the second, which was discovered by the French scientist Blaise Pascal in the seventeenth century, is that pressure applied to an enclosed liquid is transmitted with undiminished force in every direction.

To calculate the pressure exerted by a force, the value of the force is divided by the area on which it is acting. (Force is measured in such units as *Newtons*. One Newton or 1 N is the force required to move a 1 kg mass with an acceleration of 1 m/sec^2. The *pound-force* is also used and is the force exerted by gravity on a 1 lb mass.) Pressure can thus be expressed as Newtons per square metre (N/m^2) or pounds-force per square inch (or psi). For example, if two cylinders, each containing a piston, are connected by a pipe filled with a liquid, a downward force on one piston will create pressure which will be transmitted through the liquid to the other piston, exerting an upward force on it. If the area of the first piston is 10 cm^2 and the force on it is 10 N, the pressure in the liquid will be 1 N/cm^2. This pressure will be transmitted to the other cylinder, so the pressure under the second piston will also be 1 N/cm^2.

The pressure on the second piston is the same regardless of its area, a fact which leads to the astonishing power potential of hydraulic mechanisms. By making the area of the second piston ten times that of the first one, any force acting on the first one produces ten times that force on the second one. Thus if the area of the second piston is 100 cm^2, a pressure of 1 N/cm^2 acting on it will push it upwards with a force of 100 N (calculated by multiplying the pressure in the liquid by the area of the piston).

Some research into the principles of hydraulics was carried out by Archimedes as early as 250 BC, but it was not until the late eighteenth century that the first hydraulic mechanism was made. This was a hydraulic press built by Joseph Bramah, which consisted of a large cylinder containing a piston to which a ramrod (or ram) was attached. A small hand-operated pump was used to pump water, under pressure, into the cylinder. The water drove the piston along the cylinder, pushing the ramrod against the material to be pressed.

Since that time the use of hydraulic machinery has expanded rapidly to every industry, chiefly because of the simplicity of the components required and because the liquid can be carried through small bore (narrow) piping to operate mechanisms at a distance from the source of pressure. This latter feature is a great advantage on aircraft and ships. Water was used in the early hydraulic mechanisms, which is why they are still called 'hydraulic', from the Greek words *hudor* (water) and *aulos* (a pipe). Light mineral oils or castor-based oils are now used as the liquid because of their low freezing point and their lubricating properties.

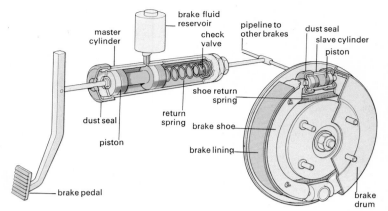

HYDRAULIC DRUM BRAKE

brake fluid reservoir — master cylinder — check valve — pipeline to other brakes — dust seal — slave cylinder — piston — shoe return spring — dust seal — return spring — piston — brake shoe — brake lining — brake pedal — brake drum

Left and below: One of the simplest hydraulic systems in everyday use is that used to operate the brakes of a car. A master cylinder, primed with hydraulic fluid from a small reservoir, is connected by tubing to a slave cylinder at each of the four wheel brakes. The master cylinder contains a piston which is operated by the footbrake pedal. When the pedal is depressed, pressure is created in the fluid, and this pressure is transmitted to the slave cylinders at the wheels, where it pushes on a pair of pistons. In drum brakes, the pistons force the brake shoes against the inside of the drum. In disc brakes, the pistons are forced inwards to make pads grip the brake disc.

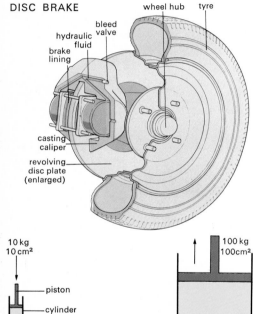

DISC BRAKE

wheel hub — tyre — bleed valve — hydraulic fluid — brake lining — casting caliper — revolving disc plate (enlarged)

10 kg 10 cm² — piston — cylinder — hydraulic fluid — pressure 1 kg/cm² — 100 kg 100 cm²

Above: This drawing shows how a hydraulic system can multiply a force. The large cylinder has 10 times the area of the smaller one, so a force exerted on the smaller piston will result in a force 10 times greater on the larger one. The smaller piston, however, must move 10 times as far as the larger one.

Above left: The nosewheel of the BAC TSR2 supersonic strike and reconnaissance aircraft was operated hydraulically, as are all modern retractable undercarriages. Early hydraulic undercarriages were operated by hand pumps, but these were soon replaced by high pressure pumps driven by the aircraft's engines.

Left: On this hydraulic car jack the pump is operated by pushing the handle up and down, which forces oil from the reservoir within the jack body through a non-return valve and against a piston. The piston is linked to the lifting arm, and as the pressure increases it pushes the arm upwards, tilting the car clear of the ground.

Photri

Zefa

Jacks

Most hydraulic systems now use power-driven pumps to pressurize the liquid and ensure an adequate supply, but hand pumps are still used for servicing and testing components and in case of emergency if the main supply fails. They are also used in many simple mechanisms such as the lifting jacks used to raise vehicles when a wheel is being changed.

The pump is incorporated in the jack body, the lower part of which is used as a reservoir for the liquid. The upper part of the body forms a cylinder containing a piston, and it is the upper end of the piston which is placed under the vehicle. Operation of the hand pump transfers the liquid from the reservoir to the cylinder where it is applied to the piston, lifting it and the vehicle. The jack is lowered by opening a needle valve which allows the liquid to by-pass the pump and return to its reservoir.

Pressure control

When power-driven pumps are used in hydraulic systems, additional components are required to safeguard the system against excessive rises in pressure when the mechanisms have reached the end of the operation they are performing, or when they are not being used. In these circumstances provision must be made for off-loading (disconnecting) the pumps when the maximum pressure is reached, in order to prevent overheating of the liquid and undue wear on the pumps.

The section of a hydraulic system concerned with the supply of liquid under pressure is termed the power system. In certain industrial applications it is supplied by the manufacturers as a separate unit called a *power pack*. Present day hydraulic systems operate at pressures from about 68 to 340 bar (1000 to 5000 psi) and power packs are made in various sizes to suit the pressure and volume of liquid required to operate the mechanisms. The function of the components is the same whether they are supplied as a power pack or incorporated in the hydraulic system as a whole.

Above left: Simple hand-operated hydraulic mechanisms have many applications in addition to the common hydraulic car jack. This picture shows a hydraulic roof support being positioned in a uranium mine. These roof supports work on a similar principle to the car jack, having a pump mechanism operated by a hand lever.

Above: Excavators make extensive use of hydraulic systems. The arms and buckets are operated by hydraulic rams, and hydraulic motors are used to drive the wheels or tracks. The pumps are driven by the machine's diesel engine; the selector valves are operated by levers and pedals in the driver's cab.

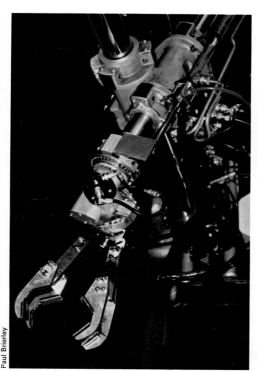
Paul Brierley

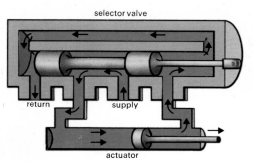

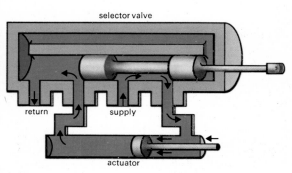

Left: Remotely controlled mechanical arms can be operated by means of hydraulic rams and motors. Devices of this type are used in automatic machine tools for transferring the workpiece from one operation to the next. They are also used for handling dangerous substances such as nuclear fuels.

Above: These two diagrams show how a selector valve controls the movement of an actuator in a hydraulic system. The position of the selector valve determines whether the actuator will move to the right, as in the upper diagram, or to the left as in the lower diagram. The arrows indicate the fluid flow.

35

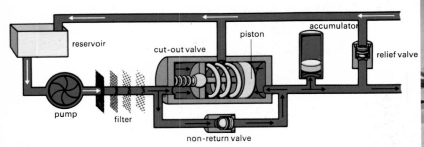

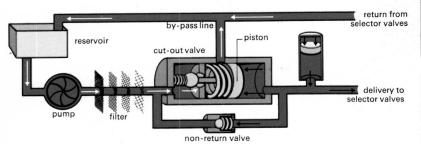

Above: Some of the complex hydraulic systems used to fold back the wings of a carrier-borne jet fighter so that it takes up less space on the ship. Aircraft use a great deal of hydraulic equipment for operating the flight control systems, such as the rudder, flaps and elevators.

Above: In a hydraulic power pack, fluid from the reservoir is pumped into the delivery line through a non-return valve, as shown in the upper diagram. If the pressure exceeds a certain value the piston in the cut-out valve moves to the left, allowing the fluid to return to the reservoir, as in the lower diagram.

Below: This 1889 photograph shows the hydraulic lift on the Eiffel Tower, Paris. During the late nineteenth century many cities installed systems of hydraulic mains, using water as the fluid, which customers used to drive machinery like lifts or cranes, in the same way as electric mains are used today.

Power systems

A typical power system or pack contains a reservoir, one or more power-driven pumps, a filter, a relief valve, an accumulator, a check valve (non-return valve) and either a cut-out valve (pressure regulator) or a pressure switch.

The reservoir contains a supply of liquid for the pumps and accommodates the returning liquid from the system. The pumps deliver liquid under pressure into the system, and the filter keeps the liquid clean. The accumulator smooths out any fluctuations in pressure. It stores a supply of liquid under pressure for emergency use or to supplement the main supply.

The cut-out valve off-loads the pumps by automatically re-routing the liquid from the pumps back to the reservoir when the maximum system pressure is reached. The non-return valve holds the pressurized liquid in the system when the pumps are off-loaded, and the relief valve is provided as an additional safeguard should the cut-out valve fail to operate.

The pressurized liquid is piped from the power system to a selector valve and then to the *actuator* or *hydraulic motor* which operates the mechanism that the system is powering. A pipe carries the returning liquid back to the reservoir.

Where pumps are driven by electric motors a pressure switch may be used to stop the motors when the maximum pressure is reached. This enables the cut-out valve to be dispensed with and saves electricity. The switch is designed to start the motors again when the pressure drops.

On aircraft and vehicles the pumps are usually driven by the engines, but on stationary equipment they are invariably driven by electric motors. The most common pumps are the *gear pump* and the *radial cylinder pump*. The gear type pump has two intermeshing gears within a close-fitting casing, which draw the liquid in through one port and force it out through another.

The radial cylinder type has an odd number of cylinders (usually from 5 to 11) arranged in a block around a driving shaft. The shaft operates pistons inside the cylinders. Oil enters through a port in the side of each cylinder and the piston forces it out through a valve in the top.

Actuators and motors

If the mechanism being driven by the hydraulic system has a reciprocating action or requires lifting or lowering, it is operated by an actuator or jack, which consists of a cylinder having a piston and ramrod. The cylinder is fixed to the main structure and the ramrod extends or retracts to operate the mechanism. In cases where continuous rotary motion is required, however, it is usual to employ a hydraulic motor. Some tracked vehicles, for example, use hydraulic motors to drive their tracks.

Hydraulic motors are similar in design to rotary pumps, except that the operation is reversed. Pumps are rotated by a mechanism to pressurize fluid, whereas motors are rotated by pressurized fluid to operate a mechanism.

Two types of motor are in common use, the *gear motor* and the *vane motor*. The gear motor has a pair of gears like those of the gear pump, and the fluid is forced between them to make them revolve and drive the mechanism, the fluid being expelled into the return line.

The vane motor has a rotor fitted with a number of movable, radially extending vanes which are spring loaded to press against the motor housing. The rotor is eccentrically mounted in the housing so that when liquid under pressure is fed through an inlet on one side of the rotor it passes between the rotor and the housing, turning the rotor as it goes. The outlet to the return pipe is on the opposite side of the rotor to the inlet.

Applications

The range of applications for hydraulic power is enormous. Hydraulic systems are used on ships, railway locomotives, aircraft, computer disc drives, earthmoving machines, refuse trucks and factory equipment. On a modern 250,000 tonne oil tanker, for example, there may be some 35 km (22 miles) of piping connecting over 100 actuators which open and close the various valves used for loading and unloading the oil. The selector valves are mounted on a huge console and each one has an indicator to show whether the valve is open or closed. This system enables the tanker to be loaded or unloaded using a minimum of personnel with the maximum of efficiency.

Energy, Work and Power

There is a considerable difference between the common usage of the words energy, work and power, and their strictly scientific definitions. The scientific meaning of the word 'energy' is founded on the idea of movement; anything that moves is said to have *kinetic* energy because of its motion. This idea is then extended to allow the definition of the word to include the capability of producing movement. An object which, because of its circumstances or position, can produce motion if required is said to have *potential* energy.

A fully-wound clockwork spring, for example, has potential energy. This is converted into kinetic energy when the spring unwinds and drives the gears of a clock mechanism or a clockwork toy.

Forms of energy

Defining energy as either potential or kinetic may at first glance appear quite straightforward. An object has kinetic energy if it is moving, and potential energy if it is capable of producing motion. In practice, however, this distinction is less clear, as in the case of a gas under pressure.

If this gas is free to push a piston it will expand and produce motion, but before it expands it can be said to have potential energy. After it expands, the piston that it moves then has kinetic energy, and the whole action could be said to represent an energy conversion from potential to kinetic.

In fact the 'potential' energy in the compressed gas existed because the molecules of the gas were in continuous motion, hammering against the piston to produce the effect we call pressure. Thus the gas actually possessed kinetic energy and all that happened during the 'conversion' was that the kinetic energy of the random movement of countless molecules of gas became the kinetic energy of the ordered movement of one solid object in one particular direction.

The definitions of the various forms in which energy can be found therefore depend largely upon the manner in which we wish to consider them. In the example above, the 'potential' energy of the compressed gas can be increased by raising its temperature—this causes the molecules to move faster, so that they each possess a higher kinetic energy. However, to be more specific, the energy of the gas can be said to consist of heat or *thermal* energy. Other forms of energy include *radiation* energy, such as light, radiant heat, radio waves and X-rays, *chemical* energy, and *nuclear* energy.

Chemical energy is energy given off by a chemical reaction, such as the heat given off when a fuel is burned. For example, when methane gas burns, the carbon and hydrogen atoms in the methane molecules combine with the oxygen molecules in the air to form carbon dioxide and water. A certain amount of the energy that was holding the original molecules together is not needed to hold the new ones together and is given off as heat. This kind of reaction is the basis of the power of all explosives.

Aspect

Picturepoint

Du Pont

Above: An atom has a central nucleus, made of protons and neutrons, with electrons in orbit around it. In a fission reaction, a free neutron (shown here in black) penetrates the nucleus (shown here in red) of a suitable fuel, such as uranium-235, and splits it, releasing more neutrons which then split neighbouring atoms. This process spreads throughout the fuel, giving off vast amounts of energy.

Left: In the uncontrolled chain reaction in a nuclear bomb, all the energy is given off in a fraction of a second, with terrible results.

Above: The chain reactions within a nuclear reactor are basically the same as those in an A-bomb, but they are controlled so that the energy is given off gradually in the form of heat. This heat is used to raise steam to drive electricity-generating turbines.

Left: Explosives such as gelignite or TNT work by rapidly releasing large amounts of chemical energy—the product of a chemical reaction during which the atoms which make up molecules recombine to form different ones. Nuclear energy, on the other hand, is a result of the re-arrangement of the particles which make up the atoms themselves.

This chart show energy conversions involved in the generation and use of electricity. The two pictures on the right show a water turbine under construction and the turbine hall of a coal-fired power station. In a hydroelectric power station, the potential energy of the water

behind the dam is converted into kinetic energy as the water runs through the turbines. The turbines convert this kinetic energy into mechanical energy, and drive the generators that convert it into electrical energy. In both conventional and nuclear power stations, (left and below left) chemical and nuclear energy are converted to heat energy, producing steam. The turbo-generators convert the steam's heat energy into mechanical, and then electrical energy.

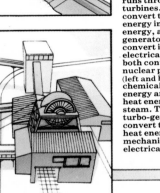

Electricity is a convenient form of energy which can easily be converted into many other forms, for example light, heat, mechanical and sound energy. Many devices employ more than one conversion, for example the bell converts electricity to mechanical energy and then to sound.

Work

Work can be defined as movement against a force; for instance, lifting an object involves doing work against the force of gravity. The work done on an object by a force is calculated by multiplying the value of the force by the distance through which it moves the object.

Energy is the capacity to do work; it can be converted into work, and work can be converted into energy. A good example of this is the operation of a drop-hammer piledriver, where a crane lifts a heavy weight then drops it to drive a pile into the ground.

Energy is produced by burning fuel in the crane's engine, and this is converted into work to lift the weight. At the top of the weight's stroke, the work done on it has been converted into potential energy. When the weight is dropped, the potential energy is converted into kinetic energy, and when it hits the pile this kinetic energy is converted back into work to drive the pile into the ground.

Thermodynamics

The conversion of work to energy, or energy to work, leads to scientific facts that make nonsense in everyday language. For example, a sack of flour resting on the

floor has zero potential energy. If a man lifts it, he will have done work on it and given it potential energy. If he then puts the sack gently back on to the floor, he takes its potential energy away from it again.

Since he has lifted the sack and given it potential energy, then put it down and taken the energy away again, scientifically speaking the net energy input to the sack, and thus the net work input, is zero. The man has done no 'work' in lifting the sack and putting it down again, even though he has actually used energy.

All energy changes (such as from chemical to mechanical or from electrical to mechanical) result in a certain amount of energy being 'lost' during the change, as though it had drained away into a universal lake of unusable energy. This is known as increasing *entropy*, since the energy 'lost' cannot be regained for further use.

For example, an electric motor which converts electrical energy into mechanical energy, actually delivers less energy that it receives. The 'missing' energy is used up in several ways; for example, in overcoming the electrical resistance of the wiring of the motor, and in counteracting the friction of the bearings. This

energy is wasted in the form of heat and sound, and in wearing away the bearings. It is, in fact, dissipated in such a way that it can never be recovered.

A little of the energy in the Universe is lost every time an energy change occurs, as in the case of the electric motor. It has been predicted that eventually all the energy will have drained away and become unusable. This will be the 'end' of the Universe—still a long way off yet—sometimes called the 'heat death' of the Universe because then everything will be at the same temperature. As all energy derives ultimately from a flow of heat, without temperature differences there can be no such flow, and thus no more usable energy can be obtained.

The relationship between thermal (or heat) energy and kinetic (or dynamic) energy is explained by two laws, the *First and Second Laws of Thermodynamics*, which were formulated during the nineteenth century. The First Law, also known as the *Law of Conservation of Energy*, states that the total amount of energy is constant, and energy cannot be created or destroyed, only converted from one form to another.

The second law implies that energy will not flow 'uphill'; it must be pushed up,

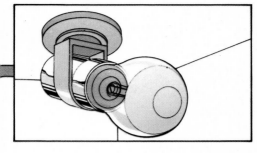

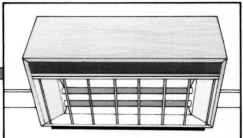

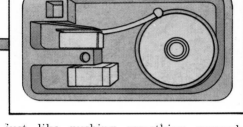

Above: Current passing through a light bulb filament raises its temperature so that it gives off light.

Above right: When a car battery is charged, electrical energy is converted into chemical energy and stored. When the battery is used, this energy is converted back into electricity.

Right: The term 'horsepower' was devised by James Watt in the eighteenth century. One horsepower is the power needed to raise 550 lb through a height of 1 foot in 1 second, that is, 550 ft.lb/sec. It is about 50% more than a horse can maintain over a period of time.

1 ft

550 lb

Above: Measuring engine power on a hydraulic dynamometer. The engine drives a rotor which forces fluid against a casing. The force on the casing is measured and multiplied by the speed of the engine to calculate the power.

Right: A simple dynamometer. The flywheel tends to lift the weight, causing a reduction in the spring balance reading from which the torque can be calculated.

just like pushing something upwards against the force of gravity. One result which is relatively obvious is that heat cannot flow from a body of lower temperature to one of higher, unless work is done on it. But a more far-reaching example brings home the full impact of the Second Law and its relationship to entropy.

A warm object which is at rest may have the same energy as a cold object which is moving, the energy in both cases being the total kinetic energy of the molecules of the object. In the first case, the molecules are moving at random within the object, and in the second case they are all moving in an orderly manner in one direction.

However, there is an essential difference between, for example, a warm brick which is static and a cold one which is moving (and so possessing the same amount of energy). Eventually the cold brick will hit the ground and come to rest, becoming warm as the kinetic energy of the orderly motion of its molecules is converted (when the molecules are 'shaken up' by the impact) into the kinetic energy of random molecular motion within the brick. The entropy of the brick, which is a measure of the randomness or disorder within it, has inevitably increased.

On the other hand, the reverse cannot happen; the random motion of the molecules of a warm brick cannot by chance become an orderly motion, so that the brick suddenly becomes cold and throws itself into the air. An input of energy is necessary to change the random motion into an orderly motion, in other words to decrease the entropy of the brick.

It is clear from these examples that the natural tendency is for entropy to increase; and work must be done in order to decrease it.

The Second Law of Thermodynamics dictates that a block of ice (in which there is little molecular motion, and low entropy) may not spontaneously form itself from water vapour in the air in the Sahara Desert at noon. Similarly, a refrigerator must be supplied with energy in order to withdraw heat from within it, in other words to decrease its entropy.

Power

Power is the rate at which work or energy is supplied, transferred or consumed. The relationship between energy and power is a simple one—power is energy divided by time. For example, if a machine has a power output of one horsepower, it can deliver 550 ft.lb. of energy per second.

Electrical Machines

The basic principles behind such electrical machines as motors, generators and transformers were discovered by Michael Faraday (1791-1867) during the first half of the nineteenth century. Faraday discovered that if a piece of a conducting material, such as copper wire, was moved in a magnetic field, an electric current would flow in it. In addition, if current was passed through a piece of copper wire which was within a magnetic field, forces would be set up which made the wire move. These two discoveries led to the development of dynamos and motors.

Faraday also found that if a varying electric current was passed through a coil of wire, a similarly varying current would be induced to flow in a second coil placed next to it. This was the basis of the transformer.

Dc machines

The simplest type of direct current (dc) machine consists of three main components, the *stator*, the *rotor*, and the *commutator*. The stator is a horseshoe-shaped permanent magnet, and the rotor is mounted on a shaft, free to rotate, between the two poles of the magnet.

The rotor has a coil of copper wire, through which the current flows, wrapped around a soft iron core. The ends of the coil are connected to the commutator, which acts as a sort of rotating switch to reverse the direction of the current within the coil twice per revolution of the rotor.

When direct current is passed through the coil, a magnetic field is produced. The coil in effect becomes a magnet, suspended within the field of the horseshoe magnet. It is then forced to turn so that its lines of magnetic flux line up with those of the horseshoe magnet, with its north and south poles next to the south and north

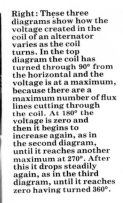

Right: These three diagrams show how the voltage created in the coil of an alternator varies as the coil turns. In the top diagram the coil has turned through 90° from the horizontal and the voltage is at a maximum, because there are a maximum number of flux lines cutting through the coil. At 180° the voltage is zero and then it begins to increase again, as in the second diagram, until it reaches another maximum at 270°. After this it drops steadily again, as in the third diagram, until it reaches zero having turned 360°.

Left and below: In a hydroelectric power station, the alternators are driven by water turbines which are turned by the force of water passing down through them. The picture on the left shows the tops of the generating sets at a modern hydro station in Scotland, while the picture below shows the water pipelines supplying a small hydroelectric power station in the Pyrenees mountains in south-west France.

Below right: Most power stations use steam turbines to drive the alternators. This is a turbogenerator at a nuclear power station, where the steam is produced by the heat from a nuclear reactor. This alternator generates 22 kV at 50 Hz. The power is developed in the stator, and the dc supply which creates the magnetic field of the rotor is generated by the small machine at the near end of the unit.

Below left: One of the earliest electrical machines was the Wimshurst machine. It generated static electricity by means of the friction between a rotating glass disc and a stationary metal one.

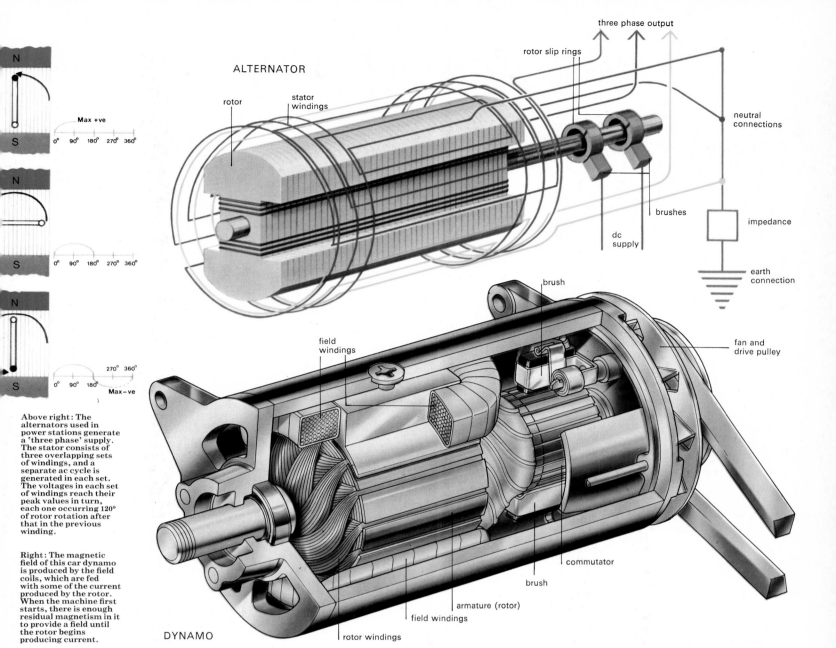

ALTERNATOR

rotor

stator windings

three phase output

rotor slip rings

neutral connections

brushes

dc supply

impedance

earth connection

Above right: The alternators used in power stations generate a 'three phase' supply. The stator consists of three overlapping sets of windings, and a separate ac cycle is generated in each set. The voltages in each set of windings reach their peak values in turn, each one occurring 120° of rotor rotation after that in the previous winding.

Right: The magnetic field of this car dynamo is produced by the field coils, which are fed with some of the current produced by the rotor. When the machine first starts, there is enough residual magnetism in it to provide a field until the rotor begins producing current.

brush

field windings

fan and drive pulley

commutator

brush

armature (rotor)

field windings

rotor windings

DYNAMO

poles respectively of the magnet.

Just as the coil reaches the position where its field aligns with that of the magnet, however, the direction of the current flow within it is reversed by the action of the commutator. Its magnetic field is thus also reversed, and the coil then has to move around another 180° to keep its field in line with that of the magnet. Already moving when its field was reversed, the coil continues moving in the same direction. By reversing the current flow each time the coil is about to line up its field with the magnet's, the coil can be made to rotate continuously.

In practice, dc motors have a number of separate coils, wound round the core in sequence, and the commutator is a series of copper strips to which the ends of the coils are connected.

A simple dc machine like this can also be used as a dynamo to produce dc electricity. The rotor is turned mechanically, and as the coils turn they cut through the magnetic flux lines of the stator magnet so creating a current within them. This current is collected from the commutator by carbon brushes and taken away by wires to supply an electric circuit. A common example of this is the dynamo driven by a car engine,

which supplies the electrical system and charges the battery. Large dc machines often use electromagnets in place of permanent magnets to provide the main magnetic field.

Alternators

To produce an alternating current (ac), another principle of electromagnetism is employed. This is the fact that the current induced in a coil rotating within a magnetic field is proportional to the rate at which the coil cuts through the lines of flux of the magnetic field.

These lines of flux pass from one pole of the magnet to the other and as the coil passes near the poles it is almost in line with the flux lines. At this point it cuts them at a maximum rate. On the other hand when the coil is at right angles to the poles it is also at right angles to the flux lines and cuts through a minimum number of them.

The result of these different rates is that the voltage induced in the coil at any one time depends on its position in relation to the magnetic field. The voltage is at a maximum when the coil is in line with the poles, it falls to a minimum when the coil is at 90° to the poles, and then it rises to a maximum again as the coil once more

lines up with the poles. After a further 90° of rotation the coil is again producing a minimum voltage.

At the second maximum, however, the coil is the opposite way round in relation to its position at the first maximum. As the direction of the magnetic field remains unchanged, this reversal of the coil means that the current induced in it will flow round it in the opposite direction and the voltage will have the opposite polarity, that is, negative instead of positive or vice versa.

In effect the voltage and current produced by such a coil build up smoothly to a maximum in one direction, fall to zero, and then build up to a maximum in the other direction, with each 180° of its rotation. In 360° of rotation this alternating voltage (and current) goes through one whole *cycle*, from one maximum to the other and back again.

The *frequency* of an ac supply is the number of complete cycles per second, one cycle per second being known as 1 *hertz* (1 Hz), named after the German physicist Heinrich Hertz (1857-1894). For example, if the coil rotates at 50 revolutions per second (3,000 rpm), the frequency will be 50 Hz.

In Europe, the frequency of the mains

41

supply is 50 Hz, produced by *alternators* (mostly driven by steam turbines) running at 3,000 rpm. In North America the mains frequency is 60 Hz and the alternators run at 3,600 rpm.

On most small alternators the current produced by the rotor is collected by brushes from a pair of copper rings, called *slip rings*, mounted on the rotor shaft, each ring being connected to one end of the coil. Other alternators, including the large ones used in power stations, avoid having to collect large amounts of power through brushes and slip rings by keeping the coil stationary and rotating the magnetic field within it. The power developed in the coil (or stator, as the stationary part of any motor or generator is known) can then be collected by fixed connections. In this case the rotor may be a permanent magnet or an electromagnet fed with a relatively small amount of dc power through brushes and slip rings.

Ac motors

There are several types of ac electric motor, of which the *induction motor* is the most widely used in industry, largely because of its simplicity of design. This type uses a rotating magnetic field produced in the stator to induce *eddy currents* in the rotor which in turn produce their own magnetic field. These currents are produced whenever a magnetic field is moved relative to a conductor. And as long as there is a difference in speed of rotation—that is, as long as the rotor is moving more slowly than the stator field

—eddy currents are created and the attraction between the two magnetic fields effectively pulls the rotor round.

The stator consists of a series of electromagnets, and these are connected in such a way that an alternating current passing through them creates a pattern of north and south poles which move around the stator in sequence. The rotor is made of a slotted steel core, with bars of low-resistance copper or aluminium in the slots making a kind of 'cage'. The bars are connected together at the ends of the core and provide paths for the induced eddy currents.

The *synchronous motor* uses the same kind of rotating field as the induction motor, but the rotor is made of permanent magnets or dc electromagnets. The field of the magnetic rotor is synchronized with the rotating field. It follows it at exactly the same speed, since no relative motion is needed to produce its magnetism.

If the stator is arranged so that a single pair of poles appears to rotate around it, the motor will run at the same speed as the supply frequency—50 revolutions per second for a 50 Hz supply, or 60 rps for a 60 Hz supply. Doubling the apparent number of poles will give a third of the speed. Electrical machines of the synchronous type are more often used as alternators than as motors, as the simpler, more robust induction motor is usually preferable for most applications.

Two other forms of synchronous motor are the *reluctance motor* and the *hysteresis motor*. In the reluctance motor the rotor

DC MOTOR

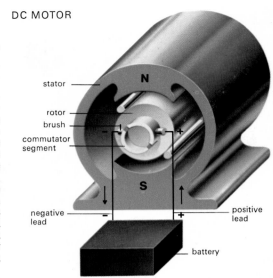

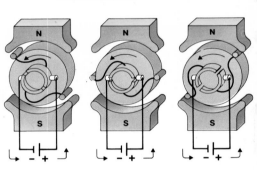

SYNCHRONOUS MOTOR

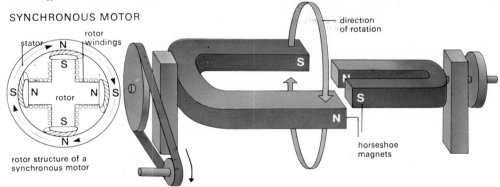

rotor structure of a synchronous motor

horseshoe magnets

direction of rotation

SQUIRREL CAGE MOTOR

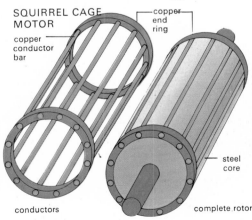

copper end ring

copper conductor bar

steel core

conductors

complete rotor

Above: The synchronous motor has a rotating magnetic field in its stator which attracts the field in the rotor and pulls it round with it, just as the magnet on the right will turn if that on the left is rotated. The diagram on the far left shows the way this happens in an actual motor. The rotor is fed with dc.

Right: A great deal of heat can be generated within big transformers, and so a cooling system is necessary. This transformer, at a 400 kV substation in England, has a special insulating oil circulating through its windings to carry away the heat, which is then dissipated by the banks of cooling radiators on its right.

Above: Many induction motors are called 'squirrel cage' motors because of the way the rotor conductors are arranged. Eddy currents induced in the rotor by the rotating magnetic field of the stator produce forces which drag the rotor around, trying to make it catch up with the rotating field.

Right: In a normal induction motor the field travels in a circular path around the stator windings, pulling the rotor with it. A linear motor is like a normal one which has been unrolled. The field travels along the windings, carrying a suitable conductor, such as an aluminium plate, with it.

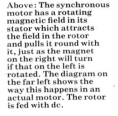

conventional motor

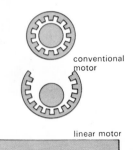

linear motor

position of maximum field travels around motor attracting the rotor

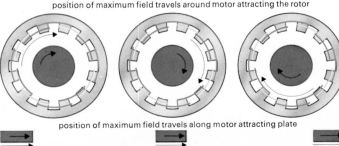

position of maximum field travels along motor attracting plate

Paul Brierley

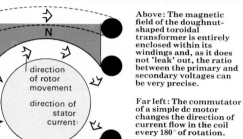

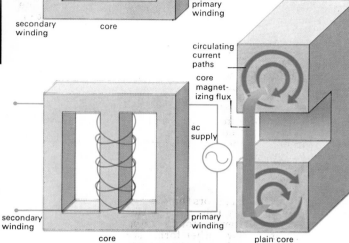

1 volt 2 amp

1 : 1

1 volt 2 amp

step-up transformer

1 : 2

2 volt 1 amp

step-down transformer

2 : 1

ac supply

secondary winding   core   primary winding

circulating current paths

core magnetizing flux

ac supply

circulating current paths

secondary winding   core   primary winding

plain core   laminated core

TRANSFORMERS

Above: The magnetic field of the doughnut-shaped toroidal transformer is entirely enclosed within its windings and, as it does not 'leak' out, the ratio between the primary and secondary voltages can be very precise.

Far left: The commutator of a simple dc motor changes the direction of current flow in the coil every 180° of rotation.

Left: Many dc motors have electromagnets instead of a permanent magnet stator to provide the stationary magnetic field.

N

direction of rotor movement

direction of stator current

S

CEGB

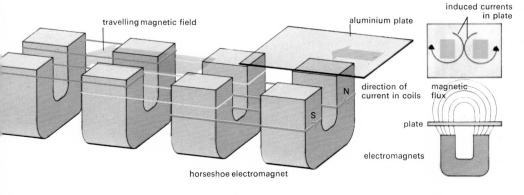

ASEA

Above: In a transformer, the ratio between the primary and secondary voltages is the same as the ratio between the numbers of turns of wire in the primary and secondary windings. The ratio between the primary and secondary currents, however, is the inverse of this winding ratio. The diagrams also show the two main winding layouts for power transformers, and the way a laminated core reduces the induced circulating currents which cause power losses. Two main kinds of power loss occur: the 'iron loss' is power used in magnetizing and demagnetizing the core; the 'copper loss' is power used in overcoming the electrical impedance of the windings.

Left: This transformer produces 600 kV output for testing heavy electrical equipment. Voltage is discharged from the plates making up the sphere at the end of the long, ribbed insulator.

is an unmagnetized piece of steel with a toothed circumference, and the stator has a correspondingly toothed inner surface. The rotor moves so as to line its teeth up with those of the stator, as this provides the path of minimum *reluctance*, or resistance to the passage of magnetic flux, between the stator and the rotor.

The rotor must be given a spin to start it, but once it is moving it will keep going at a synchronous speed because the magnetic polarity of the teeth of the stator changes every half cycle of the ac supply. Each rotor tooth is pulled round from one stator tooth to the next by this constantly reversing magnetic field. Because they run at the precisely controlled speed of the ac mains, these cheap and reliable motors are widely used to drive electric clocks.

The hysteresis motor has a smooth steel rotor which is capable of being permanently magnetized. As the moving magnetic field of the stator passes a point on the rotor, that point becomes a small permanent magnet which follows it round. It eventually catches up with the moving field and locks on to it, so that the rotor behaves like the rotor of a synchronous motor.

All types of ac electric motor can be made in linear form, that is, with the stator windings arranged in a line rather than in a circle. This arrangement produces a magnetic field which moves along the line of windings and will carry any suitable piece of conducting material along with it. *Linear motors* thus produce straight-line motion instead of rotary motion and so are becoming popular for driving travelling cranes, sliding doors and baggage handling systems as well as passenger transport systems such as that at the Birmingham (England) International Airport.

LINEAR MOTOR

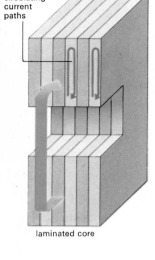

induced currents in plate

aluminium plate

travelling magnetic field

N

S

direction of current in coils

magnetic flux

plate

electromagnets

horseshoe electromagnet

The Internal Combustion Engine

The internal combustion engine was one of the most important inventions of the nineteenth century. Its development and its applications have had far-reaching effects throughout the world—its use has revolutionized transport, its manufacture has spawned vast new industries and its technology has inspired developments in many other fields of engineering.

The internal combustion engine is so called because the heat energy that it converts into mechanical energy is produced within it by the repeated explosion of a mixture of fuel and air. For instance, if petrol gasoline vapour is mixed with the right proportion of air, the resulting mixture can be ignited by means of a spark. As it explodes it expands rapidly, and this expansion is what drives the pistons.

Early designs of these engines used coal gas as the fuel and were based on steam engine technology. The first reasonably successful engine was built by the Frenchman J. J. E. Lenoir in 1859. The Lenoir engine, however, suffered from a low power output and high fuel consumption, so many attempts were made to produce a more efficient design. This was eventually achieved in 1876 by Nikolaus Otto in Germany and his company, Otto and Langen, produced about 50,000 engines during the following 17 years.

Petrol engines

The basic components of an internal combustion engine are the cylinder, closed at the top by the cylinder head, and the piston which moves up and down within it. The piston is connected to a crankshaft by a connecting rod, so as the piston moves up and down the crankshaft is turned.

The fuel and air are mixed by the carburettor and this mixture is then drawn into the cylinder by the suction created during a downward stroke of the piston. When the piston rises again, the mixture is compressed as the space between the top of the piston and the cylinder head decreases. This compression raises the temperature of the mixture, making it more explosive.

Just before the piston reaches the top of its travel, the mixture is ignited by an electric spark created by current jumping across the gap between the two electrodes of a spark plug, screwed into the cylinder head.

By the time the piston has reached the top of its travel, the explosion which began in the mixture around the spark plug has spread rapidly throughout the rest of the mixture in the cylinder. The resulting expansion of hot gases created by the burning mixture drives the piston down again.

The power of the explosion is thus converted into a downward movement of the piston, and this motion rotates the crankshaft. The rotation of the crankshaft is then used to drive, for example, a car or a motorcycle.

The simplest form of petrol engine is the two-stroke engine, in which there are

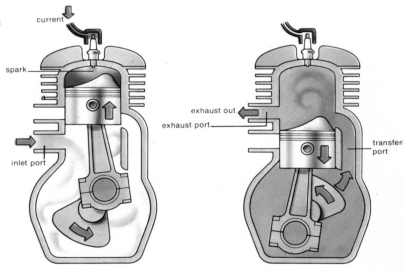

Above: A two-stroke outboard motor engine. It is a V-6 engine, having two banks of three cylinders set at an angle to each other to form a V-shape. The total cylinder capacity is 2448 cc (149.9 in³), and the power output is 149 kW (200 hp).

Right: The two-stroke cycle. As the piston moves up to compress the fuel/air mixture in the cylinder, the next charge of mixture is drawn into the crankcase via the inlet port. After the compressed mixture in the cylinder has been ignited by the spark plug, the expanding gases drive the piston down the cylinder. As the piston descends it pushes the mixture in the crankcase up the transfer port and into the cylinder. The mixture entering the cylinder pushes the exhaust gases out through the exhaust port, then the piston starts to rise and the cycle begins again.

two strokes of the piston, one up and one down, for each ignition of fuel. On a two-stroke engine the mixture is drawn into the cylinder via the crankcase, the casing below the cylinder which encloses the crankshaft.

As the piston rises to compress the mixture in the cylinder, the low pressure created in the crankcase below it sucks in fresh mixture through an opening, the inlet port, in the side of the bottom of the cylinder where it meets the crankcase.

Meanwhile, the mixture already in the cylinder has been compressed and ignited, and the piston is on its way down again. As it descends it uncovers two other openings in the cylinder wall, which were closed off by the sides of the piston during its upward compression stroke.

One of these ports is the exhaust port, through which the burned exhaust gases escape, and the other one, on the opposite side of the cylinder, is the transfer port. The transfer port is the top opening of a passage leading down to the crankcase, and as the piston moves down it pushes the mixture in the crankcase up the transfer port and into the cylinder. As the mixture enters the cylinder it pushes the remaining exhaust gases out through the exhaust port.

The piston now rises again, covering the exhaust and transfer ports· and so sealing the cylinder, compressing the mixture ready for ignition. The impetus required to push the piston back up the cylinder is provided by a relatively heavy flywheel, fitted to the end of the crankshaft, whose inertia keeps it turning after it has been set moving by the down-

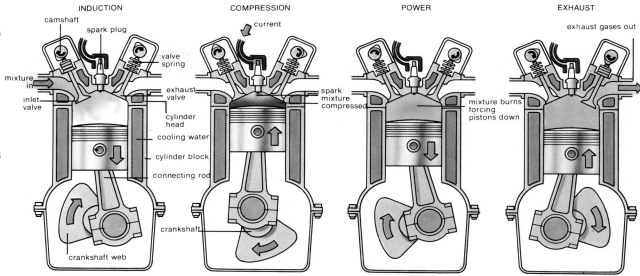

| INDUCTION | COMPRESSION | POWER | EXHAUST |

Right: The four-stroke cycle. On the first stroke, the induction stroke, the piston moves down and the inlet valve opens, allowing mixture to enter the cylinder. On the second stroke, the compression stroke, both valves are closed and the piston moves up to compress the mixture. After the mixture has been ignited the piston is driven back down on its power stroke. As it rises again on its exhaust stroke the exhaust valve opens and the exhaust gases are driven out of the cylinder. The exhaust valve then closes, the inlet valve opens, and the next induction stroke begins.

Below: A four cylinder, four-stroke petrol engine used in Ford Transit vans and light trucks.

ward power stroke of the piston.

The four-stroke engine is more complicated than the two stroke because there is a separate stroke of the piston for each of the four stages of the combustion cycle. In addition, cam-operated valves are used to control the entry of the mixture and the exit of the exhaust gases, the mixture entering the cylinder directly and not via the crankcase.

The first stroke of the cycle is a downward stroke of the piston, during which the inlet valve is open to allow mixture to be drawn into the cylinder. The inlet valve then closes and the piston moves up on the second stroke, the compression stroke, to compress the mixture which is then ignited by the spark plug. The expansion of the burning mixture drives the piston back down on its power stroke.

The cycle is completed by the next upstroke of the piston. As the piston rises, the exhaust valve opens and the exhaust gases are forced out of the cylinder. Then the exhaust valve closes and the cycle begins again.

Carburation
As the air is drawn through the carburettor by suction from the engine, it passes through a narrow passage called a *venturi* or *choke* (barrel). This narrowing of the air's path causes an increase in its velocity, and this increase in velocity causes a decrease in the air's pressure.

A small nozzle or *jet*, connected to the fuel supply, is positioned at the venturi, and the low pressure air flow sucks a fine spray of fuel out of the jet. This fine spray vaporizes and mixes with the air, in a ratio (by weight) of approximately 15 parts air to 1 part fuel. The amount of mixture drawn into the engine, which determines its speed, is controlled by a flap-like *butterfly valve* or *throttle* connected to the accelerator control.

On engines with more than one cylinder, the carburettor feeds the mixture into a *manifold*, a set of pipes connecting it with each of the cylinder inlets. Each cylinder draws mixture from the carburetor in turn. Many large engines have more than one carburettor, or a carburettor with more than one choke, to improve the flow of mixture to the cylinders.

A high voltage of up to 30,000 volts is needed to create the spark across the spark plug gap, and this voltage is supplied by the *ignition coil*. Current from a low voltage supply (such as the 12V supply from a car's battery) is fed into the low tension (lt) winding of the coil, which consists of a few hundred turns of copper wire wound on a soft iron core.

The flow of current sets up a magnetic field in the coil. When the current flow is switched off by a set of contact breaker points, operated by a cam driven by the engine, this magnetic field dies away or 'collapses'. The collapsing magnetic field creates or *induces* flow of current in the high tension (ht) winding of the coil. In comparison to the few hundred turns of relatively heavy wire which make up the lt winding, the ht winding consists of many thousands of turns of fine copper wire. This also is wound around the soft iron core.

When one coil induces a current in another, as in an ignition coil, the ratio of the initial voltage to the induced voltage is the same as the ratio of the number of turns of wire on the first coil to the number of turns on the second coil. This means that if the second coil has a thousand times more turns than the first, the induced voltage will be a thousand times greater than the initial voltage.

The high voltage pulse created by the coil is fed to the spark plug, where it travels down the centre electrode to its tip, which is inside the cylinder, and then sparks across to the other electrode. On multi-cylinder engines the pulses from the coil are fed to the *distributor*, which then distributes them to each cylinder in turn.

On many modern engines the current in the low tension circuit is controlled by an electronic circuit instead of by a mechani-

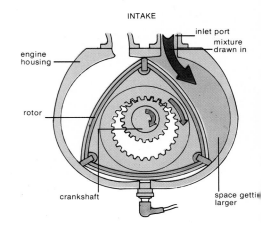

INTAKE

inlet port
mixture drawn in
engine housing
rotor
crankshaft
space getting larger

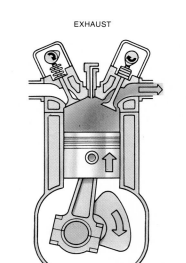

ROTARY MOTOR CYCLE ENGINE

1. Air intake for carburettor
2. Carburettor
3. Cooling passages in rotor housing
4. Thermostatic switch for radiator fan
5. Inlet port (exhaust port below)
6. Wax thermostat
7. Rotor set trochoid pump for metering oil
8. Coolant pump rotor
9. Coolant pump volute
10. Ignition contact breaker (3 sets of points)
11. Oil filter
12. Oil sump inlet strainer
13. Chain tensioner
14. Multi-plate clutch
15. Twin drive chains from engine to clutch
16. Kick starter shaft
17. Kick starter freewheel mechanism
18. 5 speed gearbox
19. Chain lubricator
20. Drive chain to rear wheel
21. Electric starter
22. Spark plug
23. Tip seal
24. Rotor
25. 3 phase alternator
26. Combustion chamber

Picturepoint

Above: A four-stroke diesel engine for use in particularly heavy commercial vehicles.

Below: A diesel draws in air, compresses it to raise its temperature to over 550°C (1022°F), then sprays in the fuel which ignites spontaneously in the hot air and drives the piston down on its power stroke.

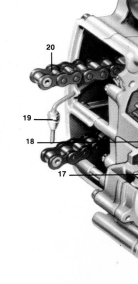

| INTAKE | COMPRESSION | POWER | EXHAUST |

air

fuel

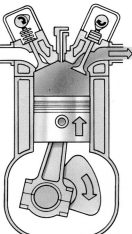

COMPRESSION AND IGNITION

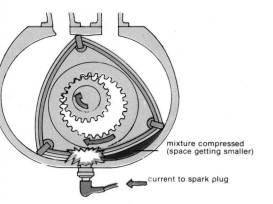

mixture compressed (space getting smaller)

← current to spark plug

POWER

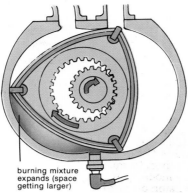

burning mixture expands (space getting larger)

EXHAUST

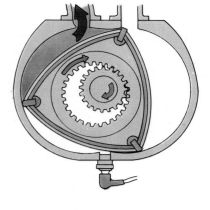

Above: A Wankel rotary engine has a three-lobed rotor which rotates eccentrically around a fixed gear. This turns a crankshaft (not shown) which passes through the centre of the fixed gear and fits into the central recess of the rotor. As each face of the rotor passes the inlet port it draws in fuel mixture. The rotor then compresses the mixture and the spark plug ignites it. The exploding gases expand and push the rotor on round. The rotor tip seals may be lubricated by oil mixed with the fuel, or by oil sprayed directly into the rotor housing.

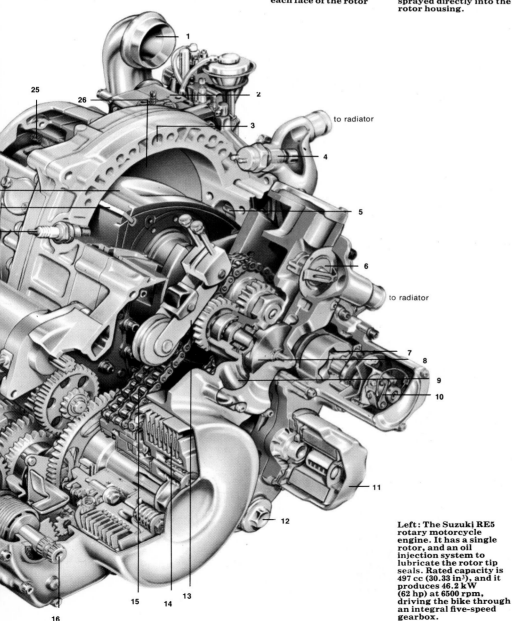

Left: The Suzuki RE5 rotary motorcycle engine. It has a single rotor, and an oil injection system to lubricate the rotor tip seals. Rated capacity is 497 cc (30.33 in³), and it produces 46.2 kW (62 hp) at 6500 rpm, driving the bike through an integral five-speed gearbox.

cal contact breaker unit. Some also use fuel injection systems instead of carburettors, the petrol being sprayed directly into the cylinder instead of being mixed in a carburettor.

Diesel engines

The first diesel engine was built by Rudolf Diesel at Augsburg in Germany in 1897. Diesel engines, which may be either two-stroke or four-stroke, differ from petrol engines in several important respects. Only pure air is drawn into the cylinder on the induction stroke of the piston, and it is compressed to a much greater degree than is the fuel/air mixture of a petrol engine.

This high compression of the air raises its temperature to well over 550°C (1022°F). As the piston nears the top of its travel a measured amount of fuel is sprayed into this hot air by an injector nozzle fed by a pump unit.

The air is so hot that the fuel ignites spontaneously as it mixes with it, without needing a spark to set it off. As there is no carburettor, the speed of a diesel engine is controlled by altering the amount of fuel delivered to the injector by the pump. There is an injector in each cylinder of a multi-cylinder diesel engine, and the pump delivers a shot of fuel to each injector. Diesel engines can be modified to run on almost any kind of inflammable fuel, but most of them run on diesel oil.

Cooling

The combustion process inside the cylinders of an engine creates a large amount of heat, so without some form of cooling the temperature of the engine would rise rapidly. This would lead to a loss of performance and possibly internal damage due to the expansion of engine components; for instance the pistons could jam or 'seize up' within the cylinders.

Air-cooled engines have cooling fins on the outside of the cylinders, which increase their surface area so that the heat is carried away quicker by the surrounding air. Greater cooling is achieved by using a fan, driven by the engine, to blow air through the fins.

Water-cooled engines have water circulating in passageways around and between the cylinders to carry the heat away, and the water itself is cooled by passing it through a radiator. Most water-cooled engines have fans to draw air through the radiator and so increase the rate of cooling of the water.

Steam Engines and Turbines

Despite a tendency to regard steam power as a symbol of obsolescence, it continues to provide much of the energy used in modern society and there is, as yet, no practical alternative. Indeed, even the most advanced nuclear power station reactor is merely a source of heat to produce the steam which drives the generator turbines. Steam engines and turbines are good examples of energy conversion systems, in this case converting heat into mechanical energy.

The heat energy in steam is in a very convenient state for conversion into mechanical energy. Steam engines and turbines do this by expanding a supply of steam from a small volume at high pressure to a large volume at low pressure, with a corresponding fall in temperature. In steam engines this expansion moves a piston to-and-fro in a cylinder; turbines use it to give velocity to a flow of steam which then turns a rotor. Both machines are *external combustion heat engines*, that is, their fuel is burnt outside the working section. This permits better control of the combustion, and so the fuel can be burned under optimum conditions for avoiding atmospheric pollution.

Steam is generated in boilers heated either by furnaces fired by any convenient fuel such as oil or coal, or by some flow of hot fluid like the coolant from a nuclear reactor or the waste gases from a metal-smelting furnace.

The main types of boiler are the *shell* boiler, the *fire-tube* boiler and the *water-tube* boiler. The shell type boiler is cylindrical with internal flues, and is often set in brickwork containing *return flues* which carry the heat round to heat the outside of the boiler shell. The 'Lancashire' boiler, with two furnaces, is typical of this class.

In fire-tube boilers, as used on locomotives, the hot gases from the furnace pass through an array of small tubes immersed in water. In the water-tube boiler, on the other hand, arrays of small tubes carry the water through the combustion chamber. Although this type is more expensive to build, it is the most suitable for high pressure work, and is commonly used to supply turbines.

Steam engines

Most steam engines are *double acting*, that is, both sides of the piston are used to produce power, one side of the piston making a power stroke during the exhaust stroke of the other. The sequence of events during one revolution begins when steam is admitted to the cylinder just before the end of the previous stroke.

Next, the inlet port closes (known as *cut-off*) and the steam expands, driving the piston back down the cylinder. Just before the end of the power stroke the exhaust port opens, (known as *release*), and on the return stroke most of the steam is driven out of the cylinder. Finally the exhaust port closes and the remaining steam is compressed until admission begins again.

In most engines the whole sequence of events for both sides of the piston is

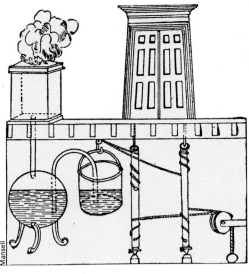

Mansell

Above: The fact that heat could be converted into mechanical energy was known almost 2,000 years ago. This system, devised before 100AD by Hero of Alexandria, used the expansion of hot air beneath the fire on the hollow altar to drive water from the container into the bucket—which then descended and opened the temple doors.

Bildarchiv

Right: Newcomen's 'atmospheric' engine of 1710. Steam from the boiler 'a' was admitted to the cylinder 'c' and this pushed the piston up. A jet of cold water was then sprayed into the cylinder, condensing the steam, and the piston was driven back down by atmospheric pressure acting on its top surface.

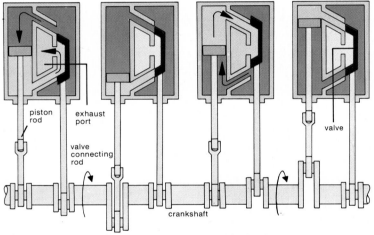

piston rod

exhaust port

valve connecting rod

valve

crankshaft

FOUR CYLINDER DOUBLE-ACTING STEAM ENGINE

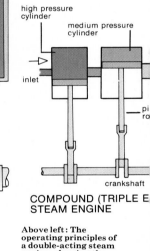

high pressure cylinder

medium pressure cylinder

inlet

piston rod

crankshaft

COMPOUND (TRIPLE E STEAM ENGINE

Above left: The operating principles of a double-acting steam engine, showing the action of the slide valve which controls the supply of steam to the cylinder.

Above: In a triple expansion engine the steam is passed from one cylinder to the next as its pressure drops.

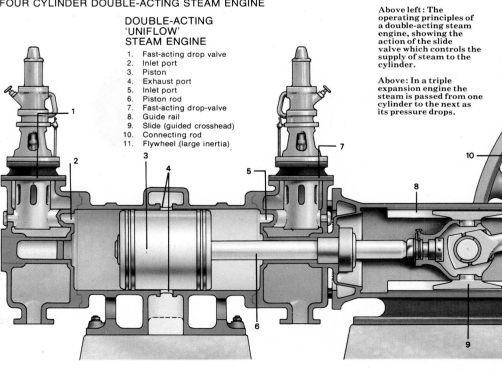

DOUBLE-ACTING 'UNIFLOW' STEAM ENGINE

1. Fast-acting drop valve
2. Inlet port
3. Piston
4. Exhaust port
5. Inlet port
6. Piston rod
7. Fast-acting drop-valve
8. Guide rail
9. Slide (guided crosshead)
10. Connecting rod
11. Flywheel (large inertia)

Left: James Watt was working as an instrument repairer in Glasgow University in 1763 when he was given a model Newcomen engine to repair. It occurred to him that the alternate heating and cooling of the cylinder was very inefficient, and so he designed an engine with a 'separate condenser'. This was a separate chamber into which the steam was led for condensation, so that the cylinder could be kept hot, and this greatly improved the engine's performance. He went on to design engines which drove rotating shafts instead of rocking beams, and he also invented the double-acting engine. The *watt*, the metric unit of power, is named after him.

John Watney

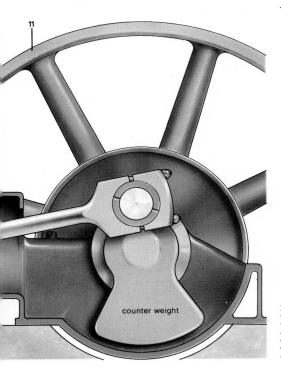

Radio Times Hulton Picture Library

Above: A two-cylinder high pressure steam engine which was installed in a small cargo boat.

Left: An early pioneer of the French motor industry, the Marquis de Dion, driving a steam tricycle which he built in 1897. The engine is at the front and drives the rear wheel.

11

counter weight

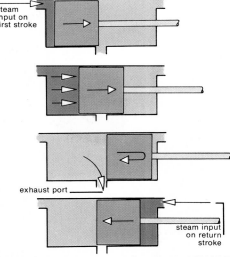

steam input on first stroke

exhaust port

steam input on return stroke

PRINCIPLE OF THE UNIFLOW STEAM ENGINE

Left: A diagram of a uniflow steam engine, which has an inlet valve at each end of the cylinder and a ring of exhaust ports half way along it.

Above: In the uniflow engine, steam is admitted at each end in turn, driving the piston up and down the cylinder and escaping through the exhaust ports.

controlled by a single D-shaped valve, which slides along the cylinder to open and close the ports in sequence. Some large stationary engines have separate inlet and exhaust valves for each side of the piston.

The to-and-fro motion of the piston is converted into rotary motion by a crank linked to the piston rod by a connecting rod. The inertia of a flywheel carries the crank on round past the places where the rod is in line with the crank arm and has no turning effect on it.

As the crank turns, the angle between the connecting rod and the piston rod is constantly changing. To allow for this, the connecting rod must be pivoted where it meets the piston rod. The most common arrangement uses a metal block which slides along guide rails at the end of the cylinder and connects the piston rod to the connecting rod. This sytem, the *guided crosshead*, is the one used on steam locomotives and in marine engines.

Some *single-acting* engines, where one side of the piston is used to produce power, have the connecting rod attached directly to the piston by a metal pin, the *gudgeon pin*, as in a petrol engine or diesel engine.

Compound engines

In a single cylinder, if the difference between the volume of the steam at cut-off and its volume at release is very large, the temperature variations of the cylinder wall which result will cause heat losses. These are unacceptable because the lost heat has to be replaced by burning more fuel, or else the temperature variations must be reduced by limiting the pressure of steam admitted to the cylinder

49

to such an extent that the power of the engine is greatly reduced.

A solution to this was found by using a small, high pressure cylinder whose exhaust steam was passed into a larger, low pressure one. Such combinations are called *compound engines* and were made in several forms, some of which are still found in industrial engine-houses.

Triple expansion engines, with high pressure (HP), intermediate (IP), and one or two low pressure (LP) cylinders were used extensively in ships. The Atlantic liner *Olympic* (1911-36) had two such engines, each with a 1372 mm (54 in) HP cylinder, a 2134 mm (84 in) IP cylinder, and two 2464 mm (97 in) LP cylinders. Each engine developed 11,185 kW (15,000 hp) at 75 rpm.

Quadruple expansion engines were also used at sea, particularly in German ships around the turn of the century. One example, the *Kaiser Wilhelm II* built in 1902, had a total of eight cylinders and produced 16,033 kW (21,500 hp).

Uniflow engines

Uniflow engines are double-acting engines which release most of the expanded steam through a ring of exhaust ports in the cylinder wall. The ports are about half way along the cylinder, so that during most of the power stroke of either side of the piston, the piston is either between the inlet valve and the exhaust ports or closing off the exhaust ports.

A total expansion greater than in most compound engines is achieved in one cylinder at an almost constant wall temperature. Many large engines were built on this principle between 1908 and

Below: The upper drawing shows the steam path through a compound turbine which has six high pressure and four low pressure stages. The lower drawing shows the steam flow in a radial flow turbine. A rotating disc carries rings of blades which move within the fixed blades, and the steam flows outwards through them.

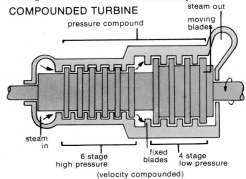

COMPOUNDED TURBINE

pressure compound

steam out

moving blades

steam in

6 stage high pressure

fixed blades

4 stage low pressure

(velocity compounded)

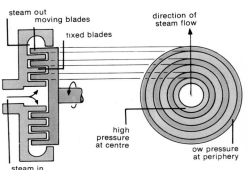

steam out
moving blades

fixed blades

direction of steam flow

steam in

high pressure at centre

low pressure at periphery

PRINCIPLE OF RADIAL-FLOW TURBINE

Right: Another of Hero's inventions, the 'Aeolipile', a kind of steam turbine. The tubes fixed to the hollow sphere had their ends bent over in opposite directions. The sphere was mounted over a boiler. Steam passed into it through the hollow bearings, to escape through the tubes and rotate the sphere.

Radio Times Hulton Picture Library

Below right: A single stage velocity-compounded turbine. The steam enters through the admission valve, and passes into the nozzle passages where it expands as its pressure drops. This expansion increases its velocity and it then passes rapidly through the blades, turning the rotor as it goes.

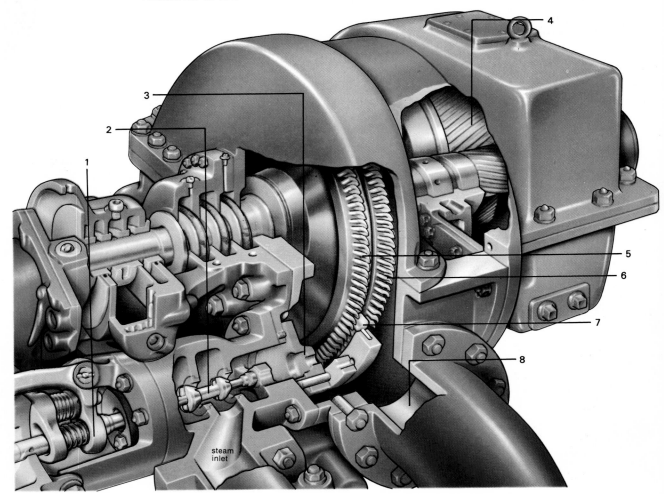

SINGLE-STAGE VELOCITY-COMPOUNDED TURBINE

1. Inlet valve governing mechanism
2. Inlet valve
3. Steam nozzle
4. Speed reduction gears
5. Moving blades (first set)
6. Moving blades (second set)
7. Intermediary fixed blades
8. Steam outlet

steam inlet

Above: The rotor and blades of the first turbine built by Sir Charles Parsons in 1884. The steam entered at the centre and flowed outwards towards the ends, turning the rotor at 18,000 rpm. The turbine was used to drive an electricity generator on board a ship and it remained in use for 16 years.

Below: This miniature turbine set was used in the Second World War to provide electricity for paratroops' radio and signals equipment. A fire was lit beneath the boiler to the left, and the steam was passed through the hoses to the generator turbine on the right. Power output was about 48 watts (8 amps at 6 volts).

Right: The rotor of a large power station turbine. As the blades used in the low pressure stages are so long, at a speed of 3000 rpm the tips of the blades may be moving at over $1\frac{1}{2}$ times the speed of sound. The blades are made of high grade steel alloy to withstand the speed, heat and erosion by the steam.

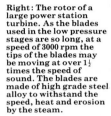

1958, several uniflow cylinders being used in parallel for the largest. A five-cylinder German engine of the 1930s produced 22,371 kW (30,000 hp) to drive a rolling mill in a steelworks, and was the most powerful steam engine ever built.

Steam engine applications

Almost every type of machine that moves has at some time been driven by steam, either directly or through shafts and belts. In Victorian times the steam engine provided the power to print newspapers, spin and weave textiles, pump water, and power washing machines in 'steam laundries'. Portable steam engines ploughed and drained the land, threshed corn, drove fairground machines and even vacuum cleaners for cleaning-contractors. There were even steam driven scalp massage brushes in some barbers' shops.

Most of these applications will never return, but one which may be revived is the steam car. Several types were built in considerable numbers before the First World War, but went out of favour as the petrol engined car grew more efficient.

Steam turbines

The first practical steam turbines were built in the late nineteenth century by Carl De Laval in Sweden and Sir Charles Parsons in England. The main working part of a turbine is a rotor, which carries a set of blades, and is contained inside a casing which has a set of fixed blades to direct the flow of steam. A rotor can be regarded as a sort of windmill, each blade being a sail and the flow of steam acting like an enormously strong wind.

Expanding steam moves very fast: for example, expansion from a pressure of about twelve times atmospheric pressure down to about half atmospheric pressure produces a velocity of about 1100 m/sec (3600 ft/sec). The optimum speed of the moving blades for the transfer of kinetic energy from the steam to the rotor is half that of the steam. For instance, in the above example the ideal rotor speed would be 550 m/sec (1800 ft/sec). This is not always possible to achieve, however, and so the turbine may not be able to extract all the available energy from the steam.

Excessive steam speeds which can lead to this kind of energy loss are often avoided by using several sets of fixed and moving blades, and allowing only a fraction of the total pressure drop to occur in each set. Such turbines are said to be pressure-compounded. The blades are made progressively longer from the inlet to the exhaust end to allow room for the greater volume of steam at the lower pressures. This is comparable to the progressive increase in the size of the cylinders of a compound steam engine, where the high pressure cylinder is smaller than the intermediate and low pressure cylinders.

When a large pressure drop cannot be avoided, the steam leaving a row of moving blades is often re-directed on to a second, and sometimes a third, row of moving blades without further expansion. This sytem is called velocity-compounding.

There are two basic classes of turbine blading: impulse, in which the steam expands only in the fixed blades, and reaction, in which the steam expands in both the fixed and the moving blades. Steam has to be admitted to the whole circumference of the rotor when reaction blading is used, but impulse blading can be worked with some of the inlet nozzles shut off if required. Large turbines often have both types of blading, carried by several rotors in separate casings.

Power station turbines

The very large turbines used in power stations run at constant speeds, the speed being determined by the mains frequency of the system for which they are generating electricity. In most European countries, for instance, the frequency is 50 Hz (50 cycles per second) and the speed of the turbines is 3000 rpm. In North America, the frequency is 60 Hz and so the turbine speed is 3600 rpm.

A single line of rotors driving one alternator (ac generator) is used for powers up to 300 MW (300,000 kW). Two lines, interconnected on the steam side but with separate alternators, are used for greater power, sometimes as much as 600 MW. Such turbines are called cross-compounded.

Double-flow rotors, in which steam is admitted half-way along the cylinder and expands outwards towards both ends, are often used. These avoid excessive blade lengths for handling the large volumes of steam at the low pressure end and balance the pressure thrusts of reaction blading. The low pressure ends of the largest turbines comprise several double-flow rotors working in parallel.

Marine turbines

Smaller turbines are used in ships than in power stations because their size and speed must suit propeller requirements. The turbine may drive the propeller shaft through a set of reduction gears, or it may drive a generator which powers an electric motor that in turn drives the propeller shaft.

Large marine turbines are cross-compounded to save length. For example, the Queen Elizabeth II has two turbines, each developing 41,013 kW (55,000 hp) from two cross-compound rotors, one impulse and one double-flow reaction.

51

Jets and Gas Turbines

The invention of the jet engine had a tremendous impact on aviation. The world's first military jet was the German Messerschmitt Me 262, which went into service as a light bomber in 1944, and the first jet airliner was the de Havilland Comet, which made its first commercial flight on 2 May 1952. The jet engine is now extremely important in the field of aviation, but the gas turbine engine from which it was derived is also important in many others areas, including marine propulsion and electricity generation.

In both the gas turbine and the jet engine, air is drawn in at the front and compressed. Then fuel is burned in the compressed air, and the resulting gases expand rapidly through a turbine section.

One of the earliest patents for a gas turbine engine operating on similar principles to modern ones was that issued to John Barber in England in 1791, but the first successful engines were not built until the early twentieth century.

The Swiss firm of Brown-Boveri ran a successful gas turbine in 1906 which was identical in principle to modern engines. This engine had an *axial* compressor, so named because the air enters and flows through it parallel to the axis of rotation of the compressor. The compressor consists of a series of discs or rings, each carrying blades projecting radially like spokes, which are assembled into a strong, light drum capable of rotating at high speed.

This compressor *rotor* revolves inside a closely fitting casing which has sets of stationary blades (*stator* blades) which just fit between the revolving blades of the rotor. When the rotor is spinning at high speed, air is drawn in and compressed as it passes through the sets or *stages* of fixed and moving blades, before being discharged at the rear of the compressor.

In early engines as many as 20 stages of blading were needed for a pressure ratio of 3:1, that is, for the outlet air to be at three times the pressure of the inlet air. Today it is possible to build compressors of much higher efficiency, which can achieve a pressure ratio of 30:1 with twelve stages.

With such high compression the air

Dave Hoskings

Right: The Rolls-Royce Pegasus vectored-thrust turbofan used by the Harrier vertical take-off jet. The jet exhaust is emitted through the ducts at the sides of the engine, which can be angled to direct the thrust downwards for take-off, to the rear for forward flight, or to the front to make the plane fly backwards.

Left: The Concorde uses four Rolls-Royce/ SNECMA Olympus 593 Mk 602 turbojet engines, each developing 17,260 kg (38,050 lb) thrust.

Right: An Olympus 593 engine. The original Olympus engines were developed in the early 1950s, and turboshaft versions are used in ships and generators.

Right: The Vickers Viscount airliner uses four Rolls-Royce Dart RDa 7/1 Mk 525 turboprop engines, each developing 1484 kW (1990 hp).

Far right: A Pratt and Whitney JT9D turbofan on a Boeing 747 airliner. The JT9D-7W version of this engine produces 21,320 kg (47,000 lb) of thrust.

Picturepoint

ZEFA

Left: A Lynx helicopter is driven by a pair of Rolls-Royce BS 360 Gem turboshaft engines mounted side-by-side behind the main rotor shaft. The engines, capable of producing 670 kW (900 hp) each, drive the rotor via a reduction gearbox, and a transmission shaft takes the drive to the tail rotor.

Right: The McDonnell Douglas DC-10 airliner is powered by three General Electric CF6-50A turbofans, two of which are mounted under the wings with the third, shown here, in the tail.

Below: Checking a Rolls-Royce RB211 turbofan with an X-ray camera mounted on a fork lift truck.

Rolls Royce

ZEFA

John Ross/Robert Harding

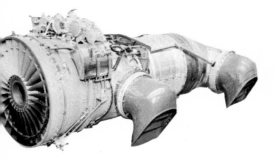

Rolls Royce

becomes so hot that the downstream stages have to be made of *refractory* (heat resistant) alloys.

From the compressor, the hot, high pressure air is fed through the combustion chamber where the fuel is added to it. A few gas turbines have run on pulverized coal or peat, but almost all use liquid fuels. An advantage of these engines is their ability to run on a wide range of fuels and, although most run on kerosene it is possible to run gas turbines on heavy oils, high-octane petrol or natural gas.

An enormous amount of heat energy can be generated within the combustion chamber of a modern engine. As much as 37,350 kW (50,000 hp) can be produced in a combustion chamber whose volume is less than that of a briefcase.

From the combustion chamber the gas, now at perhaps 1300°C (2372°F), flows at high speed through the turbine section of the engine. Like the compressor, this consists of several axial stages, each separated by a row of stator blades which direct the flow on to the row of rotor blades immediately downstream, causing the rotor to revolve at high speed.

The rotor drives the compressor, usually by means of a simple drive shaft. It may also drive the machinery that the turbine is powering, or additional turbines may be used for this purpose.

Turboprops and turboshafts

The *turboprop* engine is a gas turbine engine which drives an aircraft propeller. The drive is taken from the turbine to the propeller via a gearbox because of the great difference in the rotational speeds of the rotor and the propellor.

For example, the Canadian Pratt and Whitney PT6 engine, used on many light transport planes such as those built by de Havilland of Canada, has a drive ratio of 15:1, linking a 33,000 rpm turbine with a 2,200 rpm propeller. The latest version has a 22.74:1 gearbox ratio, the 30,017 rpm turbine driving a larger propeller at only 1,320 rpm for lower noise.

In some engines, instead of having one turbine to drive both the compressor and the propeller, there are two turbines. The gas from the combustion chamber passes first through the compressor drive turbine, and then through the *free turbine*, which is mounted on a separate shaft to the compressor and its turbine. The propeller gearbox drive is taken from this shaft.

Sometimes a free-turbine type of turbo-prop is installed 'back to front', with the compressor at the rear and an arrange-

Right: The Rolls-Royce RB211 turbofan has three shafts or 'spools', carrying the low, intermediate and high pressure turbines and compressors (the low pressure compressor being the fan). The Lockheed L-1011-200 TriStar is powered by three RB211-524 engines, which deliver 21,775 kg (48,000 lb) thrust each.

Rolls-Royce RB-211
1 ip turbine
2 lp turbine
3 hp turbine
4 annular combustors
5 bleed air cooling
6 hp compressor discs
7 hp compressor blades
8 ip compressor discs
9 ip compressor blades
10 fan casing
11 guide vanes
12 33-blade titanium fan
13 inlet guide vanes
14 lp (fan) shaft
15 shaft coupling
16 engine core
17 ip shaft
18 hp shaft
19 rear shaft bearings
20 turbine discs
21 tail cone

Below: This drawing shows how the airflow is divided in two on a turbofan engine such as the RB211. The turbofan produces a lower jet flow velocity than a turbojet, making it quieter, and the noise level is further reduced by the shielding effect of the fan airflow which encircles the exhaust from the core.

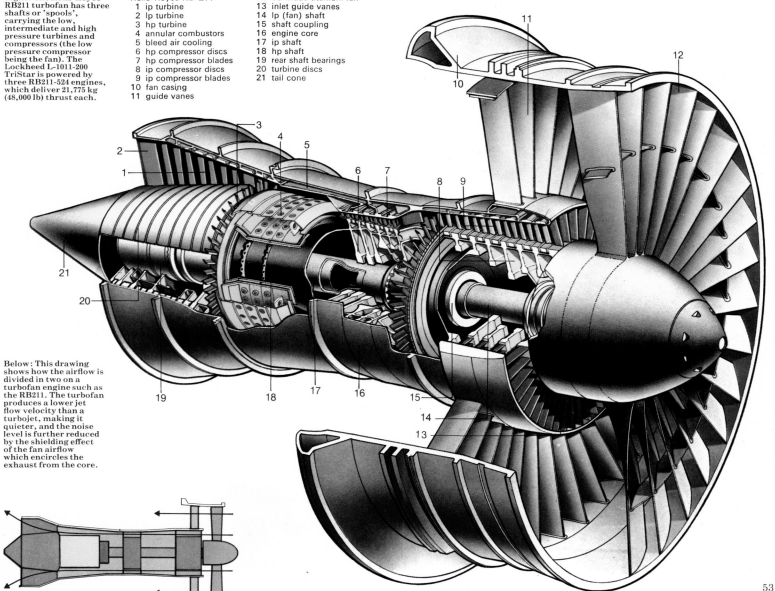

ment of ducts and vents to guide the inlet air into the compressor and deflect the exhaust gases away from the inlet. This simplifies the drive shaft arrangements which would be necessary to drive a front propeller if the engine were installed in the normal way.

Turboprops have not been produced for large aircraft since 1955, except for a small number of specialized military aircraft. Smaller turboprops, however, are being produced in increasing numbers for private and business aircraft and short-range transport aircraft. The small turboprop is gradually eating into the last remaining market for the aircraft piston engine.

Turboshafts are gas turbines used as a source of shaft power. They are used to drive naval craft of all kinds, fast container ships, hydrofoils, hovercraft, trains, electricity generators, and large-scale oil and gas pumping units. They are also being developed for use in heavy road trucks and other vehicles.

Turbojets and turbofans

The first jet engines were developed independently in the 1930s by Frank Whittle in England and Dr. Hans von Ohain in Germany. The jet is basically a gas turbine engine; the essential difference is that the turbine section extracts only a part of the energy of the gas flow. This extracted energy is just sufficient to drive the compressor in a *turbojet* or the compressor and a fan in a *turbofan*. The rest is used to accelerate the gas out through a nozzle at the rear of the engine —so driving the aircraft forward.

Newton's third law of motion states that for every action there is an equal but opposite reaction. In the case of the jet engine, pushing large amounts of gas rearwards at high velocity is the action, and the reaction to this is the forward thrust on the engine.

Whittle's first engine ran in April 1937, and the first British jet plane the Gloster E28/39 flew in May 1941. By the end of the Second World War, refined forms of this engine had been built in Britain and the USA for use in fighter aircraft.

Whittle's engine used a *centrifugal* compressor, because despite being fatter and less efficient than an axial compressor it was already well developed and easier to make. This type of compressor is essentially a spinning disc on which curved walls fling the airflow outwards at high velocity. Around the disc, often called the *impeller*, is a fixed deflector or *diffuser* in which the airflow is turned rearwards and slowed down. Its pressure rises as it is slowed.

Centrifugal compressor technology has since developed greatly, and almost all gas turbines designed for light planes, road vehicles, and small stationary power units use these cheap and robust compressors. At speeds higher than 30,000 rpm they can develop a pressure ratio exceeding 7:1.

Whittle's engines used an array of separate combustion chambers or 'cans' and expelled the gas discharged from the turbine through a simple short nozzle. Such an engine is called a *turbojet*. It is the simplest of all gas turbines, but tends to be noisy and is less efficient in aircraft propulsion until supersonic speeds are reached.

Since 1950 the gap between the noisy, high-speed turbojet and the quieter low-speed turboprop has been filled by a broad range of engines at first called *ducted fans*, but today called *turbofans*. Some early types were aft-fan engines, in which an additional turbine was added to the rear of the jet and provided with very long blades, which acted on the air flowing past the outside of the engine, rather like a multi-bladed propeller.

Nowadays the fan is mounted at the front of the engine, and it is essentially an oversized axial compressor, usually having one (but often as many as four) stages. The air it compresses is divided into two parts. That compressed by the inner part of the fan enters the main compressor and passes through what is known as the 'core' of the engine.

The core consists of the compressors, combustion chamber and turbines. In the Pratt and Whitney TFE 731 engine, for example, there is a four-stage low pressure axial compressor, a single stage high pressure radial compressor, an annular combustion chamber, then a single stage high pressure and a three stage low pressure turbine.

The rest of the fan airflow, which is usually from two to six times greater than that passing into the core, is discharged through a separate outer fan duct and used to provide forward thrust, rather like the rearward airflow from a propeller. If the fan is designed to run at a lower speed than the turbine, it is driven from a reduction gearbox mounted in front of the compressor.

The turbofan creates a greater rearward flow than the turbojet, but at a lower velocity. This reduction in the jet flow velocity makes it very much quieter. The turbofan is today by far the most important aero engine (except for light aircraft). The latest designs have three separate shafts, each rotating at its own best speed. One carries the fan, one an intermediate pressure (ip) compressor, and the third the high pressure (hp) compressor. Each shaft has its own turbine and the shafts are concentric (mounted one within the other), with the hp shaft outermost.

Afterburners

Engines for supersonic aircraft need to be slim but powerful. Most modern military aircraft compromise by using a turbofan with a low *by-pass ratio*—the ratio of the fan or secondary airstream to the core or primary airstream. In these military engines the fan airflow is not much greater than the core airflow.

Virtually all supersonic aircraft have an afterburner which adds fuel to the gas flow downstream of the turbine. The fuel burns in the gas, giving a much higher jet velocity and temperature. This gives extra thrust, but at the expense of greatly increased fuel consumption, and so it is used mainly for take-off and, in the case of military aircraft, to give more engine power during combat manoeuvres.

An engine which has an afterburning or *reheat* system has to have a propelling nozzle whose diameter can be reduced when afterburning is not in use. As the nozzle is a large item, subject to severe stresses at about 1200°C (2200°F), it is not easy to make it open and close. The most common method is to use rings of inner and outer 'petal' flaps which are accurately positioned by hydraulic or pneumatic actuators located in cooler areas away from the nozzle.

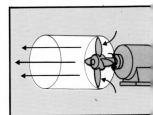

The series of six diagrams on the right show the underlying principles of the gas turbine engine, and the way it can be used to drive a car or a truck.

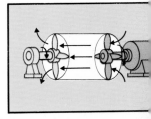

In the first diagram, an electric fan is drawing in air and blowing it through a hollow cylinder, rather like a turbine compressor blowing air through the engine core. If a freely mounted fan is placed at the end of the cylinder, as in the second drawing, the airflow from the electric fan will make it rotate, like a turbine rotor. If heat energy is added to the airflow between the two fans, the air will expand and accelerate, creating enough energy to enable the second fan to drive the first, as in the third diagram, and the electric motor can be dispensed with.

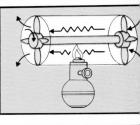

In a turbine, this heat energy is supplied by burning fuel in a combustion chamber between the compressor and the rotor, and the engine is started by an electric starter motor or by blowing compressed air through it. If sufficient energy is produced by heating the air between the fans, only part of it will be needed to drive them.

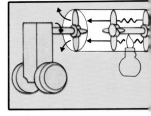

The remaining energy can be used to drive a third fan, shown in the fourth diagram, and a load. In a gas turbine, this third fan is the free or power turbine and it is used to drive, for example, an aircraft or ship propeller, the wheels of a car or a truck, or an electricity generator. Any heat energy remaining in the gas after it has driven the third fan can be used to help heat the air from the first fan before fuel is burnt in it, and thus less fuel has to be burned to raise the turbine gas to its working temperature.

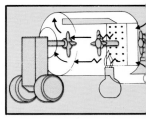

The heat from the exhaust gas is transferred to the air from the first fan in a device called a heat exchanger, as in the fifth drawing. The final drawing shows how the simple fans and other components shown in the other drawings relate to the components of an actual gas turbine engine. The advantage of having the power turbine on a separate shaft is that the speed of the compressor is unaffected by the load on the power turbine.

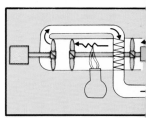

British Leyland

54

Left: The experimental Rover-BRM gas turbine engined sports car taking part in the Le Mans 24-hour race in 1965. It finished the race with an average speed of 160.6 kph (99.8 mph).

Right: A gas turbine powered frigate. Gas turbines are used in many types of ship, and are usually adapted from aero engines.

Below: A mobile gas turbine powered generating unit used to provide emergency electricity supplies.

British Leyland

Centrax

Vosper Thorneycroft

Right: The British Leyland 2S 350R gas turbine truck engine. It is started by a 24 V electric starter motor, which accelerates the compressor while fuel is sprayed into the combustion chamber and ignited by an electric ignitor plug. Once the engine has reached a quarter of its top speed the starter and ignitor are switched off, and the engine accelerates up to its idling speed, which is half its top speed.

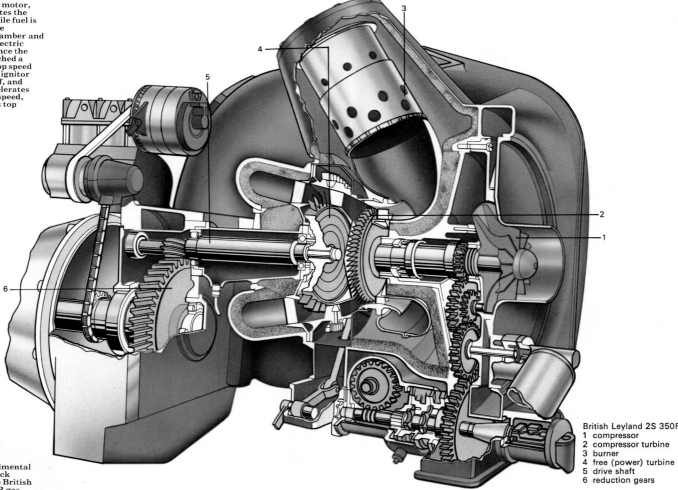

Left: An experimental articulated truck powered by the British Leyland 2S 350R gas turbine engine, a cutaway drawing of which is shown above right. The engine produces 260-300 kW (350-400 hp), can run on either petrol or diesel oil, and is designed for a life of 12,000 hours without major breakdowns.

British Leyland 2S 350R
1 compressor
2 compressor turbine
3 burner
4 free (power) turbine
5 drive shaft
6 reduction gears

Nuclear Power

The nucleus of an atom, the tiny central core around which the electrons are grouped, consists of positively charged particles called protons and uncharged particles called neutrons. The essential difference between an atom of one element and an atom of another lies in the numbers of protons and neutrons each possesses.

If the nucleus of an atom is split up, a process known as nuclear *fission* takes place, and a vast amount of energy is released as the protons and neutrons are scattered. Some of these will recombine to form fresh nuclei, creating atoms of lighter elements than the original one. For example, splitting a uranium atom may result in the formation of barium and krypton atoms and the liberation of three free neutrons. If one of these neutrons strikes the nucleus of a neighbouring uranium atom it will split it, and the process will begin again.

This sequence of a neutron striking a nucleus and splitting it, releasing more neutrons which then go on to split more nuclei, is called a *chain reaction*. In an atomic bomb, this chain reaction is allowed to proceed unchecked, resulting in a very rapid build-up of an enormous amount of energy which is released in a violent explosion. In a nuclear reactor, on the other hand, the speed at which the reaction spreads, and thus the rate at which the energy is released, is carefully controlled. The energy is given off in the form of heat, which is then used to raise steam to drive, for example, electricity generator turbines.

Only a few elements are capable of undergoing a fission chain reaction since this requires large, relatively unstable nuclei. These elements are known as *fissile* materials, and one of the most widely used is the isotope of uranium called uranium-235 (^{235}U) which has 92 protons and 143 neutrons in its nucleus.

Even with a suitably fissile material, a chain reaction will only be self-sustaining if there is a sufficient mass of the material (and thus enough fissile nuclei present) to ensure that as many neutrons as possible are able to collide with nuclei and split them, freeing more neutrons to keep the reaction going. If the mass of a piece of fissile material exceeds this mass, which is known as the *critical mass*, a self-sustaining chain reaction will begin spontaneously.

In the case of uranium-235, for example, the critical mass is about 50 kg (110 lb). Below the critical mass a reaction can only be sustained if neutrons are constantly supplied from an external source.

Fermi's pile

The first controlled nuclear reaction was created by Enrico Fermi (1901-1954) in Chicago on 2 December 1942. Fermi had already shown that neutrons could be slowed down by releasing them in a *moderator* such as water or graphite. The neutrons bounce off the atoms of the moderator, losing energy and slowing down as they do so. These neutrons are called 'thermal' neutrons because when slowed they possess about the same level of energy as the heat energy possessed by the atoms or molecules of the substance through which they are passing. The slow neutrons are more efficient at causing fission than fast ones.

Fermi's reactor or 'pile' consisted of a pile of graphite blocks, throughout which lumps of uranium were dispersed. Strips of neutron-absorbing cadmium were provided as control rods, regulating the speed at which the chain reaction could proceed by absorbing some of the free neutrons, while counters and foils were used to measure the rate at which neutrons were being produced.

At *criticality*, when enough fuel had been assembled for a chain reaction to take place, the pile was about 7.8 m (24 ft) across and 6.2 m (19 ft) high. Criticality was approached by adding successive layers of graphite and uranium to the pile, and it finally contained about 6 tonnes of uranium, of which 0.7% was the lighter isotope ^{235}U, and 99.3% was ^{238}U (92 protons and 146 neutrons).

At this time it was understood that when ^{238}U captures a thermal neutron the resulting compound nucleus ^{239}U does not undergo fission, but disposes of the energy it gained during the capture (known as its *energy of excitation*) by emitting high energy photons of the form of electromagnetic radiation known as *gamma radiation*. Later, it emits two electrons (*beta particles*) in succession as two of its neutrons decay into photons.

The resulting nucleus, with 94 protons and 145 neutrons, is ^{239}Pu, an isotope of a previously unknown element, plutonium. Like ^{235}U, plutonium-239 is a fissile material which is suitable for making atomic bombs, and is used in the new Fast Breeder reactors that are now being developed.

Above: The world's first nuclear reactor, built by Enrico Fermi in 1942.

Right: Enrico Fermi was born in Rome on 29 September 1901. He studied in Pisa, and later went to work with Max Born at Gottingen, returning to Italy in 1924. He became Professor of Theoretical Physics at Rome University in 1927, and investigated quantum statistics, beta decay and neutrinos, but his most important work was the study of radioactivity and neutron bombardment for which he received a Nobel Prize in 1938. In that year, he left Italy to work in the USA, joining the University of Chicago in 1941. He died in Chicago in 1954.

Below: A diagram showing how the fuel, moderator and control rods are arranged in a nuclear reactor. The moderator slows the fast neutrons so that they react more readily with the fuel, and the neutron-absorbing control rods control the speed of the reaction. The diagrams at the bottom show six types of nuclear power station.

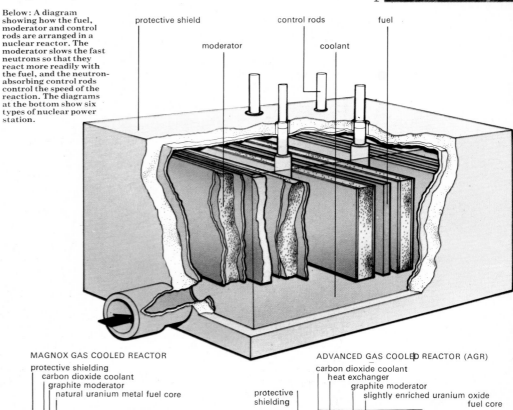

protective shield

moderator

control rods

coolant

fuel

MAGNOX GAS COOLED REACTOR

protective shielding
carbon dioxide coolant
graphite moderator
natural uranium metal fuel core

heat exchanger

pump

generator

ADVANCED GAS COOLED REACTOR (AGR)

carbon dioxide coolant
heat exchanger
graphite moderator
slightly enriched uranium oxide fuel core

protective shielding

pump

generator

Left: Loading fuel elements into an Advanced Gas Cooled reactor at Hinckley 'B' power station in Somerset, England. Each fuel element consists of 36 stainless steel fuel pins, filled with uranium oxide pellets inside a graphite sleeve. When fully loaded the reactor contains 2,464 fuel elements.

Below: The top of the experimental High Temperature Reactor at Winfrith, Dorset. This reactor, known as the 'Dragon' reactor, is a helium-cooled, graphite-moderated reactor, and is one of the projects set up by the European Nuclear Energy Agency. Supported by 12 countries, this project was started in 1959.

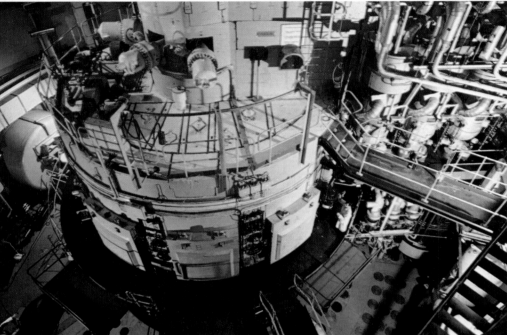

Left: Unloading pellets of uranium-plutonium oxide fuel from a furnace which forms the pellets from a powder mixture. There is a radiation-proof glass shield between the operator and the fuel, and he handles it by means of special gloves fitted into the shield. This type of fuel may be used in future Fast Breeder reactors.

Right: The coolant pipes at the bottom of the prototype Steam Generating Heavy Water Reactor at Winfrith. This prototype produces 300,000 kW of heat, which raises the steam to drive generator turbines that generate 100,000 kW of electricity for supply to the National Grid.

The bomb dropped on Hiroshima used ^{235}U as its fissile material, but the Nagasaki bomb used ^{239}Pu. In both cases, the explosion was achieved by using conventional high explosives to force pieces of the fissile material together to form a *supercritical* mass, which then exploded almost instantly as the chain reaction spread through it.

Modern reactors

Modern *thermal reactors*, so named because they use thermal neutrons, use one of three moderators to slow the fast neutrons given off by fission and make them thermal neutrons. These are graphite, which consists of pure carbon; 'heavy' water, which is *deuterium* (symbol D, an isotope of hydrogen which has one proton and one neutron in its nucleus) combined with oxygen; and 'light' water, which is just ordinary water. As they collide with the moderator nuclei, the neutrons lose energy, rather as the cue ball is slowed down by collisions on a snooker table.

Of the three moderators, graphite was originally favoured, especially in the United Kingdom, where it is used in the Magnox and Advanced Gas-cooled Reactor (AGR) power stations. Looking to the future, graphite is the moderator used in the helium-cooled High Temperature Reactor (HTR), pioneered by the international Dragon Project at Winfrith in England. The use of heavy water has been developed mainly in Canada, its particular attraction being that it is the least wasteful of neutrons.

Light water is the most compact moderator, an important consideration in nuclear power plants for submarines and surface ships. Light water reactors have been highly developed in the USA and USSR, not only for ship propulsion, but also as power station reactors. The United States' Pressurized Water Reactor (PWR) uses ordinary water as the moderator and coolant. In order to cope with the heat it is pressurized so that it equals approximately 150 atmospheres.

Magnox reactors are fuelled with uranium metal clad in a magnesium alloy, but most present-day nuclear reactors have fuel in the form of pellets of uranium oxide sealed in long metal tubes or 'pins'. These pins are grouped together in fuel 'elements', several hundred of which are required to charge the reactor. Typically, the fuel stays in the reactor for 3 to 5 years before it must be removed.

The heat which fission generates in the fuel pins is carried away by a stream of liquid or gas coolant, which is passed through heat exchangers, where steam is raised in secondary circuits for feeding the turbo-generators. In the Boiling Water Reactor (BWR) and in SGHWR, the primary coolant is water, but its pressure is adjusted so that boiling occurs in the fuel channels. The steam so generated may be fed direct to the turbine.

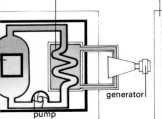

SURIZED WATER REACTOR (PWR)
ctive shielding
surised water coolant and moderator
riched uranium oxide fuel core
heat exchanger
generator
pump

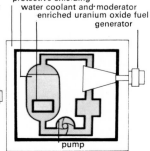

BOILING WATER REACTOR (BWR)
protective snielding
water coolant and moderator
enriched uranium oxide fuel
generator
pump

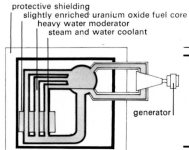

HEAVY WATER REACTOR (SG HWR)
protective shielding
slightly enriched uranium oxide fuel core
heavy water moderator
steam and water coolant
generator

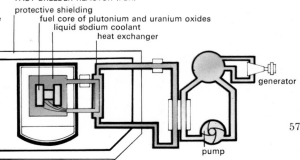

FAST BREEDER REACTOR (FBR)
protective shielding
fuel core of plutonium and uranium oxides
liquid sodium coolant
heat exchanger
generator
pump

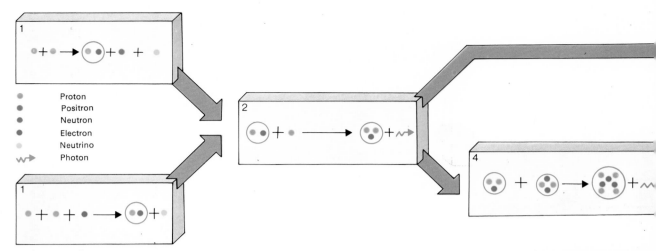

- Proton
- Positron
- Neutron
- Electron
- Neutrino
- ∿ Photon

Although in general gas-cooling offers prospects of higher temperatures, and thus higher efficiencies when generating power, it tends to be less compact than water-cooling.

Whichever coolant is used it must be maintained at high pressure, either by enclosing the fuel, moderator and coolant in a pressure vessel, or by placing the fuel elements in pressure tubes through which the coolant is forced. The reactor is surrounded by a concrete case called a 'biological shield', several feet thick, to protect the operators from radiation.

Radiation

There are three types of radiation which may be given off during atomic reactions, or when a *radioactive* element decays. The unstable nucleus of such an element achieves stability by giving off particles, gradually transmuting itself through a series of lighter elements.

Uranium, for example, decays through a series of 'daughter' elements until it eventually becomes lead. The rate of decay of a radioactive element is measured in terms of its *half life*, which is the time taken for half the atoms initially present to decay into the next daughter element in the particular series. Half life times range from fractions of a second to millions of years. For example, ^{238}U has a half-life of 4.5×10^9 years, whereas astatine has a half life of only 8.3 hours.

The three types of radiation are known as *alpha*, *beta* and *gamma* radiation. Alpha radiation is the emission of alpha particles, each of which consists of two protons and two neutrons. Beta radiation is a stream of beta particles, either negatively charged electrons or their positively charged counterparts, positrons. Gamma radiation is similar to, but stronger than, X-rays and is given off by atoms which have surplus energy following the emission of an alpha or beta particle or after the capture of a neutron. All three forms of radiation are dangerous to living things, and can cause burns, cancers, infertility and genetic damage.

Waste disposal

When fuel elements have come to the end of their useful lives, they are withdrawn from the reactor by remote control and placed in deep 'cooling ponds' nearby. There they remain for about six months, to allow much of the radioactivity of the fission products to die away. They are then transported in heavily shielded casks, which may weigh up to 100 tons, to a re-processing plant, such as that at the Sellafield (Windscale) Works of British Nuclear Fuels plc.

Here, the fuel is dissolved in acids and the residual uranium and plutonium are recovered. Of the fission products, the inert gases, krypton and xenon, and some tritium, are released to the atmosphere. The rest of the tritium and small proportions of other fission products are discharged into the sea or pumped into suitable underground strata.

Much the greatest part of the fission products is stored in jacketted stainless-steel tanks, behind concrete shielding, with arrangements to dissipate the heat released by radioactive decay. Ultimate disposal of these wastes, which will remain radioactive for many centuries, is likely to be their incorporation into insoluble glassy substances that can be stored in water-filled ponds.

Fast Breeder Reactors

Present types of thermal reactor suffer from a serious limitation; they can, at best, consume only about 1 or 2% of the uranium available, most of the ^{238}U having to be rejected as useless because there is not enough ^{235}U available to create the chain reactions necessary to consume it. World resources are uncertain, but it seems likely that uranium could be in short supply early in the next century, if the installation of these types of power plant continues at an increasing rate. Two ways around this difficulty are being explored. One is to substitute thorium for ^{238}U in a thermal reactor, in which case a new fissile material, uranium 233, would be generated. By feeding this back into thermal reactors, it should be possible to consume much of the available thorium.

The other line of development is that of the controversial *fast breeder reactor*, which should be able to consume a high proportion of the uranium reserves, through the recycling of plutonium back to the reactors. As its name implies, the fast reactor employs no moderator, so that the neutrons retain their high velocities as they move through the core of the reactor. This avoids the difficulty which restricts the usefulness of plutonium as a fuel for thermal reactors, in which it tends to form higher isotopes, such as ^{240}Pu, instead of undergoing fission, when it absorbs neutrons. Because such wasteful losses of neutrons are minimised in the gas reactor, their absorption in ^{238}U can be used to breed at least one new ^{239}Pu nucleus for each that is destroyed.

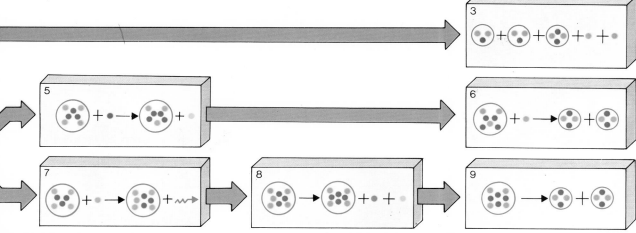

form beryllium-7 and a photon. (5) This beryllium-7 nucleus nearly always absorbs an electron and becomes the nucleus of lithium-7, emitting a neutrino in the process. (6) The lithium-7 nucleus then combines with a proton, and this makes it split up into two nuclei of helium-4. (7) Less commonly, the nucleus of beryllium-7 formed in stage (4) absorbs a proton, thus becoming a nucleus of boron-8 and emitting a photon. (8) This boron-8 then decays into beryllium-8 and gives off a positron and a neutrino. (9) In turn the beryllium-8 nucleus then splits in half to make two helium-4 nuclei Fusion reactors may be able to fuse deuterium to make helium and produce enormous energy.

Left: Loading fuel into the zero energy reactor Zenith II at Winfrith. A zero energy reactor is an experimental unit which does not produce any useful energy, but is designed to give information which can be used by nuclear power engineers in the design of full-scale reactors. This reactor uses 5 tonnes of fuel.

Right: The design and construction of fuel elements is continually being improved to ensure the most efficient, safe and reliable operation of nuclear reactors. In this test, an SGHWR fuel pin is being heated in an atmosphere of steam to simulate the conditions that would arise following the loss of coolant from a reactor core.

Below: This container, known as an Excellox 3 flask, is used for transporting used nuclear fuel by road to the British Nuclear Fuels reprocessing plant at Sellafield (formerly Windscale), Cumbria. During reprocessing any unused ^{235}U is recovered from the fuel for future use. The Sellafield plant is the biggest in the world, processing over 1,000 tonnes a year.

UKAEA

British Nuclear Fuels

Fusion reactions

The engineering and safety problems of the fast breeder reactor are formidable, so it is perhaps as well that an entirely different approach to the problem of utilising nuclear energy is being attempted. Its availability from uranium and thorium depends on the fact that these heavy elements can be split into lighter ones with an accompanying release of energy. Energy can also be obtained, however, by a sort of reverse of this process, the fusing together or *fusion* of two light nuclei to make a heavier one, a process which is accompanied by a release of nuclear energy.

The easiest fusion reaction to use a source of power is the D-T reaction. In this, the nuclei of two isotopes of hydrogen, the *deuteron* (the nucleus of deuterium) mass two, and the *triton* (the nucleus of tritium), mass three, fuse together. They form a helium nucleus, mass four, with the emission of an energetic neutron, mass one, and the liberation of energy. This is the basic reaction of the H-bomb.

Deuterium is available in almost unlimited quantities in the ocean, but tritium must be produced artificially from lithium by bombarding it with neutrons so that it absorbs them. In the H-bomb, lithium deuteride is detonated by neutrons and compression from an A-bomb trigger. In a controlled thermonuclear reactor, as at present envisaged, the reactant hydrogen isotopes would form an ionised plasma, periodically raised to temperatures at which the nuclei have kinetic energies of motion sufficient to enable them to react, despite the electrostatic repulsion of their positive charges.

The main reaction space would be surrounded by a lithium-containing blanket, in which the escaping neutrons are absorbed to maintain the supply of tritium. The technology of such reactors has yet to be successfully demonstrated, but world reserves of lithium are sufficient to provide an energy source comparable to that of uranium as it would be used in fast breeder reactors. Over the next few decades, the choice between uranium-based fission and lithium-based fusion may be dictated by environmental and economic considerations.

One great advantage of fusion is that it produces helium, a safe, inert gas, and less highly dangerous wastes than fission reactions. In the longer term, the more difficult fusion technology affords the prospect of almost unlimited energy supplies.

Fossil Fuels

The fossil fuels are so called because they are formed from the remains of plants and other living organisms that existed on earth millions of years ago. Peat, lignite and coal, for example, were formed from the remains of the trees and plants in ancient forests which sank into swamps and were subsequently covered by layers of mud which later became rock.

Petroleum (crude oil), on the other hand, probably originated from the remains of plants and animals living in seas and lakes. These remains settled on the sea or lake beds where they were gradually buried under layers of sediment. Slowly the organic remains were converted into petroleum and natural gas.

Peat

Peat is the initial stage in the formation of coal and was probably the first of the fossil fuels to be used by man. It is found in bogs, where it has formed from decayed rushes, reeds, mosses and sedges by the action of water and bacteria.

The formation of peat requires certain climatic and topographic conditions. There must be soil capable of retaining water at or near the surface, and the average temperature must be low enough to prevent rapid evaporation and decay, but not so low as to prevent the abundant growth of vegetation. The temperature best suited to the formation of peat is between 5° and 9°C (42° to 48°F), and so peat bogs are found in the temperate zones of the earth. For example, they cover large areas of swamp and fen land in northern Europe, varying in depth from 6 to 12 metres (20 to 40 ft).

Freshly cut peat contains up to 80 per cent of water, and so before it can be used as fuel it has to be dried out, either mechanically or by leaving it in the open air so that the water evaporates. When burnt in domestic fires, peat gives out a good heat and leaves a clean ash, but it produces a lot of smoke.

Properly dried peat yields almost as many by-products as coal does. Peat gas, for example, has been used successfully as a fuel for internal combustion engines and for various types of furnace. It does, however, require a longer and more complicated purification process than that needed for coal gas.

The process of extracting gas from peat also yields many valuable organic compounds, including alcohols and phenols, which are used as raw materials in a great number of industrial processes such as the manufacture of plastics, drugs, dyes and waxes.

Finely-shredded peat can be made into an exceptionally strong wrapping paper, while chemical treatment under pressure converts peat into a hard fibre suitable for making furniture and flooring.

In agriculture, peat makes a good absorbent litter for cattle, while cleaned peat is an excellent fodder. Ammonium sulphate, which can be obtained from peat, is a very good fertilizer.

Coal

Although outcroppings of coal have existed since prehistoric times, the use of coal as a source of heat is comparatively recent. To the ancient world, coal was

Picturepoint

Camera Press

Above: The Pitch Lake on the West Indian island of Trinidad. Pitch is a very heavy, semi-solid form of oil, and one of its main uses is as road tar.

Left: This power station in county Offaly, Eire, burns milled peat to raise the steam that drives its generator turbines. It produces 40 MW of electricity, and burns 280,000 tonnes of peat per annum.

Below: A crude oil distillation column. Crude oil, heated in a furnace, enters the column near the bottom. The constituent 'fractions' of the oil rise to various heights in the column; those with the lowest boiling points rise to the top.

merely a kind of black stone, and even the early metalworkers had no use for it as they did all their smelting with wood or charcoal.

There is some evidence that the ancient Britons used a certain amount of coal, and that the Romans learned of its value from them. The first definite written reference to coal, however, occurs in the Anglo-Saxon Chronicle, which was compiled in about 990AD. Among the first official references is one in a charter provided by King Henry III, in 1259, authorizing the inhabitants of Newcastle to dig coal from their fields.

During the following five centuries, the use of coal for domestic fires grew rapidly, and the soft, easily obtained coal which was used gave rise to serious pollution in the form of smoke and soot. It was heavily taxed, and in many places its burning was prohibited because of the danger to public health.

The consumption of coal increased rapidly during the eighteenth century, following the advent of the Industrial Revolution. In addition to its use as a fuel for steam engines, it became valuable as the source of coke, a hard, porous form of carbon used in steelmaking and also a fuel itself.

Shell

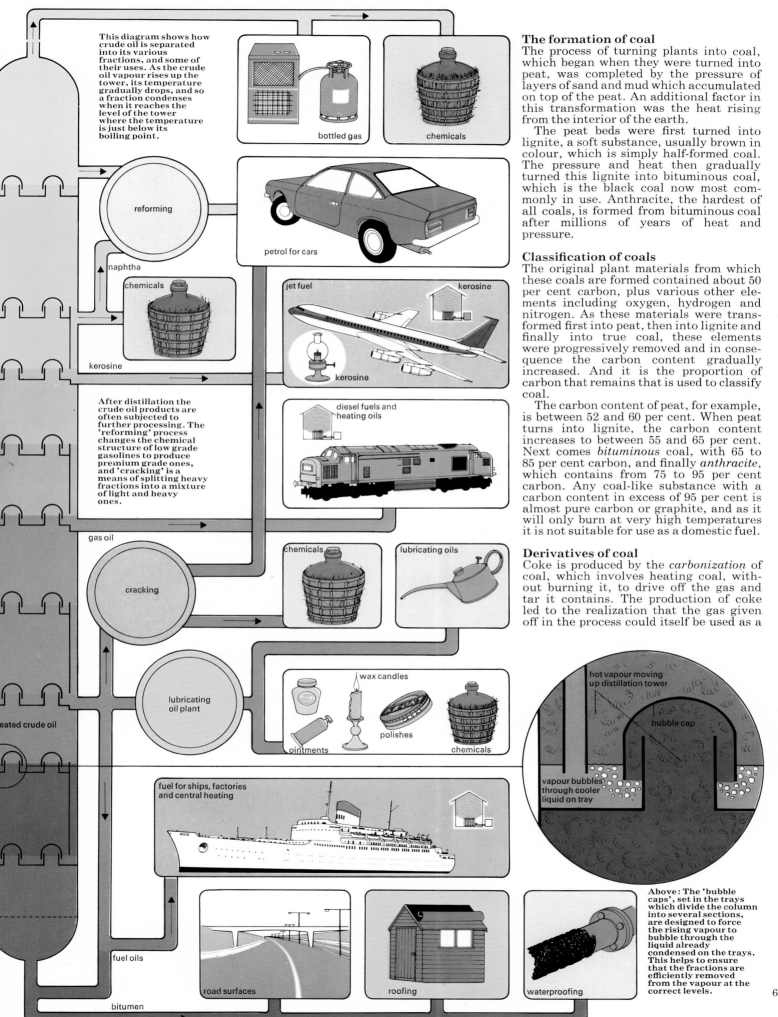

This diagram shows how crude oil is separated into its various fractions, and some of their uses. As the crude oil vapour rises up the tower, its temperature gradually drops, and so a fraction condenses when it reaches the level of the tower where the temperature is just below its boiling point.

bottled gas

chemicals

reforming

naphtha

petrol for cars

chemicals

kerosine

jet fuel

kerosine

kerosine

After distillation the crude oil products are often subjected to further processing. The 'reforming' process changes the chemical structure of low grade gasolines to produce premium grade ones, and 'cracking' is a means of splitting heavy fractions into a mixture of light and heavy ones.

diesel fuels and heating oils

gas oil

cracking

chemicals

lubricating oils

lubricating oil plant

wax candles

polishes

ointments

chemicals

heated crude oil

fuel for ships, factories and central heating

fuel oils

road surfaces

roofing

bitumen

waterproofing

The formation of coal

The process of turning plants into coal, which began when they were turned into peat, was completed by the pressure of layers of sand and mud which accumulated on top of the peat. An additional factor in this transformation was the heat rising from the interior of the earth.

The peat beds were first turned into lignite, a soft substance, usually brown in colour, which is simply half-formed coal. The pressure and heat then gradually turned this lignite into bituminous coal, which is the black coal now most commonly in use. Anthracite, the hardest of all coals, is formed from bituminous coal after millions of years of heat and pressure.

Classification of coals

The original plant materials from which these coals are formed contained about 50 per cent carbon, plus various other elements including oxygen, hydrogen and nitrogen. As these materials were transformed first into peat, then into lignite and finally into true coal, these elements were progressively removed and in consequence the carbon content gradually increased. And it is the proportion of carbon that remains that is used to classify coal.

The carbon content of peat, for example, is between 52 and 60 per cent. When peat turns into lignite, the carbon content increases to between 55 and 65 per cent. Next comes *bituminous* coal, with 65 to 85 per cent carbon, and finally *anthracite*, which contains from 75 to 95 per cent carbon. Any coal-like substance with a carbon content in excess of 95 per cent is almost pure carbon or graphite, and as it will only burn at very high temperatures it is not suitable for use as a domestic fuel.

Derivatives of coal

Coke is produced by the *carbonization* of coal, which involves heating coal, without burning it, to drive off the gas and tar it contains. The production of coke led to the realization that the gas given off in the process could itself be used as a

hot vapour moving up distillation tower

bubble cap

vapour bubbles through cooler liquid on tray

Above: The 'bubble caps', set in the trays which divide the column into several sections, are designed to force the rising vapour to bubble through the liquid already condensed on the trays. This helps to ensure that the fractions are efficiently removed from the vapour at the correct levels.

61

fuel, and that the coal tar was a valuable source of many useful organic compounds such as benzene, toluene and phenol.

Coal gas is a mixture of several gases, typically 50 per cent hydrogen (H_2), 25 per cent methane (CH_4), and 10 per cent nitrogen (N_2), plus small amounts of carbon monoxide (CO), carbon dioxide (CO_2), ethylene (C_2H_4), benzene (C_6H_6) and oxygen (O_2).

Coal tar contains over 200 compounds, many of which are important raw materials for a wide range of industrial processes. These include the production of fats, soaps, dyes, drugs, flavouring essences, solvents, tars, plastics, explosives and insecticides.

Another means of obtaining useful by-products from coal is the *hydrogenation* process. Powdered coal is processed with hydrogen gas at high temperatures and pressures, and this produces a form of oil which is then further processed with hydrogen to make petrol and diesel oil. The hydrogenation process also yields ammonia (NH_3) and a wide range of light hydrocarbons.

Petroleum

The name 'petroleum' is derived from the latin words *petra*, meaning 'rock', and *oleum*, meaning 'oil'. It thus means 'rock oil', so distinguishing it from animal or vegetable oils. Petroleum deposits are trapped beneath layers of impervious rock, but in some places they have seeped to the surface and collected in pools. The lighter constituents have evaporated out of these pools, leaving behind surface deposits of pitch or bitumen, very heavy, semi-solid forms of oil.

Only a small amount of the petroleum formed beneath the earth's crust rose through fissures in the rock to collect in pools, and most remained trapped beneath domes of impervious rock. Normally there is a layer of natural gas above the petroleum, and frequently a layer of salt water beneath it. In many cases the richest deposits of petroleum lie beneath a great depth of rock and can be reached only by massive and costly drilling operations.

Although the Chinese had been drilling for oil as long ago as 320BC, their wells were never very deep. The first serious modern attempt to drill for oil was by Edwin L. Drake, who drilled a successful well about 30 metres (100 ft) deep in Pennsylvania in 1859, and this marked the beginning of today's petroleum industry.

Petroleum from the early oilfields was primarily used for domestic lighting and heating oils, but towards the end of the nineteenth century it became very important as the source of fuel for the new internal combustion engines. Today, however, petroleum is much more than just a source of fuel, and even the natural gas associated with it, which was once considered a waste product and burnt away, is carefully collected and distributed for domestic and industrial use. Natural gas is a mixture of several gases, the principal ones being methane (CH_4) and ethane (C_2H_6).

Petroleum, often called 'crude oil' or simply 'crude', is a complex mixture of an enormous number of hydrocarbon compounds, together with small amounts of compounds of other elements. The exact composition of a crude oil depends on many factors, such as its age and the

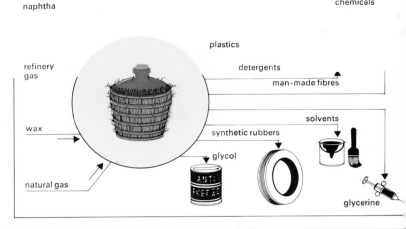

naphtha · refinery gas · wax · natural gas · agricultural chemicals · plastics · detergents · man-made fibres · solvents · synthetic rubbers · glycol · glycerine · ANTI FREEZE

types of organism from which it was formed. Every deposit of crude oil is a unique mixture, whose exact composition differs even from deposits separated from it vertically or horizontally by only a few metres of rock.

The chief hydrocarbons present belong to the *paraffin*, *naphthene* and *aromatic* groups of organic compounds. The paraffins are compounds with a general formula C_nH_{n+2}, and the carbon atoms within them are arranged in straight or branched chains. The naphthenes, also called *cycloparaffins*, are formed by the removal of two hydrogen atoms from each end carbon atom of a paraffin chain, and then joining the chain together to form a ring. The simplest naphthenes have only one carbon ring per molecule, and can be sub-divided into the *cyclopentanes*, with five carbon atoms in the ring, and the *cyclohexanes*, which have six carbon atoms in the ring.

The aromatics are compounds based on the benzene (C_6H_6) ring. They are extremely useful to the chemical industry, but they must be removed from fuel oils because they adversely affect their burning properties.

The non-hydrocarbon compounds present in crude oil are mainly compounds

Above: Measuring the sulphur content of petroleum products. The samples are burned, and the combustion gases given off are collected and analyzed so that the sulphur content can be calculated. Sulphur compounds are a source of air pollution, so they must be kept to a minimum in motor fuels.

Below: A general view of a modern oil refinery. The world's refineries produce over 3,000 million tonnes of products annually, including fuels, oils, gases, waxes, bitumen, and the chemical *feedstocks* which are the basis of the vast range of oil-based products such as plastics and detergents.

Shell

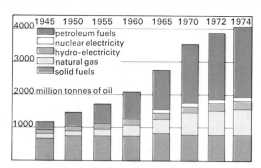

Right: The growth in world energy demand (excluding China, the USSR and Eastern Europe) from 1945 to 1974. The contribution of non-oil fuels is expressed in terms of the amount of oil which would provide the same amount of energy. In 1974, petroleum fuels provided 51% of the total energy supplied.

Picturepoint

BAC

John Goldblatt

Above left: Oil derivatives are the raw materials for some of the most important plastics now in use. Ethylene, for example, is used in the manufacture of polyethylene (better known as polythene), and benzene is one of the chief raw materials used in the production of nylon.

Above: The world's airlines are some of the biggest consumers of petroleum fuels. Jet aircraft fuels are based on a type of paraffin known as aviation kerosine, often blended with a low-octane gasoline. This picture shows a British Airways *Concorde* refuelling at Singapore.

Above: Most candles are now made from paraffin wax obtained from crude oil. They are made by pouring molten wax into a mould containing the wick, or by forcing small particles of solid wax into a mould at high pressure and compressing them around the wick, which is usually made of plaited cotton.

Right: Cattle can be protected from parasitic insects and infective organisms by passing them through a bath or 'dip' of water containing chemicals which kill off the insects and germs. Many agricultural chemicals, including such pesticides, are made from the by-products of oil refining.

Shell

of sulphur, nitrogen and oxygen. Crude oil may contain as much as 7 per cent sulphur, up to 2 per cent nitrogen, and up to 1.5 per cent oxygen. Other elements present in very small amounts include vanadium, nickel, chlorine, arsenic and lead, as well as particles of material from the rock containing the crude.

The petroleum is refined by *fractional distillation*, which involves heating it in a tall tower so that the various compounds are distilled out of it and rise to various levels in the tower. The lightest compounds such as the gases, which have low boiling points, rise to the top, and the heavier oils with higher boiling points are collected lower down.

The distillates may then be further processed by *cracking* or by *reforming*, both of which involve the use of *catalysts*. These are substances which assist in creating a chemical reaction, but which themselves remain unchanged by the reaction. Catalytic cracking, often called 'cat cracking', is a means of breaking down the heavier distillates to form lighter compounds. Reforming is used to change low-grade distillates into higher grade ones, for example a low grade motor fuel can be reformed into a higher grade one.

Petroleum derivatives have an enormous range of uses—making plastics, artificial rubber, detergents, anaesthetics, insecticides, explosives, chewing gum, wax polishes, dyes, cosmetics, food preservatives, artificial silk, adhesives, medicines, paints and a large number of chemicals. It was this enormous and important range of petroleum derivatives that prompted the Shah of Iran to comment that 'oil is too good for burning'.

63

Gas Production

The earliest users of gas were the ancient Chinese. They used natural gas, piped through bamboo tubes, for lighting; and even obtained salt from sea water by evaporating it in iron tanks heated by burning natural gas escaping through fissures in the ground. The modern use of gas, however, did not begin until the late eighteenth century, when engineers in France and Britain succeeded in building practical coal-gas lighting systems.

Experiments in producing gas from coal had been carried out by many people during the seventeenth and eighteenth centuries. But although many individual gases were discovered and analyzed, none of the experiments resulted in a practical application of gas. For example, Jean Tardier, a French chemist, published a treatise in 1618 which described how he had produced gas by heating coal in an iron pot. He had intended to use the gas for lighting, but the lamp he built was far too clumsy and dangerous for practical use.

One of the first major developments came in 1765 when a man called Spedding, the manager of Lord Lonsdale's coal mine near Whitehaven, Cumberland, tapped gas from a burning bed of coal to light the mine's offices. Despite the success of this project, however, it was almost 30 years before the next major advance in gas production.

In 1792 an engineer named William Murdock built a small iron retort in the back garden of his house in Redruth, Cornwall. Coal gas from the retort was stored in a small gasholder, and then ducted through piping to provide illumination for his combined home and offices. Some years later he built a gas lighting system for the Birmingham works of his employers, Boulton and Watt, who made steam engines and mill machinery.

Boulton and Watt subsequently began building and selling gas-making and lighting equipment, which was designed by Murdock in association with another member of the firm, Samuel Clegg. At this time each customer had an individual gas-making plant to supply the gas for the lighting, and Murdock rejected the idea of a single gas works supplying gas by pipeline to local consumers.

The founder of the modern system of gas distribution was F. A. Winsor, an international financier. He had no technical or scientific qualifications, and knew nothing of gas-making, but he was convinced that selling gas rather than gas-making equipment was financially viable. Despite bitter opposition, Winsor formed the Gas Light and Coke Company in London in 1812. Samuel Clegg, who had left Boulton and Watt and set himself up as a designer and builder of gas equipment in 1806, was appointed chief engineer.

Thanks to Winsor's energy and enthusiasm and Clegg's engineering genius, the company's first plant was built and in production within a year. Then the necessary pipelines were laid, and by the end of 1813 gas street lighting had been installed in Westminster. The success of the Gas Light and Coke Company led to the installation of gas systems in cities

Gas Council

Above: One of the last British plants for making gas from oil-based feedstocks. In 1968 oil gas plant accounted for 73.1% of the total British gas-making capacity, and coal gas plant for only 11.2%. By the middle of the 1970s, however, natural gas had almost completely replaced other forms of gas.

Left: This plant is used to make town gas from low sulphur content hydrocarbon feedstocks such as refinery gas or liquid petroleum gas. The feedstock is reformed by heating it under pressure in the presence of a nickel catalyst—this assists the process but is not itself affected by it.

Lurgi

Right: The Lurgi process for making producer gas. As the coal travels down through the gasifier the hot gases rising from below turn it into coke. As the coke descends it yields a gas consisting largely of hydrogen and carbon monoxide. Any remaining coke is burnt to provide the heat.

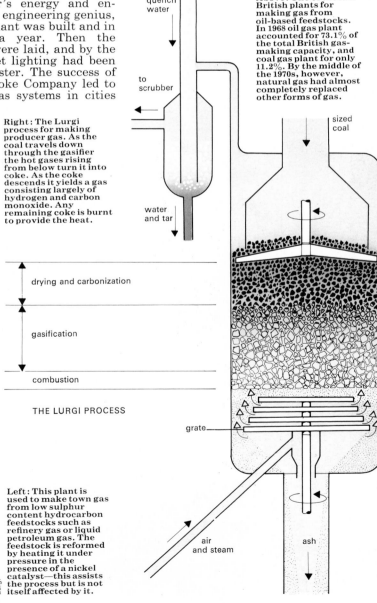

quench water

to scrubber

water and tar

sized coal

drying and carbonization

gasification

combustion

THE LURGI PROCESS

grate

air and steam

ash

Left: When a system is converted from town gas to natural gas, the pipes must be cleared of the town gas they contain before the natural gas is put into them. This picture shows town gas being burned off from a pipe in the street during North Sea gas conversion work in London.

Spectrum

Above: The first commercial gas installations had their own gas-making equipment as there was no piped distribution system. An alternative to having an individual gas plant was to have a gasholder to which gas was delivered when needed; this picture shows a French gas delivery cart.

Mary Evans

North Thames Gas Board

Above: A rail truck for collecting hot coke discharged from the retorts of a gas works. Coke was invented in the 17th century by Derbyshire brewers, who found that when they burned coal to heat the liquor from the mashed barley, the result was an undrinkable beer. This was due to the sulphur in the coal. They solved the problem by 'charring' the coal to make coke. Only later was it realized that useful gases and tars were given off during the charring.

Left: A coal gas works. In many countries coal gas production at such plants has ceased because of the availability of natural gas which also has a higher calorific value.

London News Agency

throughout Britain and abroad, and the company itself continued in operation until the British gas industry was nationalized in 1948.

The use of gas for cooking and heating began in the middle of the nineteenth century, with the introduction of gas stoves in 1840 and gas fires in 1855. The modern use of natural gas also began during this period, with the formation of the Fredonia Gas Light and Water Works Company in the US in 1858.

In addition to coal gas and natural gas, a certain amount of gas is made from oil, and processes are being developed for the manufacture of substitute or 'synthetic' natural gas from coal.

Coal gas

Coal gas is made by the *carbonization* of bituminous coal, a process involving heating coal in the absence of air. The coal is heated in retorts or ovens to a temperature of approximately 1,350°C (2,462°F), so that it softens and releases its gas.

This gas is thick and brown in colour because of the presence of coal tar vapour, and it also contains ammonia (NH_3) and hydrogen sulphide (H_2S) gases. These gases and the tar are removed by passing the gases through a series of purification processes. The purified coal gas is itself a mixture of gases, and its exact composition depends upon the type of coal used and the kind of oven or retort in which it was made.

The main constituent, however, is hydrogen which makes up approximately half the volume. It also contains 25 to 35 per cent methane (CH_4), up to 10 per cent nitrogen (N_2) and as much as 6 per cent carbon monoxide (CO). It also contains small amounts of gaseous hydrocarbons, carbon dioxide (CO_2) and oxygen. Completion of the carbonization process leaves a residue of coke, which is cooled and graded to be used again as fuel.

There are four main types of carbonization plant for the production of gas: *continuous vertical retorts*, *horizontal retorts*, *coke ovens* and *intermittent vertical retorts*. The most widely used type, however, is the first.

A continuous vertical retort system consists of a number of ovens grouped in units of four. The coal is fed in through gas-tight valves at the top of the retorts, which are heated by *producer gas* burnt in ducts around the outside. This gas is made in what are called *producers*, in which coke is heated with air and steam to yield a gas consisting mainly of nitrogen, carbon monoxide and hydrogen.

The coke formed in the retorts is extracted from them by a discharge mechanism, and fed into a sealed chamber from which it is removed at regular intervals. The coke is so hot when it leaves the retort that it would ignite spontaneously on contact with the air if it were discharged without first being cooled. This cooling is done by constantly spraying water into the coke chamber.

The gas yield from any given quantity of coal is increased by passing steam into the base of the retort. The steam provides preliminary cooling of the coke, and reacts with the carbon it contains to form *blue water gas*, a mixture of carbon monoxide and hydrogen. This gas passes up through the retort and mixes with the crude coal gas.

The mixture of gases and steam pro-

65

duced in the retorts is collected and passed to a water-cooled condensing system. Here its temperature is reduced to between 15° and 20°C (59° to 68°F). This causes most of the tar vapour to condense out, together with the steam. Most of the ammonia and other impurities are removed simultaneously as they dissolve in the condensed steam, forming what is known as *ammoniacal liquor*.

The remaining ammonia and tar are removed from the gas by passing it through washers, where it is bubbled through weak ammoniacal liquor. Residual tar can also be removed by an electrostatic system, operating at up to 50,000 volts, which separates the tar from the gas by electrostatic attraction. The hydrogen sulphide is removed from the gas by passing it over grids covered in hydrated iron oxide, which absorbs the hydrogen sulphide and is converted into iron sulphide.

To prevent corrosion of the distribution mains or user's equipment and appliances, the final purification stage removes any water. Finally the gas is dried by contact with either glycerine or calcium chloride, then piped to storage holders ready for distribution.

Most gas works also produce what is known as *carburetted water gas*. This is the result of enriching blue water gas with vaporized gas oil, a form of diesel oil. The carburetted water gas is mixed with the coal gas at the inlet to the gasholder, and the mixture is known as *town gas*.

One of the more recent developments in coal gas production is the *Lurgi process*, which can produce gas from grades of

Left: A natural gas flare at a German gas processing plant. Natural gas is composed primarily of methane and ethane, and is found beneath the earth either alone or with crude oil. There are extensive natural gas deposits in north Africa, the USSR, the USA and beneath the North Sea.

Above: Storage tanks for liquefied natural gas. Liquefaction of the gas greatly reduces its volume, making it easier to store and transport in large quantities. One of the major exporters of liquid natural gas is Algeria, and this gas is carried in the pressurized holds of specially built tankers.

Gerolf Kalt/ZEFA

Lurgi

coal formerly thought unsuitable. The coal is gasified by high-pressure streams of steam and oxygen, and as all the carbon is converted into gas there is no coke residue. The gas produced contains less impurities than ordinary coal gas, but its burning quality is lower and so it has to be enriched by the addition of butane (C_4H_{10}) or methane (CH_4).

Oil gas

Gas can also be made from mineral oils. This was originally done by 'cracking' crude oil, which meant reacting it with steam at temperatures of over 1,000 °C (1,832 °F) to split it into various liquid and gaseous hydrocarbon compounds. It was later found that most liquid hydrocarbons could be used as 'feedstocks' (raw materials) and a large number of processes were developed for making gas from them.

Oil gas is of high quality, and is low in impurities. It contains a mixture of hydrocarbons, including methane, acetylene and benzene, and it can be mixed with town gas and distributed in the normal way through a system of pipelines.

Natural gas

In many parts of the world there are valuable deposits of natural gas, either in association with oil or on their own. This gas was once considered as little more than a nuisance when discovered during drilling for oil, and was merely disposed of by burning it at the oilfields. This is still done in many areas, particularly at oilfields in remote desert areas far from any potential consumers of gas.

Today, however, oil-producing countries are beginning to collect and process this gas, either for export in liquefied form or to provide fuel and feedstocks for their own developing industries and cities. Saudi Arabia, for example, was burning off over 110 million cubic metres (4,000 million cubic feet) of gas per day in 1975, but is now building a system to collect and distribute this gas.

Natural gas has been the major source of gas in the United States since the 1930s, and gas from beneath the bed of the North Sea is now the primary source of gas for Britain and other northern European countries.

Natural gas is composed primarily of methane, together with ethane and small amounts of propane (C_3H_8), butane and nitrogen. Its *calorific value*, that is, the amount of heat that can be obtained by burning a given volume of it, is over twice that of town gas. This poses a problem when a gas network is to be changed from using coal gas to natural gas; either the natural gas must be processed to make it into a gas similar to town gas, with the same calorific value, or else all the appliances and equipment in use on the network must be converted to make them able to use the natural gas efficiently and safely.

When Britain began using gas from the North Sea it was decided to convert the system to handle natural gas, because although the cost of conversion was enormous it was estimated that the cost of *reforming* natural gas into town gas, over a period of 30 years, would be over four times the cost of a ten-year conversion programme. In addition, as the natural gas had over twice the calorific value of the town gas, the existing gas network would, in effect, be able to provide twice the amount of energy.

Deleu/ZEFA

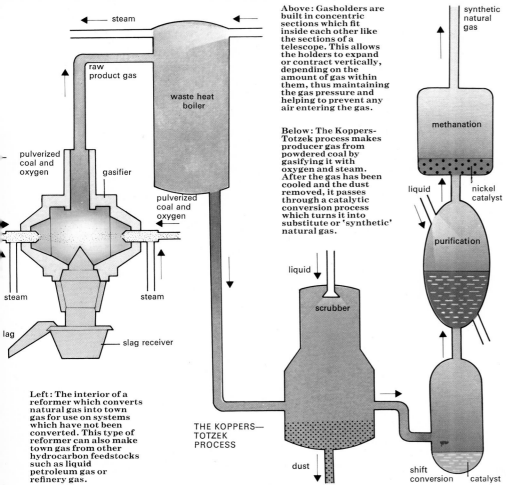

Above: Gasholders are built in concentric sections which fit inside each other like the sections of a telescope. This allows the holders to expand or contract vertically, depending on the amount of gas within them, thus maintaining the gas pressure and helping to prevent any air entering the gas.

Below: The Koppers-Totzek process makes producer gas from powdered coal by gasifying it with oxygen and steam. After the gas has been cooled and the dust removed, it passes through a catalytic conversion process which turns it into substitute or 'synthetic' natural gas.

Left: The interior of a reformer which converts natural gas into town gas for use on systems which have not been converted. This type of reformer can also make town gas from other hydrocarbon feedstocks such as liquid petroleum gas or refinery gas.

steam

raw product gas

waste heat boiler

pulverized coal and oxygen

gasifier

pulverized coal and oxygen

steam

steam

slag

slag receiver

THE KOPPERS—TOTZEK PROCESS

liquid

scrubber

dust

synthetic natural gas

methanation

liquid

nickel catalyst

purification

shift conversion

catalyst

Batteries and Fuel Cells

An electricity battery consists of one or more electric *cells*, which are devices for producing electric currents directly from chemical reactions. Electricity made in this way is much more expensive than that made by mechanical generators, but batteries, being compact and portable, are a better choice for many applications. The chemical generation of electricity is possible because many chemical reactions involve simply an exchange of electrons between atoms of different kinds.

The electrical nature of such reactions can easily be shown by passing a direct current through distilled water to which a little acid has been added to improve its ability to conduct electricity. The result is that the water splits up into bubbles of hydrogen and oxygen gases which can be collected separately.

This process of breaking down liquids by electricity is known as *electrolysis* and is widely used in industrial chemistry for separating many different compounds into their simple constituents. An electric cell performs electrolysis in reverse, forming compounds from simpler constituents in such a way that electricity is produced by the chemical reactions taking place.

In principle the action of an electric cell is simple. A current is created in a wire by feeding in electrons at one end and sucking them out at the other, causing the electrons to flow through the wire as an electric current. This is accomplished by attaching each end of the wire to a metal plate which is immersed in an *electrolyte*, a chemical solution of some *ionic* compound. When such a compound is dissolved, its molecules split into two or more parts which are kept apart by the molecules of the liquid it is dissolved in. Some parts of the dissolved molecule have a positive electric charge and are known as *positive ions*; other parts have a negative charge and are called *negative ions*.

For example, when sulphuric acid (H_2SO_4) is dissolved in water, the two hydrogen atoms are separated from each other and from the rest of the molecule. Because each loses an electron in this process, they become hydrogen ions and are denoted by the symbol H^+ to indicate that they have a positive charge. The rest of the molecule stays together as a sulphate ion, which is negative because it has gained two extra electrons (from the hydrogen atoms), and it is denoted by the symbol SO_4^-.

Sulphuric acid in water was used as the electrolyte in the first modern battery, invented by the Italian physicist Count Alessandro Volta (1745-1827) in 1800. The basic electric cell of this battery is perhaps the simplest of all. One end of the wire in which the current is to flow is connected to a plate made of zinc and the other to a copper plate. Both the plates, which are known as *electrodes*, are immersed in the electrolyte but do not touch each other.

The electrolyte reacts with the plates, feeding electrons to the zinc and extracting them from the copper in the following manner. The hydrogen ions from the sulphuric acid capture electrons from the

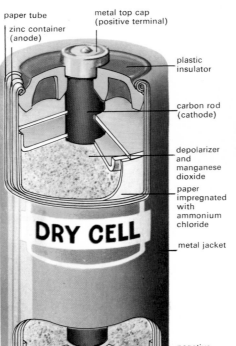

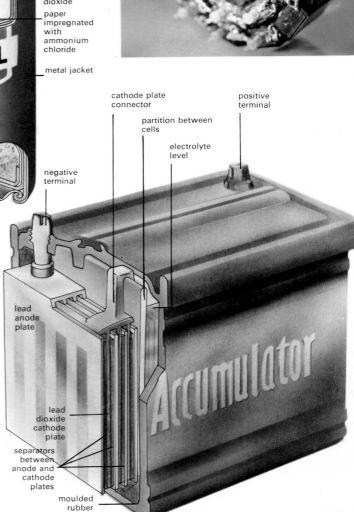

Left: This battery, comprising 200 cells, was built by Sir Humphry Davy in the basement of the Royal Institution, London, to provide electricity for experiments and demonstrations. The picture is from a French book of 1870.

Below: A battery of silver-zinc cells built for use in a satellite. Silver-zinc cells have an alkaline electrolyte and their electrodes are made of silver oxide and zinc. They give high power in relation to their size and weight when compared with other types of battery, and their high cost is considered worthwhile for such items as satellites. These batteries provide power for the satellite when it is in the earth's shadow and there is no light to drive its solar cells—or they take over if the solar cells break down.

paper tube
zinc container (anode)
metal top cap (positive terminal)
plastic insulator
carbon rod (cathode)
depolarizer and manganese dioxide
paper impregnated with ammonium chloride
metal jacket
DRY CELL
metal base (negative terminal)

Above: A dry cell of the kind used in radios and flashlights. This particular design has a carbon rod surrounded by a depolarizer and the manganese dioxide which forms the cathode (positive electrode). The rod and cathode are surrounded by paper impregnated with ammonium chloride electrolyte, and are contained within the zinc cup which is the anode (negative electrode). During operation, electrons travel from the anode, through the external circuit and into the cathode via the carbon rod.

Right: This car battery has a lead anode, a lead dioxide cathode, and a dilute sulphuric acid electrolyte.

cathode plate connector
partition between cells
positive terminal
electrolyte level
negative terminal
lead anode plate
lead dioxide cathode plate
separators between anode and cathode plates
moulded rubber casing
Accumulator

atoms of the copper plate and change into hydrogen atoms, which are insoluble and escape from the solution as gas. Sulphate ions capture zinc atoms to make molecules of zinc sulphate. The zinc atoms each abandon two electrons in favour of the two spare electrons on the sulphate ion. These two abandoned electrons move through the wire, as an electric current, to replace those lost at the copper plate.

If the external wire connection between the plates is broken (which is in effect what happens when, for example, a radio or a flashlight is switched off), so that electrons cannot travel from plate to plate via the wire, the reactions will soon come to a halt. This is because a layer of electric charge, caused by an excess or deficiency of electrons, builds up on each plate and prevents the ions of the electrolyte from approaching the plates closely enough to capture electrons or atoms. Thus the available chemical energy is held in check until the circuit is completed again and electrons can again flow through the wire.

Primary cells

The arrangement just described can only produce current as long as there is zinc available to be converted into zinc sulphate. Once the zinc plate has completely disintegrated, the reactions which drive the current can no longer proceed as there is no 'fuel' left to feed them. Such a cell, which can be used only once, is known as a *primary cell*. The commonest primary cell is the familiar 'dry' cell, which is almost universally used to power flashlights, transistor radios and other devices which need only a small amount of power.

This cell, also known as a *Leclanché* cell after its inventor, Georges Leclanché (1839-1882), is not really 'dry' at all. The active ingredient is still a solution of an ionic compound (ammonium chloride, NH_4Cl) in water, but there is so little water present that the solution is a thick paste. Into this paste is inserted a rod of carbon, which is a good conductor of electricity, and the whole is enclosed in a casing of zinc. As long as the carbon and zinc are unconnected no reactions take place in the cell, but as soon as they are connected by an external circuit a current begins to flow as electrons are extracted from the paste via the carbon rod and fed through the circuit into the zinc casing.

One product of the reactions in the Leclanché cell is hydrogen gas and, as this accumulates at the carbon rod, it begins to interfere with the operation of the cell if current is allowed to flow for very long. This phenomenon is known as *polarization* and is partly offset by including some manganese dioxide (MnO_2) in the paste. This *depolarizer* reacts with the hydrogen to remove it from the carbon surface.

Secondary cells

The principal disadvantage of a primary cell is its short life. Obviously it would be more useful to have a cell which could be restored to its original condition once it had discharged all the available chemical energy stored in it. Fortunately it is possible to do this with some types of cell. Other electric cells, however, rely on reactions which are reversible. In these, the chemical compounds whose formation gives rise to the current can be changed back to their original components simply by passing a current through the cell in the opposite direction. They are then free to recombine as before to make current.

Such cells are called *secondary cells* and a set of them is called a *storage battery* because it enables charge produced by other means (usually generators) to be 'stored' for later use.

Storage batteries may be divided into two types, acid and alkaline, according to the nature of the electrolyte. The principal acid battery is the familiar lead-acid *accumulator*, almost universally used in motor vehicles. Each cell of this battery consists of a plate of lead (Pb) and a plate of lead dioxide (PbO_2) both immersed in an electrolyte of dilute sulphuric acid.

At the positive plate, the lead dioxide reacts with the hydrogen and sulphate ions of the acid to make lead sulphate ($PbSO_4$) and water, extracting two electrons from the external wiring to balance the reaction electrically. At the negative plate, the lead metal reacts with the sulphate ions to make lead sulphate and feeds two electrons to the external wiring to maintain the electrical balance. The net effect of this is to produce a current of electrons from the negative to the positive plate.

When no more lead or lead dioxide remains the cell is exhausted. It can be regenerated (recharged) by passing a direct current through the cell from the negative to the positive plate. This induces the lead sulphate to break down again to lead on the negative plate and to lead dioxide on the positive.

During the recharging, the electrical energy put into the cell creates the chemical energy that breaks the lead sulphate into lead and lead dioxide, and combines the sulphate ions (freed from it) with the water to form dilute sulphuric acid. When the cell is subsequently used, these chemical reactions are reversed and the chemical energy is turned back into electrical energy. The electricity used in recharging the cell can thus be thought to have been 'stored' by the cell.

Alkaline batteries, as the name implies, have an alkaline electrolyte, usually 69

Above: Francis Bacon, who designed the first efficient fuel cell. The idea of combining hydrogen and oxygen in an electrolytic cell, producing water and electricity, was first demonstrated by Sir William Grove in 1838. Bacon began working on this idea in the 1930s, and in 1959 he introduced a hydrogen-oxygen cell capable of producing 6 kW of power. Bacon's work was taken up by Pratt and Whitney in the USA, who built the fuel cells used in the Apollo moon missions. Fuel cells are now being built for large-scale power production.

Below: Bacon's 6 kW fuel cell, built in 1959.

Right: Hydrogen gas, which can be used to run fuel cells producing electricity for domestic and industrial premises, could be produced by the electrolysis of water. The electricity required for the electrolysis could be generated by using natural energy sources such as the wind, waves or sunlight. The energy available from these sources is variable and unpredictable—there may be plenty at times when demand for electricity is low, and little when demand is high. Electricity itself cannot be stored, so it cannot be generated during periods of low demand and kept until it is needed. If it is used to make hydrogen, however, the gas, and in effect the energy used to make it, can be stored almost indefinitely, and distributed by pipeline in the same way as natural gas and town gas are conveyed.

Below: When dc electricity is passed through water, hydrogen gas collects at the cathode and oxygen gas at the anode.

ELECTROLYSIS CELL

dc supply

+ −

hydrogen gas

+

−

cathode (electrodes)

anode

oxygen

sea water

wind powered generators supply dc current

river water electrolysis plant

hydrogen pipeline

hydrogen storage and pressurization plant

sea-water electrolysis plant

hydrogen pipeline

hydrogen distribution network

wave powered generators

hydrogen pipeline

solar powered river water electrolysis plant

Right: In a hydrogen-oxygen fuel cell the two gases react with the electrolyte, producing water and electricity.

Below: These two diagrams show how fuel cells, running on hydrogen produced by the system shown on the left, could replace the existing electricity supply system. The cycle of events would be as follows: natural energy sources produce electricity, which is used to obtain hydrogen from water. The hydrogen is then distributed to fuel cell units, on the consumers' premises, which produce electricity by combining the hydrogen with oxygen from the air to make water.

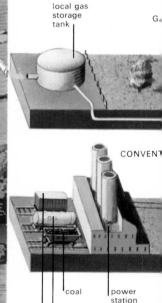

local gas storage tank

G

CONVENT

coal

oil

nuclear fuel

power station

potassium hydroxide (KOH). A common type of alkaline cell has one plate made of an oxide of nickel (Ni) and one of iron (Fe), and for this reason it is often known as the *NiFe* battery. Each cell weighs less than a lead cell but gives out only 1.2 volts. So for a 12 volt battery ten cells are needed as against six lead cells, which means that a NiFe battery ends up no lighter than a lead accumulator. Another type of alkaline cell, which has plates of silver oxide (AgO) and zinc (Zn), can give from two to ten times as much electrical energy for the same weight, but it is not widely used because of the high cost of silver.

Fuel cells

Even a secondary cell, however, cannot be used continuously. Its ability to be recharged is certainly a considerable advantage, but recharging takes several hours during which the cell cannot be used to provide current. So to obtain an uninterrupted current at least two batteries are needed and some means of recharging. All these problems are overcome in the *fuel cell*. In this, unlike any of the cells described above, the substances whose reactions drive the current are not contained within the cell but are

fed into it as required to sustain the reaction.

The first efficient fuel cell was produced, after many years of development work, by the English engineer Francis Bacon in 1959. Fuelled by hydrogen and oxygen gas, it is still the most reliable and widely used type and was chosen for the Apollo space missions.

The Bacon cell is filled with an alkaline electrolyte, potassium hydroxide in water, which is bounded by two very special electrode plates. They are made out of porous metal into which the electrolyte can penetrate, although it cannot pass right through. On the other side of one electrode is hydrogen gas, at a pressure which is carefully controlled so that the gas also can only penetrate part way into the plate. The other electrode is fed with oxygen gas in the same way.

The chemical and physical properties of the electrodes are crucial to the operation of the fuel cell, for it is only in the pores of these that the gases come into contact with the electrolyte. At the negative plate hydrogen molecules combine with *hydroxyl* ions (OH—) from the electrolyte and release electrons into the electrode. At the positive plate oxygen atoms capture electrons from the electrode

metal and combine with water molecules to make hydroxyl ions which dissolve in the electrolyte.

If the electrodes are connected outside the cell, the reactions will continue and current will flow through the external circuit as long as hydrogen and oxygen are supplied. To encourage the reactions to proceed at a reasonably rapid rate, the electrodes are made of a metal which acts as a catalyst. The best for this purpose is platinum, but since this is expensive Bacon cells use nickel which works very well at a temperature of about 200°C (392°F).

Another very promising type of fuel cell uses a metal carbonate as electrolyte. At the operating temperature of 700°C (1,292°F) the electrolyte separates into metal and carbonate (CO_3-) ions. The fuel is carbon monoxide (CO) at the negative plate, which reacts with carbonate ions to make carbon dioxide gas (CO_2) and supplies electrons as a result.

At the positive plate, oxygen combines with the carbon dioxide, extracting electrons from the plate as it does so, to make more carbonate ions. Fuel for this cell is cheap because the higher temperature allows air to be used at the positive electrode to supply oxygen, so a supply of

FUEL CELL

hydrogen   dc output   oxygen

—   +

de

de

rolyte
tion of potassium hydroxide)

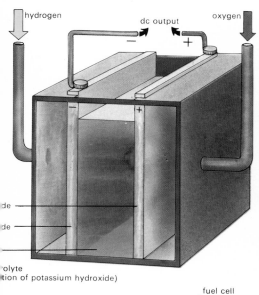

ERVICE

fuel cell
located
on site

hydrogen pipeline

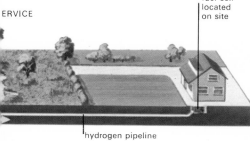

R SUPPLY

substation   transformer

United Aircraft Corporation

Electricity Council

Above: One of the fuel cell elements used in a 25 MW power unit capable of supplying the electricity for a town of 20,000 people. The power unit consists of a fuel conditioner, which produces hydrogen from natural gas, hydrogen-oxygen fuel cells, and an inverter which turns the dc output into alternating current.

Left and below left: A great deal of work is going into the development of electric cars. At present these are powered by batteries, but future designs may use fuel cells running on fuels such as liquid hydrogen, hydrazine (N_2H_4), or powdered metal-hydrogen compounds (hydrides).

pure oxygen is not required, and carbon monoxide is obtained as an inexpensive by-product in the distillation of coal tar.

Fuel cells are beginning to find more and more applications in industry and transportation. They are not at present particularly suitable for small vehicles, because the ancillary equipment needed to heat up the cell initially and remove surplus water (from the Bacon cell) or carbon dioxide (from the carbonate cell) produced by the reactions adds significantly to the weight of a small installation. However they are ideal for long-term supply of electricity in environments such as space stations and underwater habitats, where it is impractical to install conventional generating equipment.

Fuel cells are also beginning to look more attractive for some applications which have previously been the exclusive province of thermo-mechanical generators, because a fuel cell (unlike a conventional primary or secondary cell) is more efficient at converting chemical energy to electricity. Unfortunately the initial cost of a fuel cell installation on a large scale is at present far too high for it to be widely used, about ten times that of a conventional plant, even though running costs are lower.

Electricity Council

71

Scientific Method and Applied Science

One of the many uses of the laser beam-
gas velocities and turbulence being
measured within the manifold of a
car by laser anenometry.

Logic and Games

Logic and the theory of games are two fields of mathematics concerned with the study of decision-making. In logic, the object is to determine the truth or falsity of the arguments used in arriving at a decision, but game-theory deals with situations in which a decision has to be made between two conflicting requirements, both of which may be true. Logic and game-theory are closely related, and in some circumstances a combination of both may be required.

Game Theory

The theory of games was first suggested by Borel in 1921, but the basic result of the theory was proven by John von Neumann in 1928. The games in question are those of strategy, such as parlour games, chess and poker, but a complete analysis of real games such as these tends to be extremely complicated and so it is best to study the ideas of the theory in terms of very simple games.

Even simple games, however, show features which are important not only in game theory but also in its application, as suggested by von Neumann, to economics. Von Neumann argued that the social sciences had made little progress in applying mathematics to their theories because the type of mathematics available was devised with physics in mind, and thus a new kind of mathematics was needed.

The simplest form of game theory deals with two-person games such as 'showing pennies'. In this game the two players, call them 'P' and 'Q', each show a coin simultaneously. With the pay-off rules that if both have displayed heads or both tails, P pockets both, but if they have displayed different faces then Q pockets both, it is obvious that the best strategy each player can adopt is to show heads or tails at random and hope for the best.

If, however, the pay-off rule to Q is changed slightly, so that in the case of a mixed showing the player showing heads has to pay, in addition to what was to have been paid under the previous rules, an extra half the value of the coin to the player showing tails, the situation is quite different. Thus if P shows heads and Q shows tails, then P pays Q $1\frac{1}{2}$, and if P shows tails and Q shows heads, then Q receives only $\frac{1}{2}$ instead of the 1 that would have been paid under the previous rules.

The game under the new rules has, on first examination, the appearance of being just as fair as the earlier version, for Q's greater gain on one occasion is counterbalanced by a lesser gain on another. This appearance, however, is deceptive.

Suppose that P chooses to show heads on average 3 times out of 8, in a long run of games. Then, on average, by showing heads Q can expect to pay P 1 in $\frac{3}{8}$ of the games and to receive $\frac{1}{2}$ from P in the remaining $\frac{5}{8}$ of the games. This would give Q an average loss of 1/16 per game.

But if Q shows tails instead of heads, a similar calculation shows yet again an average loss for Q of 1/16 per game. From

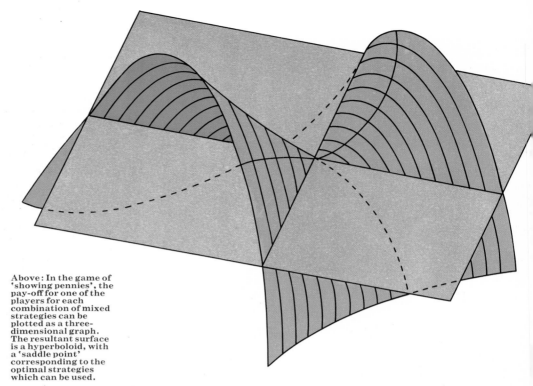

Above: In the game of 'showing pennies', the pay-off for one of the players for each combination of mixed strategies can be plotted as a three-dimensional graph. The resultant surface is a hyperboloid, with a 'saddle point' corresponding to the optimal strategies which can be used.

P's point of view, this strategy provides an expected average gain of 1/16 per game, whatever Q may do.

A similar argument for Q shows that the best strategy is to show heads for $\frac{5}{8}$ of the games in order to ensure that the loss is no worse than 1/16 whatever P may do. The game is said to have a *value* of 1/16 to P, and the strategies described are called *optimal strategies* for P and Q. Since the specification of the optimal strategies is in terms of average numbers of different moves over a large number of plays of the game, they are called *mixed strategies*. If the optimal strategy for Q had been, say, to show only heads, it would have been a *pure strategy*.

Games for more than two players

A simple analysis such as the one above would not be possible if the game were one, like chess, in which there are a large number of strategies open to each player. However, von Neumann was able to show that, in any such two-person game, there are always optimal mixed strategies and the game has a unique value.

The economic application concerns *duopolies*, situations in which two firms are competing for the same market, and the different strategies are their different promotional options. As soon as the number of players (or firms) increases to three, the situation is quite different, for now the deciding factor is which, if any, of the players agree to co-operate with each other. Moreover, von Neumann's version of the theory of three-person games is now widely regarded as being incomplete, since it excludes any discussion of what factors determine such co-operation.

Little is known of the theory of four-person games. Attempts have been made to augment von Neumann's theory of three-person games, notably by Kemeny in 1959, but the determination of the complete theory is still in the future. It is known, however, that not all games (with any number of players) will have solutions in von Neumann's sense, although

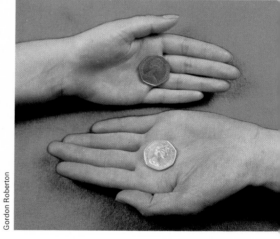

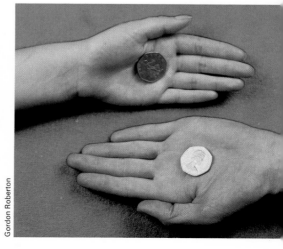

Above and below: The game of 'showing pennies' is a simple form of two-person game. The simplest pay-off rules are that when both players ('P' and 'Q') show heads, as above, or tails, as below, P wins both coins, but if one shows heads and the other shows tails, then Q wins both coins.

When playing to these rules, the optimal strategy for each player is simply to show heads or tails at random and hope for a maximum number of wins. Over a large enough number of plays each player will have won the same number, and so these rules offer no unfair advantage to either of the players.

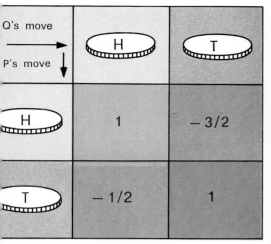

Above: The pay-off chart for the 'showing pennies' game, when in the case of a mixed showing the player showing heads has to pay an extra $\frac{1}{2}$. This chart shows the pay-offs for player 'P', the minus figures indicating payments by P to player 'Q', and the other figures payments by Q to P.

Right: John von Neumann (1903-1957), author of the *Theory of Games and Economic Behaviour*, with his wife Klara and his dog Inverse. In addition to his work on the theory of games, von Neumann was the leader of a team which built one of the first computers to use a stored program of operating instructions.

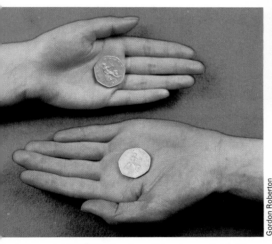

Above and below: A small variation in the pay-off rules of the game of 'showing pennies' can result in an automatic advantage to one of the players. If the rules are modified so that, in the case of a mixed showing, the player who shows heads has to pay an additional $\frac{1}{2}$ to the other player, then

if P shows heads and Q shows tails, above, P pays Q $1\frac{1}{2}$. If Q shows heads and P tails, below, then P only pays Q $\frac{1}{2}$. Under these rules, P can adopt a strategy which will provide an average gain of 1/16 per game, regardless of any attempt by Q to adopt a strategy to prevent it. The game has a *value* to P of 1/16.

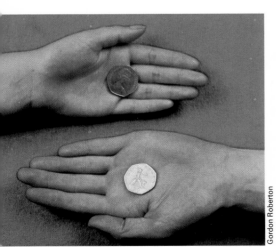

the greatest number of players for which a theory, like his 1928 one for two-person games can be determined, is still not known.

Logic

Modern mathematical logic has evolved, over the last 100 years, from the form of logic established by Aristotle in the fourth century BC. The Aristotelian logic was based on the use of *propositions*, sentences, used in arguments, which are either true or false. It made the assumption that all propositions could be put into one of four forms.

Each of these forms contained two terms, known respectively as the *subject* and the *predicate*, these terms being linked by words such as 'is', 'are', 'is not' or 'are not', with the subject being qualified by words such as 'all', 'no' or 'some'. Examples of propositions containing such terms are 'All men are mammals' (subject 'men', predicate 'mammals'), and 'No mammals are cold-blooded' (subject 'mammals', predicate 'cold-blooded').

This form of logic then went on to make the further incorrect assumption that most valid arguments could be analyzed into the form of three such propositions, namely two *premisses* and a *conclusion*. Using the two propositions mentioned above as the premisses, the conclusion would be derived by getting rid of the *middle term*, 'mammals', which occurs in both premisses, to give the conclusion 'No men are cold-blooded'.

Aristotle and his successors through the Middle Ages codified all the valid forms of this kind of argument, known as *syllogisms*, and found 19 of them.

Venn diagrams

Arguments of the Aristotelian type can be represented graphically by means of *Venn diagrams*, which were invented by the British mathematician John Venn in the nineteenth century. The argument mentioned above can thus be represented by three overlapping circles, representing men, mammals and cold-blooded animals respectively.

The areas where the 'men' and 'mammals' circles overlap the 'cold-blooded animals' circle are shaded to indicate 'emptiness', because no members of either of these groups are cold-blooded. Similarly, since no men are not mammals, the area of the 'men' circle which does not fall within the 'mammals' circle is also empty.

The diagram thus shows that all men are mammals, some mammals are men, but no men or mammals are cold-blooded.

Boolean algebra

Some attempt at making this form of logic more mathematical was made by Lully (1234-1315), a monk of Aragon, and later by Leibniz (1646-1716) in Germany, but no real progress was made until the middle of the nineteenth century. In 1847 and 1854, the English mathematician George Boole (1815-1864) published details of his work on mathematical logic. Boole was still working with syllogisms, but he invented a way of setting them out in algebraic form which later evolved into *Boolean Algebra*.

His system of notation is as follows. Each *set* of objects under discussion is assigned a letter from the alphabet, such as x, y and z. The entire range of objects under discussion, called the *universe of discourse*, is represented by the figure 1, and in addition there is a set which contains no members, called the *empty set*, which is represented by an 0.

The product of two sets, for example xy, represents the *common part*, that is, objects which are both x and y. Where xy = 0, the set 'xy' is an empty set and so x and y have no common part. In this case, x + y will be the set of objects which are either x or y. Subtraction of terms is also possible, for instance x — y is the set of objects which are x but not y, and 1 — x is the set of objects which are not x.

Using his algebraic logic, Boole was able to show that two of the nineteen forms of Aristotelian syllogism were, in fact, invalid. One of the two invalid forms is exemplified by 'All men are cowards, All men are mammals, therefore, Some mammals are cowards'. Using x, y and z for mammals, cowards and men respectively, Boole would write the premises as $z(1 — y) = 0$ and $z(1 — x) = 0$, and the conclusion as xy 0, meaning xy does not equal 0. This conclusion certainly cannot follow, since the two algebraic premises would also be true if z = 0, that is, if there were no men at all. Since we are concerned with the form of the argument and not with the particular terms involved, this possibility cannot be ruled out, and so this form of syllogism is actually invalid.

Modern logic, which deals simply with propositions, arose obscurely in the work of both Frege (1848-1925) in Germany and Peano (1858-1932) in Italy, and was brilliantly codified by Whitehead and Russell in *Principia Mathematica* (1910-1913).

Below: Simple arguments can be represented by Venn diagrams like this one, in which the relationships between sets are shown by intersecting circles which represent them.

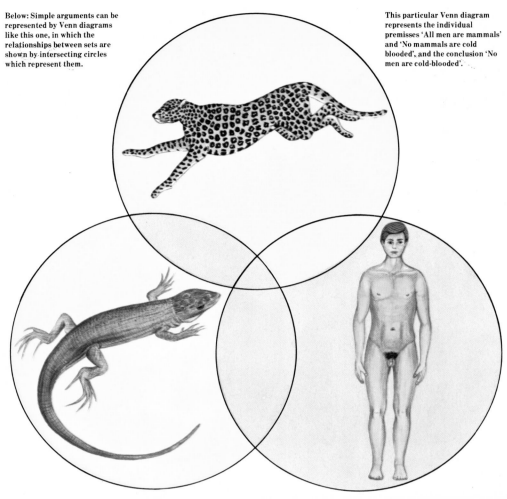

This particular Venn diagram represents the individual premisses 'All men are mammals' and 'No mammals are cold blooded', and the conclusion 'No men are cold-blooded'.

76

Left: The German philosopher Gottfried Leibnitz (1646-1716) was one of the first to attempt the formulation of a mathematical notation for logic. He also suggested that once logic could be adequately expressed mathematically, it should be possible to build a machine capable of using these mathematical equations to resolve arguments and solve problems — which, in a way, is what modern computers are doing.

Above and right: Computer technology is so advanced that anyone who wishes to can play games ranging from the traditional, such as chess, to ones designed especially for computers.

Laws of Chance

Mathematical probability provides a means of determining the likelihood of the occurrence of a particular event, given that a series of other events have already occurred. The theory can be successfully applied to an enormous range of situations, from simple ones—such as whether a tossed coin will come down showing heads or tails—to the complex and subtle probabilities involved in quantum mechanics.

Coin tossing

Suppose that a coin is tossed a very large number of times, and that after each toss the result is written down, writing 'H' if the coin lands heads uppermost and a 'T' if it lands tails uppermost. Assuming that the coin is evenly balanced, and that it never lands on its edge, we can expect a roughly equal number of H's and T's. In 1,000 tosses, a 'fair' coin will produce about 500 H's and 500 T's; if we had recorded 700 H's and only 300 T's it would look very much as though the coin were biased, so that on a single toss it would be much more likely to land head-side-up than tail-side-up. Intuitively, probability is a measure of the *likelihood* of an event.

Suppose that, over a long sequence of coin tossings, the proportion of H's in the first 'n' tosses is p_n (H), that is, the total number of H's in the first n tossings, divided by n itself. Then, as n gets very large, we find (by practical experience) that the sequence of numbers $p_n(H)$ settles down and gets closer and closer to some fixed number, called $p(H)$, which is the *probability* that on a single toss the coin will land head-up.

Since $p_n(H)$ is a proportion, it, and therefore $p(H)$, must lie between zero and one. If the coin is fair, then $p_n(H)$ will get nearer and nearer to $\frac{1}{2}$ as n increases, so that for a fair coin the probability of a 'head', $p(H)$, is $\frac{1}{2}$. If $p(H)$ is different from $\frac{1}{2}$, then the coin is biased and has a definite tendency to land with a particular face uppermost.

Since we have excluded the possibility that the coin lands on its edge, the proportion of tosses in which the result is either H or T must be 1 for all values of n, and so the probability p(H or T) must also be 1. After n tosses the number of H's plus the number of T's must be n, and therefore $p_n(H) + p_n(T) = 1$, so that $p(H) + p(T) = 1$. But since p(H or T) = 1 this means that $p(H) - p(T) = p(H \text{ or } T)$, that is, the probability of an H plus the probability of a T is equal to the probability of getting an H or a T.

Certainty

The properties that we have found for probability in the case of coin-tossing are general ones. Suppose we have any experiment, the result of which is one of 'k' possible outcomes which we label E_1, E_2, . . . E_k and call *events*. We assume that only one of these events can occur at a time. Then, if the experiment is repeated *independently* (so that the outcome of one does not affect the outcome of the next) a large number of times under identical conditions, the proportion of times the event E_i occurs will get close to the probability $p(E_i)$ for each value of

Bruce Coleman

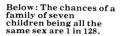

PASCAL'S TRIANGLE

Right: The figures in this triangle are arranged so that they can be used to calculate the probabilities of combinations. For example, the third horizontal row shows the odds governing the likely numbers of boys or girls in a three-child family. Adding the figures gives a total of 8; the least likely combinations, of boys only or girls only are indicated by the end figures—giving odds of 1 in 8. The chances of there being two girls and one boy, or vice-versa, are shown by the middle figures—3 in 8.

Below: The chances of a family of seven children being all the same sex are 1 in 128.

Above: Random sampling is a quality control method used by manufacturers which involves testing a small, random sample of goods from each batch produced. If the goods in the random sample are up to standard, then there is a high probability that the entire batch is satisfactory.

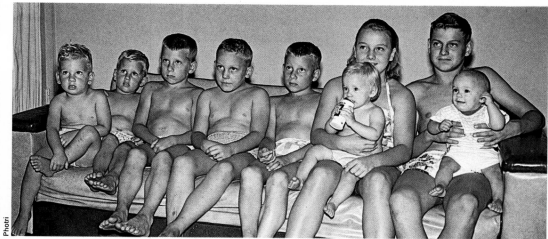

Photri

The zero on a roulette wheel ensures a balance in favour of the casino. Since it is neither red nor black, nor between 1 and 36 it is rarely bet upon, and when it does come up all other stakes are forfeit to the bank.

Conditional probability

Consider drawing a single card from a pack of playing cards (without a joker). The probability that the card is the four of diamonds is 1/52. This is because there are 52 cards in the pack, all of which are equally likely to be drawn, and so all have the same probability, p. Since some card must be drawn, the sum of these probabilities is 1, that is, $52p = 1$, or $p = 1/52$.

But suppose we are told that the card drawn is a diamond, what is the probability of it being the four of diamonds? In this case the card is one of thirteen possible cards (the number of diamond cards in the pack), and again all are equally likely to have been drawn, and so the probability is 1/13.

This is an example of *conditional probability*, and it is the probability that the card is the four of diamonds conditional on the fact that it is known to be a diamond.

Independence

When we mentioned earlier the repeating of experiments *independently* under identical conditions, we meant that the outcome of one experiment had no effect upon the outcome of the next. For example, when tossing a coin it is usually reasonable to assume that the result of one toss will not depend upon the result of the previous toss, nor will it affect the result of the next.

A well-known example of the concept of independence is as follows. If a coin is tossed twice, then, it was argued by the French mathematician D'Alembert (1717-1783), there are three possible results, namely (i) two heads, (ii) one head, one tail, and (iii) two tails, and so the probability of each of these results must be 1/3.

If you perform the experiment a large number of times, and calculate the proportions of occasions on which each of these results was obtained you will find that result (ii) occurs roughly half the time while results (i) and (iii) each occur about a quarter of the time, and this contradicts the argument that the probabilities are each 1/3. What is the explanation?

The essential part is that event (ii) splits into two parts, (iia) that the first toss gives a head and the second toss gives a tail, and (iib) that the first toss gives a tail and the second a head. Then events (i), (iia), (iib) and (iii) are really equally likely and so each have a probability of $\frac{1}{4}$. Event (ii) in fact has a probability of $\frac{1}{2}$, compared with the $\frac{1}{4}$ of events (i) and (iii).

As another example, consider families with three children. If, as is approximately biologically correct, we assume that the sexes of the different children are independent of each other and that each child is equally likely to be a boy or a girl, then the probability that a family of three children consists only of boys is $\frac{1}{8}$.

The possible families can be written as BBG, BBB, BGG, BGB, GBG, GBB, GGG and GGB, where 'G' denotes a girl and 'B' denotes a boy, and the order of the letters gives the order in which the children are born. There are thus eight different but equally likely possibilities, only one of which gives a family of boys only, and so the probability is $\frac{1}{8}$.

Alternatively, since the series of different children are independent, $p(BBB) =$ 79

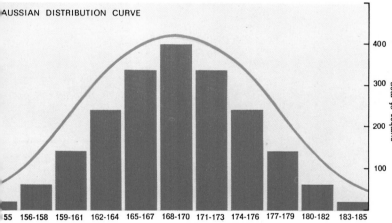

GAUSSIAN DISTRIBUTION CURVE

heights in centimetres
[x-axis labels: 55, 156-158, 159-161, 162-164, 165-167, 168-170, 171-173, 174-176, 177-179, 180-182, 183-185]
[y-axis: number of men — 100, 200, 300, 400]

Above and left: If the heights of a large number of men are measured, and plotted on a graph, the result is a diagram which shows how the number of individuals in each height category falls away smoothly to either side of the middle range of heights. The curved line is a *Gaussian curve*, and this shape of curve is obtained whenever large numbers of variations about an average point are plotted on a graph like this. For any such set of variables, once the average values and the upper and lower limits are known, the Gaussian curve can be used to find the probable distribution of individual variables within a sample group of them.

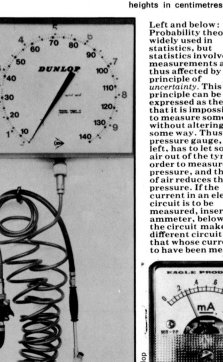

Left and below: Probability theory is widely used in statistics, but statistics involve measurements and are thus affected by the principle of *uncertainty*. This principle can be expressed as the fact that it is impossible to measure something without altering it in some way. Thus the tyre pressure gauge, on the left, has to let some air out of the tyre in order to measure the pressure, and this loss of air reduces the pressure. If the current in an electric circuit is to be measured, inserting an ammeter, below, into the circuit makes it a different circuit to that whose current was to have been measured.

i, that is for $i = 1, i = 2, \ldots i = k$.

These probabilities will always lie between zero and one; they will add up to one, that is, $p(E_1) + p(E_2) + \ldots p(E_k) = 1$; and they will satisfy the expression $p(E_i) + p(E_j) = p(E_i \text{ or } E_j)$, where '$E_i$ or E_j' denotes the outcome that 'either E_i or E_j' occurs, where E_i and E_j are any two of the possible outcomes of the experiment. The demonstration of these properties is exactly the same as in the coin-tossing, and an event which has a probability of 1 is said to be *certain*.

Some simple examples of an experiment with 'k' outcomes are:

(i) throwing a die, with event E_i defined as 'the die shows the number i' for $i = 1, 2, \ldots 6$. Here, $k = 6$ and $p(E_i) = 1/6$ for $i = 1, 2, \ldots 6$ if the die is fair.

(ii) throwing a die with E_i defined as 'the die shows the number 1 or 2' and E_2 defined as 'the die shows the number 3, 4, 5 or 6'. Here, $k = 2$ and if the die is fair $p(E_1) = 1/3$ and $p(E_2) = 2/3$.

(iii) drawing a single card from a pack of 52 playing cards, with the event E_1 being 'the card is a club', E_2 being 'the card is a diamond', E_3 being 'the card is a spade' and E_4 being 'the card is a heart'. Here, $k = 4$ and $p(E_1) = p(E_2) = p(E_3) = p(E_4) = \frac{1}{4}$.

$[p(B)]^3$, and since each child is equally likely to be a boy or a girl, $p(B) = \frac{1}{2}$, so that $p(BBB) = 1/2^3 = \frac{1}{8}$.

Simple calculations of the sort described above occur in a very wide range of 'real-life' situations. An important example of this is in the field of genetics, where probabilistic models are used in attempts to determine, for example, the chances of a child inheriting a particular disease or defect when it has occurred previously in the family.

Probability theory often produces some surprising results. A good example of this is to suppose that we have a room with 23 people in it. Since there are 365 days in an ordinary year, it would seem surprising if two of these people had the same birthday. Yet the probability of this happening is more than $\frac{1}{2}$, and if we were to look at a large enough number of rooms all containing 23 people, randomly selected from the population as a whole, then we would find that in more than half of these rooms two of the people would share the same birthday.

Determinism

We have talked above of experiments, such as coin-tossing, being repeated

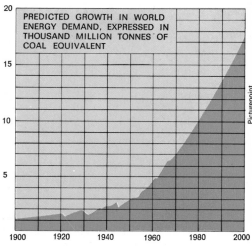

Picturepoint

Above, right and left:
Past climatic variations can be detected by studying the thicknesses of the layers of sediment deposited annually by the meltwaters from glaciers, or by measuring the thicknesses of tree rings. This form of *inductive reasoning*, the derivation of general conclusions from the study of particular items or facts, is also used by statisticians when they use a known set of facts to predict future trends, such as the growth in the world's demand for energy up to the year 2000.

Left: Harold Wilson's surprise defeat in the 1970 General Election in Britain was regarded by many observers as an example of the effect of public opinion poll forecasts upon the attitudes of voters. According to the uncertainty principle, asking someone for their opinion on something may, by making them think about it, cause them to subsequently alter it. However, in view of the relatively small sample of voters questioned by the opinion poll interviewers, this could not have accounted for the fact that the actual election result was practically the opposite of that predicted by the polls. It is more likely that many Labour Party supporters did not bother to vote because the polls predicted such an easy victory for Labour.

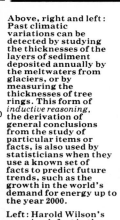

PREDICTED GROWTH IN WORLD ENERGY DEMAND, EXPRESSED IN THOUSAND MILLION TONNES OF COAL EQUIVALENT

20

15

10

5

1900　1920　1940　1960　1980　2000

Inigo Everson/Bruce Coleman

Bruce Coleman

Above: Long before the mechanism of the solar system had been realized, people 'knew' that the sun would always rise in the east and set again in the west; this conclusion had been arrived at by a crude form of inductive reasoning— it always had, and therefore it always would.

Below: Catastrophe Theory is a new mathematical technique which may provide a means of predicting sudden and dramatic changes in systems or structures. For example, it is claimed that the collapse of this bridge could have been foreseen if the theory had been used during its design.

COLLAPSED SECTION

Keystone

under identical conditions. If a card is drawn from a pack, and 'under identical conditions' means that the cards are in the same order within the pack and the chosen card is in the same position, then this experiment will always have the same result.

Similarly, any student of classical mechanics knows that if, when coins are tossed, all positions, velocities and external forces are kept the same, then it follows from Newton's laws that the final result will be the same. So when discussing repeating experiments under identical conditions, and finding the probabilities of different outcomes from the proportions of occurrences of these outcomes, it certainly does not mean that the conditions will be quite so identical. If they were, then the experiments would be completely deterministic—that is, the results would be pre-determined and there would be no need of probability.

In fact, the observed sequence of results has its origin in the *uncontrollable* variations in the initial conditions which occur when the experiments are actually performed. In the physical world, uncertainties of this sort lead to results of the type discussed. At a more fundamental level, in atomic and nuclear physics (quantum mechanics), probabilities arise which are of a totally different nature— the probabilities are *intrinsic* to the systems, and no amount of knowledge of the initial conditions can ever remove them. This possibility that the physical world contains intrinsic probabilistic aspects poses problems for philosophers who have traditionally inclined towards a deterministic, cause-and-effect view of the world.

The Nature of Mathematics

	EGYPTIAN	BABYLONIAN	GREEK	ROMAN	MAYAN	II WEST ARABIC	HINDU
1	I	▼	A	I	·	1	?
2	II	▼▼	B	II	··	2	?
3	III	▼▼▼	Γ	III	···	?	3
4	IIII	▼▼▼▼	Δ	IIII	····	?	8
5	III II	▼▼▼ ▼▼	E	V	—	9	?
6	III III	▼▼▼ ▼▼▼	F	VI	÷	6	?
7	IIII III	▼▼▼▼ ▼▼▼	Z	VII	··	?	?
8	IIII IIII	▼▼▼▼ ▼▼▼▼	H	VIII	···	8	?
9	III III III	▼▼▼▼▼ ▼▼▼▼	Θ	IX	····	9	?
10	∩	◀	I	X	=	1·	?o

Above: The modern numerals for 1 to 10, used by western cultures, compared with their counterparts from older civilizations.

Below: Three counting systems—decimal (based on the number 10), binary (based on 2) and hexadecimal (based on 16).

To ask the nature of mathematics is to pose a question to which the answer is by no means clear. The reason for this strange state of affairs is to be found in the historical development of the subject.

The origins of counting and number systems are lost in antiquity, but as long as 4,000 years ago the Akkadian arithmetic was a high point of Babylonian culture. Unlike most modern counting systems, including our own, where the number 10 plays a basic role, this Babylonian system was based on the number 60. Irrespective of the actual symbols used, or the numbers upon which they are based, all developed counting systems are precise formulations of the concept of the *natural number*.

To the obvious natural numbers, such as 1, 2, 3, 4 and so on, we now usually add the *zero*, 0, which did not in fact appear as a genuine number (as distinct from a sign to indicate a space) until the Hindu arithmetic of the ninth century AD.

In due course the ideas of space and length, that is of *geometry*, were added to those of counting. Geometry arose as a practical subject, out of such problems as those involved in the surveying of the land around the Nile delta which was subject to annual flooding, but from about 500 BC onwards it was developed as a theoretical subject by the Greeks.

Pre-eminent in early Greek geometry was the proof of the theorem of Pythagoras, which stated that the square of the longest side of a right-angled triangle was equal to the sum of the squares of the other two sides. Thus for a triangle whose sides are 3, 4, and 5 units long, the square of the longest side is 25, which equals $3^2 + 4^2$, or $9 + 16$, the sum of the squares of the other two sides.

Calculus

To the Greek mathematicians such as Pythagoras, the concept of 'number' meant natural number. Fractions were only used in commerce; in geometry a ratio was not a fraction, but a separate entity. Later mathematicians, however, adopted a more general idea of number, considering first the *rational numbers* or fractions, and then the *real numbers*, those involving decimals instead of fractions.

Whereas the natural numbers increase in definite steps of one at a time (1, 2, 3 etc), any two rational or real numbers always have a range of other numbers in between. For example, between 1 and 2 lie other real numbers such as 1.3, 1.5 or 1.875. It is thus possible to think of a *continuously varying* real number.

This opens the way for the development of *calculus* and *mechanics*, two branches of mathematics which developed together during the seventeenth century. In mechanics, the basic idea is not the *point*, as in geometry, but the *particle* or *moving point*, whose position changes with time. The new mathematics of the seventeenth and eighteenth centuries expressed this in terms of the idea of a *variable*, such as the time or the distance of a particle from a fixed reference point.

DECIMAL	BINARY	HEXADECIMAL
1	1	1
2	10	2
3	11	3
4	100	4
5	101	5
6	110	6
7	111	7
8	1000	8
9	1001	9
10	1010	A
11	1011	B
12	1100	C
13	1101	D
14	1110	E
15	1111	F
16	10000	10
8 +4 ⎯ 12	1000 +100 ⎯ 1100	8 +4 ⎯ C

Below: The Egyptians constructed right angles by laying out a knotted rope into a 3, 4, 5 triangle, which includes a right angle.

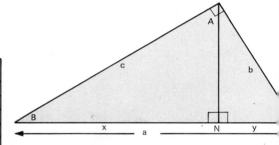

Above: Triangles ABN and ABC are *similar* triangles. Although they are different sizes, they each contain the same angles between their sides— ABC is simply a larger version of ABN.

Below: Pythagoras, one of the most famous Greek mathematicians, was born on the island of Samos in about 572 BC. He is best known for his theorem concerning right-angled triangles.

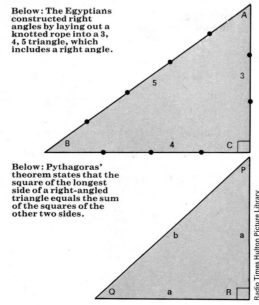

Below: Pythagoras' theorem states that the square of the longest side of a right-angled triangle equals the sum of the squares of the other two sides.

Radio Times Hulton Picture Library

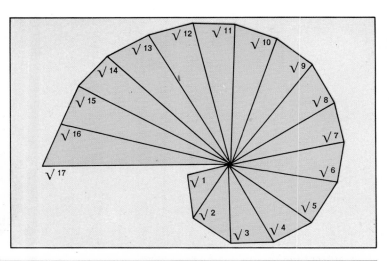

Right: A Greek geometrical construction based upon lines, radiating from a common point, whose lengths represent the square roots of the numbers 1 to 17. The lines joining the ends of these lines are all the same length, which gives the construction its shell-like shape.

Below: The shell of the pearly nautilus has a similar form of construction to the type of figure shown on the right. These creatures, which grow up to 20 cm (7.8 in) long, are found in the Indian and Pacific oceans, and as they grow they add new chambers to their shells. The animal's head is at the wide end of the shell.

Above: The work of the Greek mathematicians was known to the Arabs. This is part of a 15th century commentary on Euclid by Al-Tusi.

Below: An example of a natural geometrical construction—the cell wall structure of a micro-organism called a diatom.

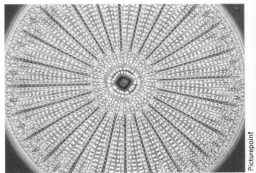

The dependence of one variable upon another, say of variable 'x' upon variable 't', was expressed in the form 'x is a *function* of t', which was written 'x = f(t)'.

The idea of *velocity* (the speed of an object *in a given direction*), which had given great difficulty to mathematicians during the thirteenth century, was now much easier to handle, for a function can be represented by means of graph. It was then possible to understand the velocity, at any instant, of a particle moving in a curved path, as that which it would have were it to continue in a straight line moving just as it was at the instant under consideration.

The velocity would be a function of the time, and if a graph showing the particle's position at various times were drawn, the velocity at any instant could be found by drawing a tangent to the curve of the graph at the time under consideration.

Infinite series

Many of the problems of calculus thrown up by mechanics would have proved too difficult without the use of the mathematical device of an *infinite series*. Some such series had been known for some time: the series '1 + ½ + ¼ + ⅛ + . . .', where each term is half the preceding one, is one example. This series may be said to have a 'sum' of 2 in the sense that, however many terms are added together they will never reach 2, but on the other hand they will get as near to 2 as desired.

But the original idea that it was sufficient for the terms to decrease in order to be able to associate a sum with a series was shattered by the series '1 + ½ + ⅓ + ¼ + . . .'. In this series, the third and fourth terms together add up to more than ½, as do the fifth, sixth, seventh and eighth. Therefore if a sum were to be associated with such a series it would be more than '1 + ½ + ½ + . . .', and so it would, in effect, have no upper limit.

Despite the difficulties involved in determining the sums of infinite series, such series were often found to be useful in solving practical problems. During the eighteenth century it was suggested that the value of an infinite series should be defined in terms of the value of the function which gives it, the term 'function' in this case meaning an algebraic expression.

The general idea of a function did not evolve until the nineteenth century, when the intuitive but clumsy idea of a 'variable' having values expressed, by an algebraic formula, in terms of the values of another variable, was finally displaced by that of a *mapping* between two *sets*.

In mechanics, for example, the relationship between time and the position of a moving particle could be expressed in this manner. The time would be represented by the set of all real numbers, and the distance at any one time between the particle and its starting point by the set of distances that it was possible for the particle to have. The mapping would then associate a unique member 'f(t)' of the second set with each member 't' of the first.

Reductionism

The concept of set was first clearly formulated by Georg Cantor in 1872, and it influenced the discussions about the philosophy of mathematics which arose in a gradual way as part of a general *reductionist* programme in the nineteenth century.

One instance of this programme is the clarification of the status of *non-Euclidian geometry*, a form of geometry not based upon the traditional form of geometry established by the Greek mathematician Euclid around 300 BC. Such geometries had been produced in earlier times, and the question arose whether it was con- 83 sistent to suppose, for example, a plane geometry in which from a point outside a line, no parallel to the line could be drawn.

This can be seen to be consistent (if ordinary geometry is consistent) by exemplifying it as the geometry of *great circles* on the surface of a sphere. A great circle is one whose diameter is the same as that of the sphere itself, and it is impossible to draw two great circles on the surface of a sphere without them intersecting. For the reductionist programme, the consistency problem in non Euclidian geometry was *reduced* to that of ordinary, Euclidian geometry.

There were other fields in which a reductionist programme was carried out. For example, ordinary geometry can be reduced to algebra by the use of a *co-ordinate system*. In this system, which was largely due to the French philosopher René Descartes (and is thus known as *Cartesian*), the position of any point can be fully described by means of its distances from two lines or *axes*, one vertical and one horizontal. Using Cartesian co-ordinates, any geometrical relationship between two points can be expressed in terms of algebra.

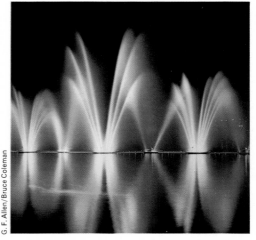

G. F. Allen/Bruce Coleman

Right: The curved path of a jet of water from a fountain forms a type of curve known as a *parabola*, and the outline of each group of jets is itself a parabola.

Below: 1. Instead of the older, graphical representation of a function, the modern picture is of two *sets*, T, called the *domain*, and X, the *range*, with a *mapping* 'f = T — X' between them.
2. Three possible geometries of parallels. Top: Euclidian—only one possible parallel to a line can pass through point 'P'. Centre: hyperbolic geometry—two parallels can pass through 'P'. Bottom: elliptic geometry—no parallel can be drawn.

Above: The two large squares represent the infinite series '1 + ½ + ¼ + . . .', which never quite adds up to exactly 2.

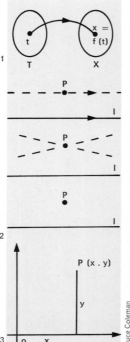

Bruce Coleman

Left: 1. A graph of the position, x, at any time, t, of a moving particle which was originally at rest at x = 0, and then gradually accelerated. The velocity at point T can be thought of as that which the particle would have if its position graph were a straight line at a tangent to the curve at point T.
2. In a velocity/time graph of a moving particle, the shaded area is of size hv, and represents the approximate distance the particle travelled during time h.

Right: 3. The reduction of geometry to algebra employs a pair of fixed co-ordinate lines to describe the position of any point 'P'.

ZEFA

84

Syndication International

Left: The woman's body and its distorted mirror image are *topologically* identical because the 'surface' of the image, although

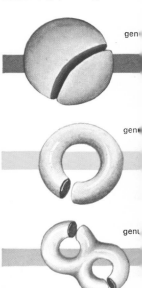

gen
gen
genu

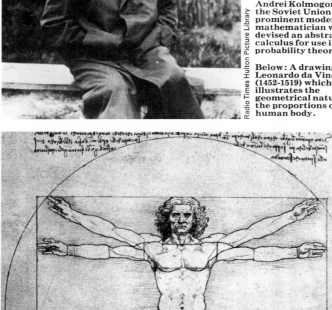

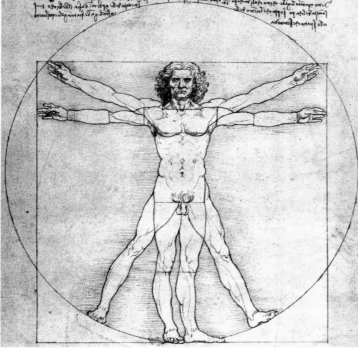

Below: Parallel lines often appear to converge, but, like an infinite series and its 'sum', they never actually do.

Left: Albert Einstein (1879-1955), whose mathematical theories of relativity were proven only later by practical experimental results. The concept of relativity is an example of the way in which mathematics is used to discover more about the physical universe.

Right: Academician Andrei Kolmogorov of the Soviet Union, a prominent modern mathematician who devised an abstract calculus for use in probability theory.

Below: A drawing by Leonardo da Vinci (1452-1519) which illustrates the geometrical nature of the proportions of the human body.

distorted, has the same mathematical properties as the body's surface.

Below: the topological *genus* of an object is

the number of times it can be cut without dividing it into two parts—none for genus 0, one for genus 1, and two for genus 2.

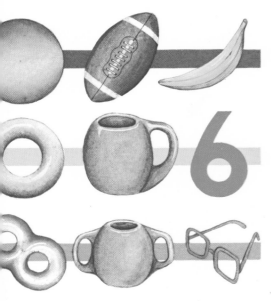

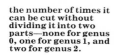

Set theory

Every attempt at a thorough reductionist programme since the work of Gottlob Frege in 1879 has depended upon the idea of a set. A set is simply a collection of all its members, and its members themselves may be sets. For example, the set of all people includes the set of all men, the set of all women, and the set of all children—and these in turn can be sub-divided into other sets.

Cantor had concluded that every well-defined decidable property defines a set, that is, the members of a set are just those possessing that property. In 1899, however, Cantor discovered to his surprise that his theory was plagued with contradictions. Russell attempted to resolve these contradictions in 1903, but with no real success.

The foundations of mathematics had suddenly been shown to be quite unsure. Russell and Whitehead, in 1919, suggested that a sure foundation was to be found in logic, but when they looked for it there they found that the logic which was taught at the time was a tissue of trivialities and nonsense that had been handed down almost unchanged from the Middle Ages, and so they had to begin again.

Their greatest triumph was the precise formulation of arithmetic, including a formula for the definition of the number 1. Another approach to the problems of the foundations of mathematics was begun by Hilbert in 1899. He was able to formulate geometry in better terms than those used by Euclid, and he turned his attention to the concept of truth, which is essential to both mathematics and logic.

The difficulties encountered in discussions about truth are exemplified by: (The sentence in these brackets is false). If we suppose this sentence to be true, then it asserts its own falsehood, which contradicts our supposition; but if we assume it to be false, this assumption is exactly what the sentence is saying, so that the sentence is therefore true and our assumption is again contradicted.

During the first 30 years of this century it became apparent that the consistency of much of classical mathematics depended upon the corresponding result for the arithmetic of natural numbers. As a result of this, Gödel, in 1929, devised a way of expressing the letters of the alphabet, and combinations of them such as words and sentences, by a numerical code. By this means, the truth or falsity of sentences could be determined arithmetically.

Gödel was able to prove that any system that was rich enough to describe elementary arithmetic, the arithmetic of natural numbers, would inevitably be either inconsistent or incomplete. Using his numerical code, he could construct an arithmetic statement which was essentially equivalent to: (The statement in these brackets is unprovable.)

There is no paradox as there was in the previous example. But if the sentence is true, it is an example of a true but inprovable sentence, so the system is uncomplete. If, on the other hand, it is false, it is an example of a false but provable sentence, and so the system is inconsistent. So, although the technical achievements of mathematics are not in question, its real nature still remains in doubt.

Time Measurement

Throughout the ages, concepts of the nature of time have been governed by spiritual and physical requirements. Until comparatively recently, natural rhythmic patterns such as life and death, day and night, winter and summer, led to the conception of time as a *cyclic* quantity, one that repeated itself at regular intervals.

The first methods of keeping track of the passage of time were based on observations of the movements of the sun, moon and stars. As the cyclic nature of these movements became apparent, it was realized that they could be used to indicate such things as, for example, the right times to plant crops. The Egyptians also used the rising of the star Sirius to predict the beginning of the annual flooding of the Nile, which occurred (coincidentally) a few days later.

From their astronomical observations, the Egyptians produced a calendar based on a 365 day year. Their studies of Sirius, however, indicated that the length of the *solar year* (the time taken for the Earth to orbit the Sun) was, in fact, 365¼ days. The Romans, who had been using a calendar based on the *lunar month* (the number of days between full moons), adopted a 365¼ day calendar in 45 BC. This was the *Julian Calendar*, introduced by Julius Caesar and calculated by Sosigenes of Alexandria.

The Julian Calendar, to avoid the problem of having to fit a quarter of a day into each year, ran for three years of 365 days then one of 366, a *leap year*, to give an average year length of 365¼ days. The solar year, however, is only 365.242199 days long, not 365.25, and so the Roman year was, in fact, 11 minutes too long. This gave a cumulative error to the Julian Calendar, which was eventually rectified by Pope Gregory XIII in 1582.

By this time the Julian Calendar was ten days out, and Gregory decreed that 5 October 1582 should become 15 October. In addition, he ordered that century years would only be leap years if they were divisible by 400, a ruling which reduced the number of leap years sufficiently to keep the calendar in step with the solar year. Gregory's calendar, known as the *Gregorian Calendar*, is the one used in Western countries today, and it is only out by 26 seconds per year.

The Egyptians astronomers noticed that the time taken for one revolution of the Earth about its axis was constant if measured against a star, but varied throughout the year if measured against the Sun. They therefore used the stars as the basis for their time measurement. Time based on star observations is known as *sidereal* time, whereas time measured against the Sun is known as *solar time*.

There are two reasons for the irregular length of the solar day. Firstly, the Earth is in an elliptical orbit about the Sun, and as a result is moves faster when near the Sun, in January, than it does when it is farther away, in July. Secondly, the Earth's axis is inclined at an angle of 23½°, causing a variation in the angular velocity of the equator relative to the Sun.

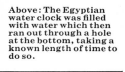

Above: The Egyptian water clock was filled with water which then ran out through a hole at the bottom, taking a known length of time to do so.

Above: The sundial is one of the oldest devices for measuring time. As the Sun travels across the sky, the shadow of the sundial's *gnomon* moves around the face of the dial to indicate the time.

Right: A model of a pendulum escapement mechanism designed by Galileo Galilei (1564-1642). The fact that the time of one swing of a pendulum was dependent on its length, and not on the angle through which it swung, was first discovered by Galileo in 1581. It was not until 1656, however, that the first really satisfactory pendulum escapement was designed, by the Dutch astronomer Christiaan Huygens (1629-95).

Below: Sand glasses were simple timing devices designed so that it took a certain time for all the sand to fall from one half into the other.

Right: The first of four chronometers built by John Harrison between 1728 and 1759 to provide accurate timekeeping for ship navigation.

The average or *mean* solar day was devised to accommodate this irregularity. Mean time varies from actual solar time by anything up to about 16 minutes. The difference between solar time and mean time is called the *equation of time*, the word 'equation' in this context being used to mean 'that which is needed to make things equal'.

Early clocks

The linear concept of time, in which time is considered as an independent, continuous function in its own right, was made possible by the invention of mechanical clocks. The first mechanical clocks were probably invented in the late thirteenth century, but it was not until the seventeenth century that reasonably accurate models were produced.

The earliest devices for measuring the passage of time were sundials, the first known forms of which were made by the Egyptians. In its simplest form, the sundial consists of a stick or *gnomon* which casts a shadow onto a scale marked off in hours. As the Sun moves across the sky during the day, the shadow cast by the gnomon moves around the scale, indicating the solar time.

The determination of time at night or

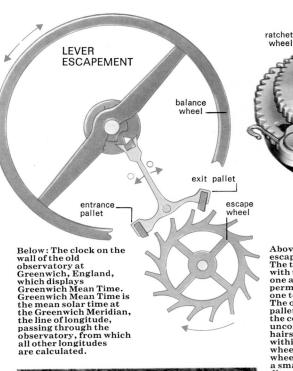

LEVER ESCAPEMENT

balance wheel

exit pallet

entrance pallet

escape wheel

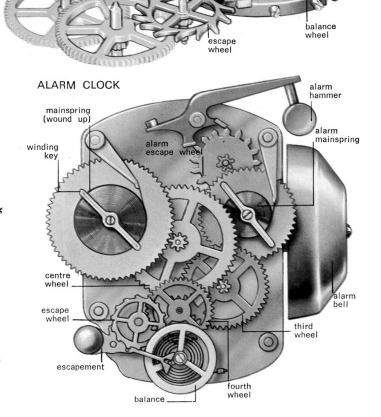

ratchet wheel

WATCH MOVEMENT

centre wheel

balance spring

mainspring

balance wheel

escape wheel

Below: The clock on the wall of the old observatory at Greenwich, England, which displays Greenwich Mean Time. Greenwich Mean Time is the mean solar time at the Greenwich Meridian, the line of longitude, passing through the observatory, from which all other longitudes are calculated.

Above left: A lever escapement mechanism. The two pallets engage with the escape wheel one at a time, permitting it to turn one tooth at a time. The oscillation of the pallets is produced by the coiling and uncoiling of a hairspring mounted within the balance wheel, and the escape wheel gives each pallet a small push as it disengages from it so as to keep the oscillations going.

Above right: A watch mechanism incorporating a lever escapement mechanism. The speed of the watch is adjusted by increasing or decreasing the tension of the hairspring, which alters the rate at which the balance wheel oscillates. The escapement controls the speed at which the mainspring unwinds to drive the hands of the clock, and the ratchet wheel stops the mainspring from unwinding without driving the mechanism.

Right: The mechanism of an alarm clock, which has an additional spring for driving the alarm hammer.

ALARM CLOCK

mainspring (wound up)

winding key

alarm escape wheel

alarm hammer

alarm mainspring

centre wheel

escape wheel

escapement

balance

alarm bell

third wheel

fourth wheel

SHEPHERD PATENTEE
53 LEADENHALL LONDON
GALVANO MAGNETIC CLOCK

87

in cloudy weather was not possible with a sundial, and so a variety of devices were developed which used forms of observable regular motion or changing circumstances. These devices included the *clepsydra* or water clock, in which time is indicated by the gradual flow of water from a bucket-shaped container with a small hole in its base.

The basic components of a mechanical clock mechanism are a source of rotational force, a means of regulating the speed of the rotation produced by this force, and a system of gears to transmit this regulated motion to the hands of the clock. The first clocks were driven by weights. A falling weight was attached to a rope wound around a horizontal drum, so that as the weight fell the drum was turned.

The speed at which the drum turned was regulated by a *foliot* and *verge escapement*. The foliot was a horizontal rod with a weight attached to each end, and fixed at its centre to a vertical rod, the verge, which was pivoted so that it, together with the foliot, could oscillate about its long axis.

As the foliot and verge oscillated, two short projections or *pallets* engaged, one at a time, with the teeth of a crown wheel. The crown wheel was driven by the weight drum, and the motion of the pallets allowed it to turn a distance of one tooth at a time. The crown wheel gave a small push to each pallet as it left its teeth, and this maintained the oscillation. The speed at which the crown wheel, and the associated gearing which drove the clock hands, could turn was determined by the rate of oscillation of the foliot and verge.

Clocks driven by springs instead of weights first appeared in the late fifteenth century, but speed regulation by means of a pendulum was not introduced until the middle of the seventeenth century. The period of swing of a pendulum depends upon its length, and so the speed of rotation of a toothed wheel can be regulated by the action of a pair of pallets connected to a swinging pendulum. The pendulum, whose length is carefully

Omega

Above: The photofinish camera records the finish of a race on a moving strip of film, on to which the finishing times are projected. The timing begins at the start of the race, and is initiated by a signal from the starting mechanism, for example from a contact linked to the trigger mechanism of a starting pistol.

Above right: An example of a photofinish picture. The timing is accurate to 1/1,000th of a second.

Right: An attendance recorder is a clock, used in many factories and offices, which records the times at which the employees arrive and leave. Upon arriving or leaving, an employee inserts a card into the machine, which stamps it with the time and the day of the week. The cards provide a record of the hours worked, and can be used in calculating wages.

Below: The world is divided into time zones, shown here as either ahead (—) or behind (+) Greenwich Mean Time.

Blick

Above: The type of watch used by American astronauts, which was also used by the Russians during the Apollo-Soyuz mission.

Below: An experimental hydrogen maser atomic clock. These devices use the natural vibrations within hydrogen atoms to control the frequency of a quartz crystal clock and maintain its accuracy. Hydrogen maser clocks have an accuracy of within one ten thousand millionth of a second per day.

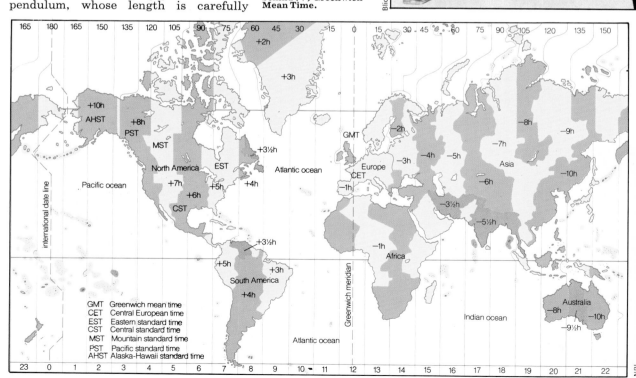

GMT Greenwich mean time
CET Central European time
EST Eastern standard time
CST Central standard time
MST Mountain standard time
PST Pacific standard time
AHST Alaska-Hawaii standard time

NPL

calculated to give the required rate of operation of the pallets, is kept swinging by impulses given to the pallets by the weight or spring driven wheel.

Another form of escapement control, now widely used in clocks and watches, was invented by Robert Hooke in the middle of the seventeenth century. This is the *spiral balance spring* or *hairspring*, a fine coiled spring mounted within a wheel, which when set in motion coils and uncoils to create continuous oscillations analogous to those of a pendulum. These oscillations are used to operate a pair of pallets, usually via a lever arrangement, which control the speed of the main mechanism.

Chronometers

The expansion of trade and the increase in the numbers of long sea voyages during the sixteenth and seventeenth centuries encouraged the production of more accurate clocks, which were essential to accurate navigation. The main problem was the determination of longitude, which could only be achieved with a clock that would keep accurate time aboard ship.

By the eighteenth century, the pendulum clock had become accurate to about one second per day, but it was useless at sea because the regular swing was upset by the motion of the ship. Large inaccuracies were also likely with spring balance clocks due to the considerable temperature variations often encountered.

In 1714, the British Government set up a Board of Longitude, which offered a prize of £20,000 to anyone who could devise an accurate means of determining a ship's longitude. If this was to be done by means of a clock, it would have to be accurate to within three seconds per day, anywhere in the world.

The prize was won by John Harrison, who between 1728 and 1759 constructed four *chronometers*, accurate clocks for use in navigation. His fourth model won the Board's prize; on a voyage of 156 days it showed an error of only 54 seconds.

Modern clocks

Although most clocks and watches are still mechanically-driven, electric clocks and electronic watches are becoming increasingly popular. Electric clocks may be battery-powered, having a small motor controlled by a balance spring, or driven by a mains-powered motor. The speed of these mains motors is precisely controlled by the frequency of the mains supply, and a simple gear mechanism takes the drive directly from the motor to the hands of the clock.

Just as the mechanical clock uses regularly oscillating functions, such as those of a balance spring or a pendulum, to control its movement, the *quartz crystal* clock uses the electrically-induced vibrations of a piece of quartz crystal. Quartz crystal is *piezo-electric*; that is, when a voltage is applied to it it will distort slightly, and conversely if it is distorted it will produce a small voltage.

In a clock, the crystal is stimulated electrically to make it vibrate at its *resonant frequency*, the frequency at which it will vibrate the most easily. This frequency, which can be maintained very accurately, is determined by the size and shape of the crystal. When the crystal has been made to vibrate at its resonant frequency, it produces voltages at that frequency, and these can be used either to drive a small motor geared to the indicating mechanism of a clock, or to drive circuits controlling a liquid crystal or light-emitting diode display. A small amount of the crystal output is fed back to it to keep it vibrating. Quartz crystal clocks can be built to have an accuracy of less than 1/30 second per day.

Another form of natural resonance which is used for time measurement is that of atoms such as those of caesium. The caesium atom can be at one of two energy states, depending upon the direction of spin of its outer electron. If the atom is passed through an electromagnetic field whose frequency is 9,192 MHz, it will change its energy state.

In the caesium clock, a beam of caesium atoms given off by caesium heated in a small oven is directed through an electromagnetic field. The 5 MHz output from a quartz clock is multiplied to give the 9,192 MHz that controls the electromagnetic field. If the quartz clock is producing exactly the right frequency, a maximum number of atoms will change their states, and this is registered by a detector. The frequency of the clock is automatically adjusted to produce the maximum number of changes, which means that it is kept as close as possible to 5 MHz.

Part of this 5 MHz output is used to drive a clock display unit, which indicates the time to within one second in 1,000 years. A newer type of atomic clock, the hydrogen maser clock, is even more accurate.

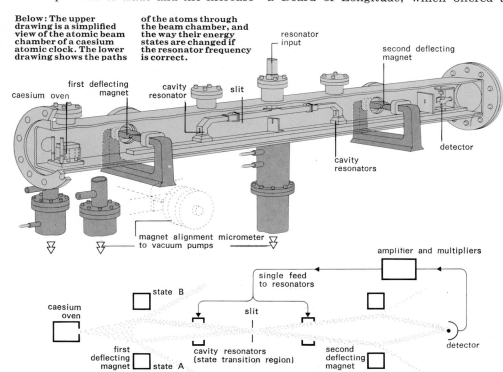

Below: The upper drawing is a simplified view of the atomic beam chamber of a caesium atomic clock. The lower drawing shows the paths of the atoms through the beam chamber, and the way their energy states are changed if the resonator frequency is correct.

resonator input

second deflecting magnet

first deflecting magnet

caesium oven

cavity resonator

slit

detector

cavity resonators

magnet alignment micrometer

to vacuum pumps

amplifier and multipliers

single feed to resonators

state B

caesium oven

slit

first deflecting magnet

state A

cavity resonators (state transition region)

second deflecting magnet

detector

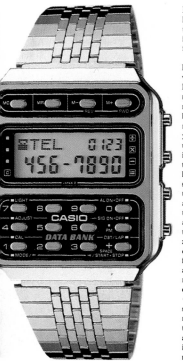

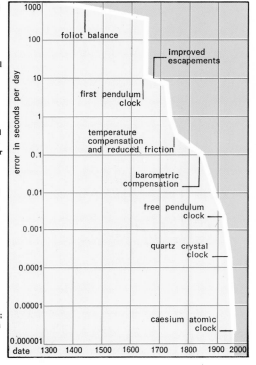

Right: This chart shows how the accuracy of time-keeping has improved since the fourteenth century.

Left: The modern digital watch is a marvel. This Data Bank Tele Memo model will run for 15 months on a lithium battery. It indicates the month, date, day and year and is programmed until the year 2099, and in addition has a regular time mode which is in hours, minutes and seconds and can run on the 12- or 24-hour clock; an hourly time signal; three independent daily alarms. It can also give the time in 20 time zones, programmed by capital city. Special features of this model are: the stop-watch mode; the 8-digit calculator in four + or − functions (addition, subtraction, multiplication, division); the memory mode which allows you to store important telephone numbers.

error in seconds per day

1000
100
foliot balance
improved escapements
10
first pendulum clock
1
temperature compensation and reduced friction
0.1
barometric compensation
0.01
free pendulum clock
0.001
quartz crystal clock
0.0001
0.00001
caesium atomic clock
0.000001
date 1300 1400 1500 1600 1700 1800 1900 2000

89

Weighing and Measuring

An organized system of weights and measures is fundamental to many human activities, particularly those associated with science, industry and commerce. Any comprehensive system must include the three basic quantities of mass, length and time, and should also cater for the measurement of temperature, electricity and magnetism, and light.

Two measuring systems have been of major importance during the last few hundred years. These are the *metric* system, used by most European countries, and the *imperial system*, used by Britain and those countries which were once part of the old British Empire. In most countries, however, the old metric and imperial weights and measures are being phased out, and the *SI system* of units (Système International d'Unités), a more accurately-defined version of the old metric system, is being adopted.

The SI system has six basic units. These are the *metre* (m), the unit of length; the *kilogram* (kg), the unit of mass; the *second* (s), the unit of time; the *kelvin* (K), the unit of temperature; the *ampere* (A), the unit of electrical current; and the *candela* (cd), the unit of luminous intensity.

Units and standards

Measurement involves the comparison of an unknown quantity with a similar known quantity. For example, the measurement of length with a ruler is a visual comparison of the unknown length with a scale of known lengths marked on the ruler. The basis for any measurement is the direct or indirect reference to some definitive standard. It is important to distinguish between 'units' and 'standards', a unit being in itself an abstract conception which is meaningless unless it is referred to the primary standard for the quantity to be measured. This primary standard may be an arbitrary material standard such as the international prototype kilogram, or a naturally-occurring invariable phenomenon such as the wavelength of the radiation from a krypton-86 lamp.

Length

Early units of length were based on the dimensions of the human body, and many of the imperial units of length were derived from such units. For example, the yard was the distance from the spine to the fingertips (with the arm outstretched), and the foot was the length of one foot. A yard was also taken to be the length of one stride, and the word 'mile' came from the Latin for 'a thousand paces'. A cubit was half a yard, the distance from the elbow to the fingertips.

The first official standard yard, established by King Edward I of England in 1305, was an iron bar subdivided into three feet of twelve inches each. Fortunately for his subjects who were unable to obtain access to this standard, the inch was also defined as the length of three grains of barley laid end to end.

Subsequent standard yards were also made of metal, Britain and the US

Above: Part of the 'Nilometer' on the southern tip of Roda, an island in the Nile near Cairo. The Nilometer, which is a form of depth gauge, was used to measure the rise of the Nile during its annual flooding, which begins in late June and reaches its maximum rate of flow in September.

Right:Stonehenge, which stands on Salisbury Plain in southern England, is one of the best known of the many neolithic structures found in north west Europe. It has been suggested that the builders of these structures used a standard length unit, the 'megalithic yard' 82.9 cm (2.72 ft) long.

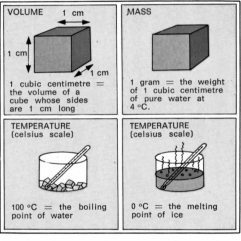

VOLUME 1 cm	MASS
1 cubic centimetre = the volume of a cube whose sides are 1 cm long	1 gram = the weight of 1 cubic centimetre of pure water at 4 °C.
TEMPERATURE (celsius scale)	TEMPERATURE (celsius scale)
100 °C = the boiling point of water	0 °C = the melting point of ice

Left: The cubic centimetre is the volume of a cube whose sides are 1 cm long, and one gram is the mass of 1 cubic centimetre of pure water at a temperature of 4°C. The Celsius temperature scale uses the melting point of ice as its zero and the boiling point of water as its 100° point.

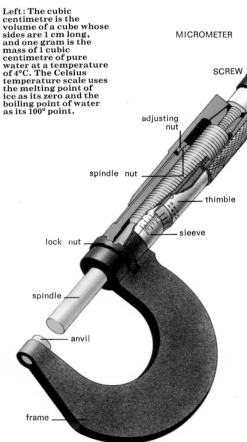

MICROMETER

SCREW

adjusting nut

spindle nut

thimble

sleeve

lock nut

spindle

anvil

frame

Above: The micrometer, a precision measuring device used in engineering. When the thimble is turned, the spindle is moved towards or away from the anvil, and the distance between them is indicated by the scales engraved on the thimble and the sleeve.

Right: The international prototype kilogram, and the platinum-iridium bar which was formerly the standard metre.

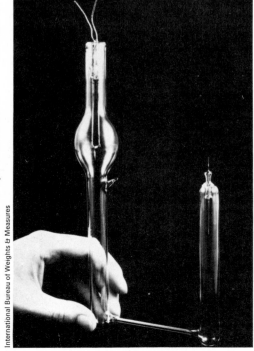

Left: A krypton-86 lamp of the type used to produce the light whose wavelengths are used to define the metre. The lamps used can produce the specified wavelength to an accuracy of 1 part in 100 million (1 part in 10^8), but the standard may eventually be re-defined in terms of the wavelengths of a stabilized helium-neon gas laser, which can be reproduced to an accuracy of 1 part in 10^{10} (10,000 million).

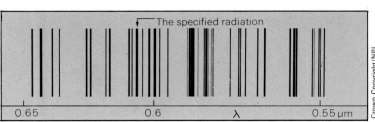

Above: Part of the spectrum of the light obtained from a krypton-86 lamp. The metre is now defined as that length which is equal to 1,650,763.73 of the wavelengths of the specified radiation, which has a wavelength of approximately 0.60578 microns (millionths of a metre).

Above: Three views of the tower of the Deutches Museum in Munich. The tower carries three large weather instrument displays: a hygrometer, which measures humidity; a wind speed and direction indicator; and a thermometer and barometer which measure air temperature and pressure.

Below: The bimetallic strip thermometer is operated by a coiled strip of two metals, one of which expands or contracts more with changes in temperature than the other one, bending the strip as shown. The clinical thermometer contains mercury which expands along the tube when heated.

ROTARY AND CLINICAL THERMOMETERS

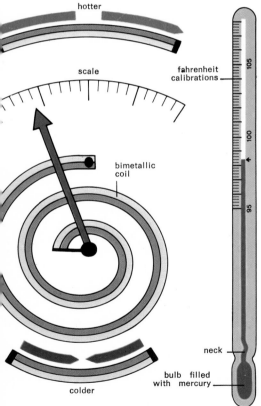

hotter

scale

fahrenheit calibrations

bimetallic coil

neck

bulb filled with mercury

colder

Above: A rotary thermometer, calibrated in degrees Fahrenheit, being used to measure soil temperature. The Fahrenheit scale was invented in Holland in 1724 by Gabriel Fahrenheit, but most countries adopted the Celsius scale devised in 1742.

Mass and volume

The metric system was first formulated on the basis of natural quantities. The metre was based on the size of the Earth, and the gram, the unit of mass, was based on the weight of pure water. The original definition of the gram was that it was the mass of one cubic centimetre (1 cm = 1/100 m) of pure water at a temperature of 4°C. A platinum cylinder, weighing the same as 1,000 cubic centimetres of water, was adopted as the standard kilogram.

There was now a neat relationship between length, mass and volume. A litre was defined as the volume of a cube whose sides were 0.1 m long, a volume of 1,000 cubic centimetres. However, due to the difficulty, at that time, of obtaining a really precise measurement of volume, the standard kilogram did not in fact weigh precisely the same as 1,000 cubic centimetres of water.

It was therefore decided to define one litre as the volume of one kilogram of water (at 4°C), and so the litre became, in fact, 1,000.028 cubic centimetres. In 1964, however, the litre was redefined to be the exact equivalent of the cubic decimetre (precisely 1,000 cubic centimetres).

The current standard kilogram, known as the international prototype kilogram, is a cylinder made of 90 per cent platinum and 10 per cent iridium, and it is kept at the International Bureau of Weights and Measures (the BIPM) at Sèvres, near Paris. Duplicate standards are kept at national standards offices throughout the world, the British national copy, for example, is copy number 18 and it is kept at the National Physical Laboratory near London.

Temperature

The primary unit of temperature is neither material nor reproducible, being a measure of heat intensity. Its nature dictates that the unit should be defined in terms of a scale relative to the difference between two standard temperatures. As it is not possible to compare directly two temperatures in the same manner as two lengths or masses can be compared, some indirect effect of heat must be used to provide a measurable quantity.

The earliest method of doing this was to employ the expansion of a liquid, contained in a glass tube, when it was heated. In this method, two fixed standard points, an upper one and a lower one, are marked on the tube. The range between these fixed points is called the *fundamental interval*, and it is divided into a scale of units or *degrees*.

A number of these *thermometer* scales have been devised, using a variety of easily-obtained natural temperatures to provide the upper and lower fixed points. Gabriel Fahrenheit (1686-1736) used a mixture of ice and salt to provide his zero or lower fixed point, and human body temperature to provide his upper fixed point. He originally divided this range

adopting bronze and brass standard yards respectively in the first half of the nineteenth century. In 1893, however, the US decided to define the yard as 0.9144 of a metre, and this definition was adopted in 1959 by Britain, Canada, Australia, New Zealand and South Africa.

The metre, the basic unit of the metric system—which was devised in France at the end of the eighteenth century—was originally defined as one ten millionth of the distance from the North Pole to the equator, along a line passing through Paris. When the length of the metre had been calculated, a standard metre in the form of a bar of platinum was made, one metre being the distance between the end faces of the bar.

This standard was replaced by a bar of platinum-iridium alloy in 1889, but the metre is now defined in an altogether different manner. Since 1960, the metre has been defined as the length equivalent to 1,650,763.73 wavelengths of the orange radiation corresponding to the transition of a krypton-86 atom from energy level $2p_{10}$ to energy level $5d_5$. This radiation is produced by a krypton-86 lamp, an electric lamp filled with krypton-86 gas, enclosed in a vacuum chamber at a temperature of 63 K (—210°C).

Alphabet & Image

ZEFA

Left: Oil prospectors using a gravimeter to detect local changes in the force of gravity due to changes in the density of the underlying rock. The gravimeter contains a weight suspended from a delicate balance mechanism which indicates changes in the pull of gravity on the weight.

Above: The speedometer and rev counter are tachometers, which measure rotational velocity. The rev counter is calibrated in revolutions per minute, but the speedometer indicates the car's speed although in fact it is responding to the rotational velocity of a gearbox shaft.

Below: A speedometer mechanism. A flexible drive cable, connected to a gearbox shaft, turns a permanent magnet. The magnet drags the stator and pointer assembly round against the force of a spring; the distance the pointer moves depends on the speed at which the magnet is turning.

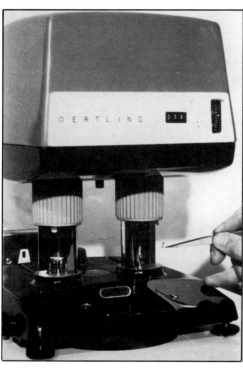

COI

Left and below left: Two precision weighing instruments. The one on the left, a deci-microbalance, is accurate to one tenth of a microgram (one microgram is one millionth of a gram). The machine below has an electronic digitali display, and a printer to record its measurements.

Below right: Aircraft speed is measured by comparing the air pressure created, by the forward motion of the aircraft, in an open, forward-facing tube (the *pitot*) with the ambient still-air pressure (the *static* pressure). This is a helicopter system; the smaller dial shows the lateral airspeed.

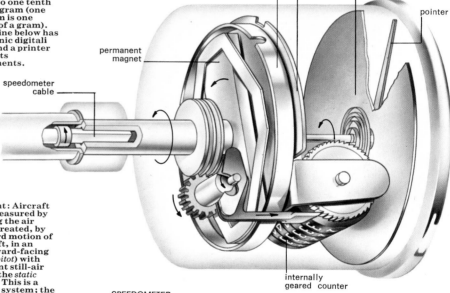

drag cup   stator   hairspring

pointer

permanent magnet

speedometer cable

internally geared counter

SPEEDOMETER

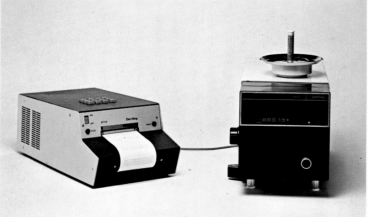

Oertling Ltd

GEC-Marconi

92

into 96 degrees, but later adjusted it so that he obtained an exact 180° between the freezing and boiling points of pure water. On his revised scale, which was adopted by many countries in 1724, the freezing and boiling points of water are 32° and 212° respectively, and body temperature is 98.6°.

The Swedish astronomer Anders Celsius (1701-44) proposed a scale of temperature with 100° representing the freezing point and 0° the boiling point of water His scale was quickly adopted as the *centigrade* scale, but the values 100 and 0 for freezing and boiling were reversed. In 1948 the centigrade scale was officially named the Celsius scale.

The SI unit of temperature is the kelvin, which is named after the physicist Lord Kelvin (1824-1907). A Kelvin is the same size as a degree Celsius, but the zero point on the Kelvin scale is a much lower temperature than that on the Celsius scale. In 1787 Jacques Charles discovered that when the temperature of a gas was altered by 1°C, its volume changed by 1/273 of its volume at 0°C. Kelvin proposed that this change in volume was due to a change in the energy of motion of the molecules of the gas. Continuing this line of thought, he went on to suggest that this change in energy of motion applied to all molecules, whether in solids, liquids or gases.

The heat energy possessed by an object or substance, of which its temperature is a measure, is retained in it as the kinetic energy possessed by its molecules due to their motion. Kelvin predicted that, since 1/273 of the energy at 0°C was lost for every 1°C drop in temperature, then at —273°C there would be no heat energy left in a substance. Therefore, —273°C was the lowest possible temperature, and should be considered as *absolute zero* and used as the zero point for an absolute scale of temperature. Absolute zero has been found to be slightly less than —273°C, and as a result degrees Celsius are converted to kelvins by adding 273.15.

Electricity and light

Electrical units are based nowadays on the definition of the ampere, which is the unit of electrical current. The ampere is defined as that current which produces a force of 2×10^{-7} newtons per metre of length between two parallel, infinitely long conductors of negligible cross-sectional area, when the conductors are placed 1 m apart in a vacuum and the current is passed through them. The newton is the SI unit of force, being the force required to give a mass of 1 kg an acceleration of 1 m/sec².

Luminous intensity is measured in candelas, which have replaced the older units such as the *international candle*. The candela is the luminous intensity of 1/600,000 square metre of the surface of a black body which is at the temperature of freezing platinum (2042 K), under a pressure of 101,325 newtons per square metre.

Time

The basic unit of time is the second. This was originally defined simply as 1/86,400 of a mean solar day, but it was re-defined in 1955 as 1/31,556,925.9747 of the year 1900. With the development of atomic clocks, however, it became possible to provide an even more precise definition of the second.

Between 1955 and 1958, the National Physical Laboratory in England, in collaboration with the US Naval Observatory, obtained a definition of the second based upon the natural resonances within caesium atoms. This definition, adopted as the SI unit of time in 1967, is that one second is the duration of 9,192,631,770 periods of the radiation given off during transitions between two energy levels of the caesium-133 atom.

Derived units

From the basic SI units, the metre, kilogram, second, kelvin, ampere and candela, all other units of measurement may be derived. Examples of derived units are the square metre (m²), a unit of area, the metre per second (m/sec), a unit of linear velocity and speed, and the newton (N), a unit of force.

A seventh basic SI unit, which is rarely encountered in everyday life, is the *mole*. The mole is used as a measure of the amount of substance present in a given sample or system. One mole of a substance is the amount present when it contains the same number of *entities*, which may be atoms, molecules, electrons, or other specified particles, as there are atoms in 0.012 kg of carbon-12.

Keystone

Above: HRH Princess Anne weighing in during a three-day equestrian event. This type of weighing machine is a form of beam balance. The weighing platform is connected to one side of the beam, very close to the pivot, so that it can be counterbalanced by the comparatively small weights hung at the other end, a long way from the pivot. Exact balance is obtained by moving the sliding weight along the calibrated beam.

Right: These Roman bronze scales also have a movable weight on one side of the beam. The object to be weighed was placed in the left hand pan, and a weight was placed in the other. The movable weight was then positioned to give an exact balance.

Below: The pitot tube on the nose of an experimental jet. Pitot tubes are either mounted on the nose, the wing, or fuselage of aircraft, and the static vents are usually fitted on the fuselage.

Michael Holford

Photri

93

Scientific Analysis

Scientific analysis represents a composition of procedures and techniques associated with man's enquiry into the physical substance of his environment. Early practical demands probably originated from metallurgists needing some method of determining the percentage purity of gold and silver. Since then a wide variety of analytic instruments of observation and measurement have been developed to satisfy the demands of all branches of science. These may be of direct application such as the chemical balance and the microscope, or they may use some property of matter to provide results indirectly—for example, the spectrometer.

Analyses fall broadly within two categories: *qualitative* analysis which encompasses the detection of what a material is made of; and *quantitative* analysis which determines how much of the material is present.

Microscopy

Microscopy is an analytic process which had its origins among biologists, although its potential in the fields of crystallography and metallurgy was soon realized. In 1683, Anton van Leeuwenhoek (1632-1723) was the first to set eyes on bacteria, using a *simple microscope*, one fitted with a single lens.

There is a limit to the magnification obtainable with a simple microscope, however, and for further resolution of detail a *compound microscope* is necessary. The compound microscope, which is the type generally used, consists of two powerful converging lenses of short focal length.

Microscope use is very diverse; from its origins as a tool of direct observation it is now essential in many fields of qualitative and quantitative analysis. Physical observations are generally of colour, optical density, size, shape and surface characteristic. Chemical observations are mainly the study of precipitation reactions where a material is brought into solution and the colour and form of the precipitate crystals are noted when a test reagent is added.

Electron microscopes

No matter how well an optical microscope is made, there is a limit to the amount of detail it can resolve, and this limit cannot be overcome optically because it is due to the nature of light itself. In order to be able to distinguish between two closely-positioned particles, the light source used must have a wavelength of not more than twice the distance between them.

Visible light is restricted to a small band of wavelengths of the electromagnetic spectrum, its wavelength being of the order of about 0.5 microns (1 micron = 1 millionth of a metre). This means that an optical microscope cannot resolve details of less than about 0.25 microns. During the 1920s it was discovered that when electrons are accelerated, they travel with a wave-like motion similar to that of light, but with a wavelength over 100,000 times shorter.

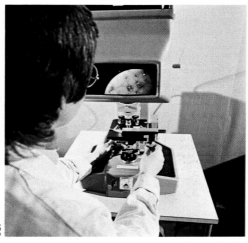

COI

Above: The microscope is one of the basic tools of scientific analysis. This one is fitted with an optical projection system which projects the image of the specimen on to a screen, instead of the user having to peer into the eyepiece. This makes it easier to use and produces a clearer image.

Right: Crystalline tartaric acid (dihydroxy-succinic acid) viewed through a microscope at x 30 magnification in polarized light. The polarized light creates these coloured effects in the crystal which enable its structure to be seen more clearly than in ordinary non-polarized light.

ZEFA

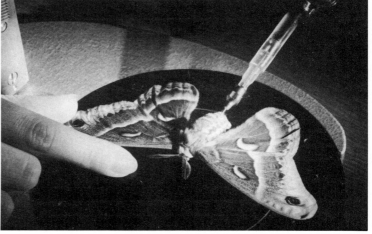

Shell

Left: A male silkmoth being injected with a radioactive substance as part of a biochemical analysis of its metabolism. The way in which the substance is broken down or metabolized, and distributed through the insect's tissues, can subsequently be analyzed by tracing the radioactivity.

Right: This apparatus is used for the microdistillation of weighable amounts of substances. This involves heating them to separate off their constituents, which vaporize at different temperatures and so can be collected separately for subsequent analysis. This enables the composition of the substances to be found.

This led to the invention of the electron microscope during the 1930s. The electron microscope uses a beam of electrons in place of light, and the beam is either directed right through the specimen, or reflected off its surface.

In the *transmission electron microscope*, an ultra-thin specimen is placed in the path of an electron beam, which passes through it and produces an image of it on a phosphorescent screen. The *scanning electronic microscope*, on the other hand, scans a fine beam of electrons across the surface of a specimen. As the beam hits the surface of the specimen it drives off 'secondary' electrons from it, which are drawn towards a detector. The detector produces a signal which is amplified, and used to drive a cathode ray tube that produces an image of the specimen.

A third type of electron microscope, the *scanning transmission electron microscope*, uses a similar scanning and detection principle to the scanning instrument, but the electrons are beamed right through the sample as in the transmission instrument. Modern electron microscopes can resolve details as small as 0.0002 microns.

Chromatography

Chromatography was initially developed as a means of separation of complex mixtures in the fields of organic chemistry and pharmacology, where chemical differences are so slight as to be insufficient to afford a means of separation, whereas molecular physical differences exist which are used as a means of resolution. Although several investigators applied chromatography more or less accidentally during the nineteenth century the Russian Mikhail Tswett (1872-1920) was the first to appreciate the underlying principles.

Chromatographic techniques involve manipulation of a few of the general properties of molecules. These are: first, solubility, the tendency of the molecule to dissolve in a liquid solvent; secondly, adsorption, the tendency for a molecule to attach itself to a finely divided solid; and thirdly, volatility, the tendency for a molecule to evaporate.

Tswett was interested in separating the pigments contained in the leaves of plants which he dissolved in ether. He then poured this solution into a vertical glass column filled with calcium carbonate and, as he continued to wash the solution through the column with more solvent, he found that it separated into a series of coloured bands which travelled slowly down the column to the bottom, where

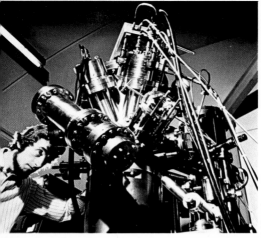

Left: Optical microscopes are limited to a useful maximum magnification of about x 2,000 because the wavelength of visible light prevents the resolution of details below 0.25 microns apart. Electron microscopes, on the other hand, can produce magnifications as high as x 1,000,000.

Right: A small transmission electron microscope like this one is usually mounted on a desk-type console. The electron beam, generated by a 60 kV electron gun, passes through the specimen and creates an image of it on the screen. The largest transmission microscopes, nearly three storeys high, operate at 3 MV.

1. 60 KV Electron gun
2. Steel frame
3. Specimen stage
4. Condenser control
5. First condenser lens
6. Second condenser lens
7. Cooling jackets
8. Specimen holder
9. Objective lens
10. First projector lens
11. Specimen rotation control
12. Cooling jackets
13. Camera shutter
14. Phosphor coated screen
15. Exposure meter
16. 70 mm camera
17. Camera retraction lever
18. Vacuum chassis
19. Second projector lens

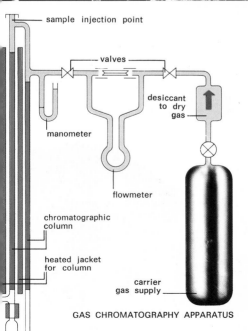

GAS CHROMATOGRAPHY APPARATUS

Labels: sample injection point; valves; desiccant to dry gas; manometer; flowmeter; chromatographic column; heated jacket for column; carrier gas supply; detector unit

Left: A basic gas chromatograph. The gas is dried by the dessicant, and its flow rate and pressure are monitored by the flow meter and manometer. The constituents of the sample are identified by the different times at which they emerge from the column. Gases used include argon, nitrogen and hydrogen.

Below: Chromatographic equipment in use in an oil company laboratory. Chromatography, particularly gas chromatography, is used extensively in the petrochemical and pharmaceutical industries, and throughout the chemical industry generally. It also has applications in forensic science.

they could be individually collected.

As the dissolved chemical compounds constituting the pigments were washed through the column, the ones that had an affinity for the large surface area of the finely divided calcium carbonate, the *adsorbent*, had their progress delayed. The ones completely inert to the surface passed through the column at the same rate as the solvent.

Not only do different substances have widely varying adsorption characteristics but differing solubility tendencies as well. As it is highly unlikely that two different substances will exhibit quantitatively the same pair of physical properties, an interaction of these features will lead to the band separation of the compound, which will have their own characteristic rate of downward migration. These bands can be detected as they emerge from the column, isolated, and identified. Modern column chromatography, as it is called, is little different from the method used by Tswett, but alumina and silica gel are the most commonly used adsorbents.

Since its inception chromatography has been continuously modified but the basis remains the same, that of two *phases* with a substance distributed between them, separation requiring one of the

95

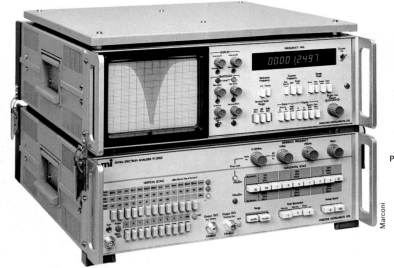

Right: This electronic spectrum analyzer is used to examine the component frequencies and waveforms of electronic signals.

Below: The *nuclear magnetic resonance* **(NMR) spectrometer is used to analyze the structure of molecules. The sample to be analyzed is placed in a strong magnetic field and exposed to radio-frequency radiation. It will absorb radiation energy at frequencies corresponding to the magnetic resonance frequencies of its atomic nuclei, those at which they change their direction of orientation within the magnetic field. The frequencies at which energy is absorbed indicate the types of atoms present.**

pyrolytic release
illuminator assembly

labelled release
carbon-14 detector

PYROLYTIC RELEASE EXPERIMENT

dump cell

test cell

organic vapour trap

dump cell

heaters

test cell

LABELLED RELEASE EXPERIMENT

nutrient
reservoir

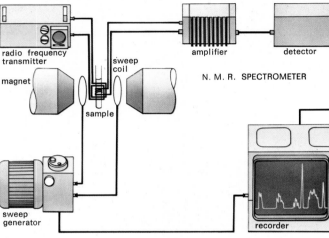

radio frequency transmitter

sweep coil

amplifier

detector

magnet

N. M. R. SPECTROMETER

sample

sweep generator

recorder

Right: The equipment used in the life detection experiments carried out by the Viking 1 and Viking 2 spacecraft on soil taken from the surface of Mars. There were three sections to these experiments: the *pyrolytic release* **experiment, which looked for evidence of photosynthesis; the**

labelled release **experiment, which looked for signs of metabolic activity; and the** *gas exchange* **experiment, which looked for changes in the composition of the gases surrounding a soil sample that would indicate that some form of respiratory activity was taking place within the soil.**

module
enclosure

phases to be moving over the other, stationary phase. The moving phase may be a liquid or a gas; the stationary phase may be a solid adsorbent or a liquid film, the former being called *adsorption chromatography* and the latter *partition chromatography*.

Partition chromatography depends on the difference in solubility a compound may have in two different liquids. One of the liquids is kept stationary as a liquid film by impregnating it in an inert support, such as kieselguhr, cellulose or some other finely divided solid. The substance to be separated is dissolved in the moving phase, its progress being delayed according to its relative solubility in each of the liquids. Substances with different solubilities may be separated, the solutes more soluble in the moving phase progressing faster.

Gas-liquid chromatography (a form of partition chromatography) apparatus consists of a liquid film support packed in a small diameter tubular column, usually several metres long. The moving phase, an inert gas such as argon, is allowed to flow through the column, which is generally placed in an oven so that it can be heated to facilitate separation of high boiling point materials. The sample mixture is injected into the head of the column and passes down the tube under the influence of the carrier gas.

The individual compounds proceed at a rate dependent upon their affinities for the stationary phase, those with a strong affinity being retained longer than those with a weak affinity. A detector at the column exit produces a signal as the compounds emerge, which is amplified and displayed on a chart recorder.

Right: The size of the equipment used by the Viking landers in their search for life on Mars can be seen from this picture of the assembly of one of the complex miniature laboratories. Each one contained three automated units which performed the life detection experiments, plus associated equipment for handling the soil samples and a computer. The soil samples were dug from the Martian surface by a telescopic digging device and transferred automatically to the three experiments. The control analysis was carried out by repeating the experiments with soil samples that were sterilized to kill off any organisms present.

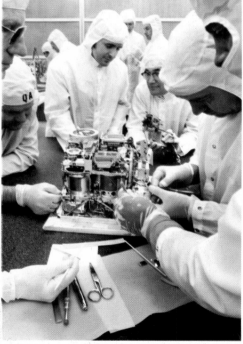

TRW Inc

Below left: The biological experiments performed by the Viking spacecraft. In the pyrolytic release experiment, a soil sample was kept in a container in which the Martian atmosphere was supplemented with carbon dioxide containing ('labelled with') radioactive carbon-14. The sample was bathed in light similar to Martian sunlight then the gases surrounding the sample were removed. It was then heated to see if it gave off any carbon-14, which would indicate that carbon had been removed from the gases by a photosynthetic organism. In the labelled release experiment, the sample was treated with a nutrient containing carbon-14, so that any living organism present to absorb the nutrient would give off carbon to the surrounding air, including carbon-14 which could be detected. In the gas exchange experiment, a gas chromatograph was used to detect any changes, caused by the respiration of a living organism, in the gases around the sample.

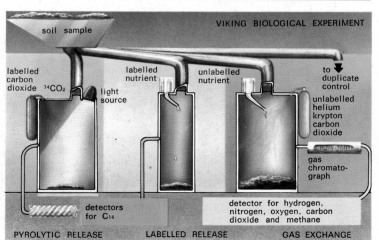

soil sample

VIKING BIOLOGICAL EXPERIMENT

labelled carbon dioxide $^{14}CO_2$

light source

labelled nutrient

unlabelled nutrient

to duplicate control

unlabelled helium krypton carbon dioxide

gas chromatograph

detectors for C_{14}

detector for hydrogen, nitrogen, oxygen, carbon dioxide and methane

PYROLYTIC RELEASE

LABELLED RELEASE

GAS EXCHANGE

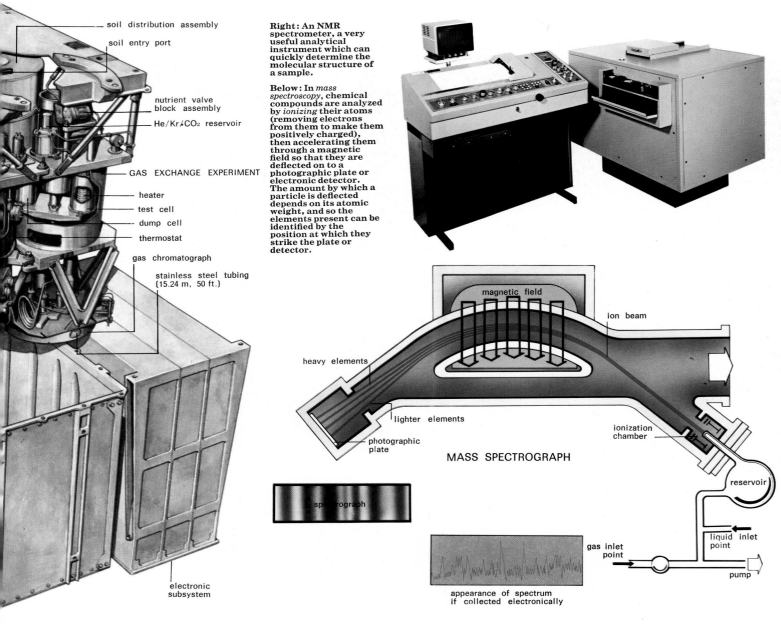

Perkin-Elmer

soil distribution assembly

soil entry port

nutrient valve block assembly

He/Kr/CO₂ reservoir

GAS EXCHANGE EXPERIMENT

heater

test cell

dump cell

thermostat

gas chromatograph

stainless steel tubing (15.24 m, 50 ft.)

electronic subsystem

Right: An NMR spectrometer, a very useful analytical instrument which can quickly determine the molecular structure of a sample.

Below: In *mass spectroscopy*, chemical compounds are analyzed by *ionizing* their atoms (removing electrons from them to make them positively charged), then accelerating them through a magnetic field so that they are deflected on to a photographic plate or electronic detector. The amount by which a particle is deflected depends on its atomic weight, and so the elements present can be identified by the position at which they strike the plate or detector.

magnetic field

ion beam

heavy elements

lighter elements

photographic plate

ionization chamber

MASS SPECTROGRAPH

spectrograph

reservoir

liquid inlet point

gas inlet point

pump

appearance of spectrum if collected electronically

This display is called a *chromatogram* and ideally takes the form of peaks, each indicating the presence of a particular component. The retention time in the column is characteristic for each compound, allowing qualitative analysis to be made upon comparison with a standard sample chromatogram.

Spectroscopy

Newton was the first to discover that when a beam of white light strikes one of the faces of a triangular glass prism, the beam is bent or deviated from its straight path and resolved into a series of rainbow-coloured bands called a spectrum. Newton's spectrum, however, was impure, as the colours overlapped. An instrument for producing and measuring a pure spectrum is called a *spectrometer*, which by focusing the light admitted via a narrow slit or *collimator* on to the prism produces a series of distinct or *monochromatic* colours.

The spectrum produced by the white light of the Sun is a series of closely-adjacent radiations called a *continuous spectrum*. By contrast elements, when incandescent, produce light of distinct colours of particular wavelengths called a *line spectrum*.

The study and analysis of spectra is called *spectroscopy*, which involves observing and measuring the radiations emitted by atoms and molecules when they are excited by means of energy which is normally thermal or electro-magnetic in nature. Atoms consist of a nucleus surrounded by electrons moving in certain orbits corresponding to levels of energy. If supplied with an amount of energy at an appropriate frequency the electron will jump to another orbit, where it will have a higher energy level.

The difference between the energy states is equal to the energy supplied. Conversely, under favourable circumstances an electron may jump from a high to a low energy orbit, emitting energy in the form of electromagnetic radiation. The frequency of this radiation is proportional to the amount of energy it contains.

In a hot body, thermally excited atoms emit and absorb visible and invisible radiation of discrete and characteristic wavelengths due to energy changes between electron orbits, normally producing a radiation spectrum of more than one wavelength.

The first known spectroscopic observations to distinguish individual atomic

transmissions were those of Josef von Fraunhofer (1787-1826) in 1814. Fraunhofer developed a spectrometer capable of resolving the spectral lines named after him, which arise from the absorption of solar radiation by the atoms in the cooler gas surrounding the Sun and by atoms in the Earth's atmosphere. The same spectroscopic techniques were soon applied to the analysis of other atomic emissions, for every element has a unique electronic structure, capable of producing a specific and identifying spectrum. Furthermore, the intensities of the lines of emission indicate the concentrations of the atoms present in the sample, so that a quantitative analysis is possible.

Any substance will absorb radiation of the particular wavelength that it emits at a high temperature. Thus, if radiation from a hot source emitting a continuous spectrum is passed through a transparent sample or vapour, the *absorption spectrum* is deficient in the wavelengths that the sample would emit if it were raised to the same high temperature. Absorption spectroscopy is a valuable analytic tool as it is easy to control and does not destroy the sample. By measuring the proportion of incident light absorbed the molecular concentrations may also be determined.

Navigation

Navigation probably originated on the waterways, such as the Nile and the Euphrates, around which the first major civilizations developed. From these simple beginnings, navigation became steadily more complex as the distances travelled and the speeds and numbers of craft increased with the spread of civilization and trade. Although the basic principles remain the same, the intervening centuries have provided a host of navigational aids and techniques to match the development of transport technology.

Navigation is a composite problem requiring the establishment of position, speed and direction. It is characterized by four main aspects: the determination of the destination; the choice of a suitable route; the estimation of course and speed; and a regular or continuous monitoring of the progress of the craft.

Early navigation

Early navigation in rivers, or in coastal waters in sight of land, was a relatively simple process, using landmarks and coastal features as visual references. Out at sea, however, the early mariners used the Sun and the stars to determine the direction in which they were heading.

The mapping of the heavens was started by the Babylonians, who regarded the heavenly bodies as being mounted on a celestial sphere, a hollow globe of great size which surrounded the Earth and rotated around it from east to west. In the north of the celestial sphere, around its upper pivot as it were, the stars did not change position as much as stars at other parts of the sphere, so a bright star near the centre of this pivotal area could act as an almost-stationary visual reference. In the northern hemisphere, the star occupying this position at present is the Pole Star (Polaris), which is part of the constellation of the Little Bear (Ursa Minor).

Gradually, the positions of celestial bodies were tabulated, and in conjunction with a calendar men could make observations with simple instruments to ascertain their latitude. One of the earliest instruments was the Greek astronomers' *astrolabe*, simplified for use by mariners and developed by the Portuguese in the 15th century for their oceanic voyages. Latitude could be found by observation of the angles between the horizon and the sun or certain stars, the simplest being the angular altitude of the Pole Star, as this angle approximately equals the latitude of the place of observation.

Solar observations were also useful in determining the time, the sun reaching its highest altitude at noon. This altitude also provided latitude, if combined with data (listed in simplified astronomical tables) concerning the angles and position of the Sun throughout the year. By comparing the local latitude with that of an already tabulated latitude of their destination, they were able to deduce their distance north or south of the destination. This furnished them with the rudiments of setting and maintaining course by sailing to the appropriate latitude and then running east or west to their destination, but without a knowledge of longitude a 'fix' of position was impossible.

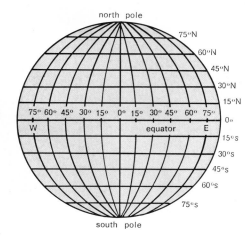

Above: Any point on the Earth's surface can be identified by its latitude and longitude. Lines of latitude are imaginary circles drawn round the Earth, the *Equator* being the line of zero latitude (0°). Lines of longitude are circles drawn through the poles, zero longitude (0°) being the *Greenwich Meridian*.

Right: A pair of seventeenth century Arabian *astrolabes*. The astrolabe had many uses including finding the time of day, and the rising and setting times of the Sun and stars. The Portuguese version, the *mariner's astrolabe*, measured the angle of the Sun or stars to indicate latitude.

Radio Times Hulton Picture Library

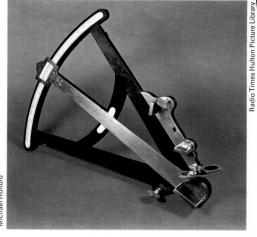

Michael Holford

Above: James Hadley's *octant* enabled navigators to make accurate measurements of the altitude of the Sun or stars, so that they could find their latitude. The observer viewed the horizon through a sight, and adjusted the movable central arm of the instrument until the reflected image of the Sun or star appeared in a mirror placed in line with the horizon. The altitude was indicated on the curved scale.

Below: A *sextant* made by Hadley in 1785. The sextant, a more accurate version of the octant and capable of measuring a greater angle, was invented in 1757 by John Campbell.

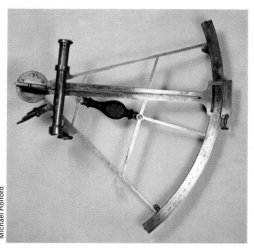

Michael Holford

SHIP'S COMPASS

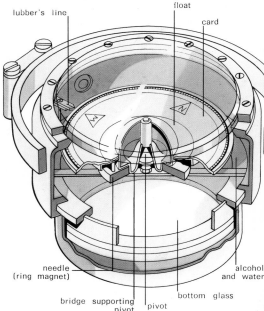

lubber's line — float — card — needle (ring magnet) — alcohol and water — bridge supporting pivot — pivot — bottom glass

Above: A mariner's compass. A magnet is attached to the bottom of the compass card, which is mounted on a float in water and alcohol so it stays horizontal as the ship moves. The 'north' on the card points to magnetic north, and the ship's direction is indicated by the *lubber's line*.

Right: The type of gyroscope used in many gyrocompasses. The gyroscope is a rapidly-spinning wheel which is controlled in such a way that it keeps itself pointing towards true north (the geographic north pole, as opposed to the magnetic one). It is unaffected by movement or by magnetism.

Left: The D-shaped scanner of a ship's radar system. Radar is a valuable navigation aid, providing information on the range and bearing of the coastline and other vessels. It is particularly useful at night and in bad weather when visual observations are not possible.

Right: Checking the accuracy of the *precision approach radar* at an RAF airfield in England. Precision approach radar is one of the many navigational aids used to guide aircraft safely down to the runway; the most advanced *instrument landing systems* can land an aircraft fully automatically.

Right: The operations room of the Thames Navigation Service in Gravesend, which is run by the Port of London Authority to ensure the safe navigation of vessels using the River Thames. The operations room is equipped with seven radar sets and several vhf radio consoles. Tide gauge readings obtained **automatically from five separate points are displayed on tv monitor screens. The service broadcasts half-hourly bulletins on the state of the tides, the weather, ship movements and other navigational information. Over 1,000 ship movements per week are monitored and assisted by this service.**

GYROCOMPASS

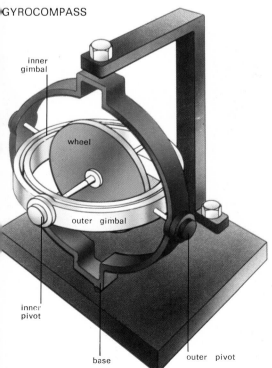

inner gimbal

wheel

outer gimbal

inner pivot

base

outer pivot

Dead reckoning

The mariner's compass, first known in Europe in the 13th century, introduced navigation as a science. The discovery of the directional properties of the lodestone, or of a magnetized needle, which if freely suspended appeared miraculously to point towards the Pole Star, even when she was invisible, made all-weather voyages possible. The compass depends upon the horizontal component of the attraction of the earth's magnetism for its directive force and thus by being free to rotate in a horizontal or *azimuth* plane determines bearing relative to the magnetic pole.

As the magnetic poles are moving slowly about the geographic poles, the compass does not show true North but aligns itself at an angle to it. This difference is called the *magnetic variation* and alters daily, but it is predictable and is listed in almanacs.

The discovery of the compass facilitated steering a course but ignored the vagaries of the wind, the tide and the current. It was therefore impossible to reckon accurately how far and on what bearing the ship lay from its destination.

The process of estimating position based on a record of known progress is known as *dead reckoning*, from the practice of throwing a log overboard (from the bow of the ship) which was assumed to be 'dead' in the water. By noting the time for the log to pass the length of the ship an estimate of speed could be made.

The English adapted this to the *log and line*. A log thrown overboard into the water was attached to a line knotted at regular intervals, and the line was paid out for about half a minute, timed on a sandglass. The length between each successive knot was chosen so that during the timed interval the number of knots paid out represented the number of nautical miles per hour (Knots) at which the ship was travelling. The speed was regularly recorded so that the distance travelled could be calculated. A record of the ship's direction of travel was also kept, and so by drawing a line on a chart which corresponded to the direction and distance travelled, the ship's position could be ascertained.

The ambitious voyages resulting from the expansion of trade created a demand for accurate maps, so that bearings from port to port could be known with some precision. Sailor's charts at this time mapped the world as plane and flat, and 99

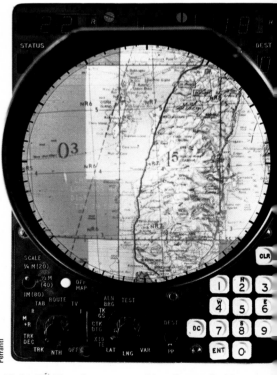

Within the diagram:

red slave
intersection of lines
gives fix of position
green co-ordinate 35.80
purple slave
red co-ordinate 116.30
master
green slave
red decca co-ordinate
green decca co-ordinate

marked with *rhumb lines*. A rhumb line, also known as a *loxodrome*, is a line which crosses every line of longitude at the same angle. Lines of latitude are rhumb lines, as they cross every line of longitude at an angle of 90°. By using the rhumb lines, routes could be planned along lines of constant direction.

The inaccuracies caused by ignoring the convergence of the meridians at the poles was acceptable in the low latitudes of the Mediterranean, but introduced large errors when sailing further North or South.

The great Flemish mathematician Gerardus Mercator (Gerhard Kremer, 1512-94) devised a projection in which straight line rhumbs were true. In this projection, while the meridians remained parallel and equidistant the lines of latitude, although parallel, were spaced in inverse ratio to the convergence of the meridians. Rhumb lines drawn between points with a ruler were correct, crossing every meridian at an equal angle. Such routes could be simply maintained using a compass on a constant course.

The position of a craft is known when both its latitude and longitude have been defined. Latitude and longitude are both measured in *degrees*, and for greater accuracy one degree can be divided into 60 *minutes*, and each minute into 60 *seconds*. The determination of longitude is inseparably associated with the measurement of time. As the earth rotates on its axis, successive meridians pass beneath the sun at an interval of four minutes for every degree of longitude. By comparing local time with a standard time at a reference meridian, say Greenwich at 0° (Greenwich Mean Time), the time divergence gives the difference in longitude, one hour forward or backward equalling 15° East or West.

Astronomical observations give local time but to deduce standard time some predictable phenomenon was required, which was independent of, and could be seen from, the observer's position on earth. The obvious answer was a clock, although it was not until the eighteenth

100

Above left: A Decca Navigator Mk21 receiver in use on a lifeboat. The Decca system uses groups of 'master' and 'slave' transmitters, operating in the 70-130 kHz band, which are positioned so that phase differences are created between the signals from the master and those from the slaves.

Above: The signals from a Decca master/slave combination produce hyperbolic lines along which the signal phase differences are zero. The receiver detects these phase differences and also responds to signals which are transmitted at one minute intervals to identify the individual Decca 'lanes', the areas

between the hyperbolic lines. The receiver displays the Decca co-ordinates and lane numbers, which are then used in conjunction with a lattice overlaid on a standard navigational chart to establish the ship's exact position. The Decca system has a range of about 480 km (300 miles).

Below: A map display of an aircraft *inertial navigation* (IN) system. An IN system computes an aircraft's speed and position by data obtained from *accelerometers*, which register its horizontal and vertical accelerations, and gyroscopes, which register changes in direction and attitude.

century, when John Harrison succeeded in designing a marine timekeeper (or chronometer) that was sufficiently accurate, that one could be carried on ship.

In addition to the chronometer, a method involving lunar distances relative to celestial bodies was proposed, for in principle any fast-moving object can be used for timekeeping provided its motion is predictable and it can be accurately observed. However, the existing instruments lacked the precision required and the method only became practicable with the invention of James Hadley's *octant* in 1731. The octant was the fore-runner of the modern sextant, and was designed for measuring the angle between a celestial body and the horizon to determine latitude.

It could also measure the angle between the Moon and a given star, and once this angle was known the exact time, and the longitude, could be calculated from astronomical tables.

Radio navigational aids

As radio waves, under perfect conditions, travel as a wave about a straight line axis their reception with a suitable receiver, or *Direction Finder* (DF), may be considered analogous to a line of sight bearing. By noting the bearings of two or more shore based stations a position fix may be obtained.

If a loop aerial of a receiver is placed at right angles to the direction of radio waves, the wavefront will strike each side of the loop simultaneously and there will be no signal. If the loop is aligned parallel to the path of the wave it will strike the two sides at slightly different instants of time and a difference signal

Right: The Transit satellite navigation system is based on eight satellites travelling in polar orbits around the Earth (orbits which pass over the north and south poles). As a satellite passes overhead, a ship using the system receives three separate transmissions from it. As the satellite's

position changes during the intervals between the signals, the receiver can compute the ship's position in a similar way to taking a fix from three separate ground-based transmitters. The ground system computes the details of the satellite's orbit and transmits this data to it every 12 hours.

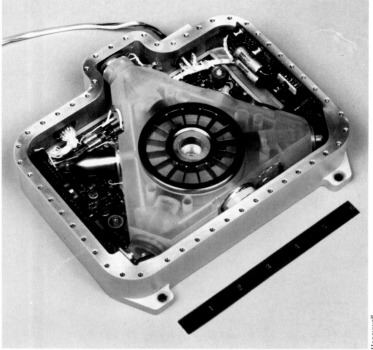

Honeywell

Above: A laser gyro developed for use in navigation systems. Instead of using a rapidly-spinning wheel, the laser gyro has two laser beams, one moving around clockwise and the other one anti-clockwise. If the gyro is rotated about its axis, the frequencies of the beams alter, and these changes in frequency are used to compute rotation rate.

Left: The sensing element of the inertial guidance system built by Ferranti for the European Launcher Development Organization satellite launch vehicles. The element contains three gyros and three accelerometers which sense the vehicle's motion.

Ferranti

will appear. Thus the signal intensity in the receiver alters from a maximum to a minimum as the aerial is rotated relative to the bearing of the transmitting station. Marine radio beacons along the coast or in lightvessels transmit a steady signal on which the bearing is taken, and a morse signal for identification.

A sophisticated omnidirectional version of marine DF is *vhf omnirange* (VOR). A beacon transmits two signals, one omni-directional and one rotating, and the bearing of the beacon relative to the receiver is indicated by phase differences between the two received signals.

Most civil air traffic is routed along busy airways in controlled airspace. These airways are separated into height bands as well as different headings. The position of the aircraft in space is pre-scribed by ground authorities by means of radio and radar contact. At present the most widely used navigation aid is VORTAC, a radio system in which numerous ground beacons along airways send out signals that enable aircrews to check their bearing and distance to the next station. The bearing is checked against a VOR transmitter while distance is estimated using *Distance Measuring Equipment* (DME), which transmits a pulse from the aircraft to interrogate a responsive ground beacon called a *trans-ponder*, which in turn transmits a signal back to the 'plane. The total time (measured from the aircraft) for the sequence to occur defines the distance from the plane to the beacon.

More flexible use of the total airspace is obtained with a phased group of ground stations that send out interlocked signals to create a hyperbolic pattern of position lines. There are a variety of systems available, which are in wide use by both shipping and aircraft. *Decca*, highly accurate to within a few yards up to 480 km (300 miles), from a Decca trans-mitting station, covers busy coastal shipping areas but is not suitable for ocean position finding and *Loran C*, although primarily designed for aircraft, can be used by ships.

'Transit' satellite

satellite orbit

position 3

position 2

position 1

tracking station, Minnesota

injection stn. California

time signal from US Naval Observatory, Washington DC.

computer centre at Point Mugu, California

ship's aerial receiving unit

TRANSIT SATELLITE NAVIGATION SYSTEM

Courtesy of Redifon

101

Relativity

The publication of Albert Einstein's Theory of Relativity in the early years of this century marked a great advance in man's understanding of the physical world. Unfortunately, the theory has a reputation for incomprehensibility, partly because of the complexity of some of the mathematics, but also because its conclusions seem to contradict common sense.

Relativity is primarily a theory about the motions of moving bodies. It was formulated in two stages: the *Special Theory* (1905) considers only bodies moving at a constant velocity relative to each other, while the *General Theory* (1915) also deals with acceleration and gravity.

The Special Theory
Einstein was led to the Special Theory by a crisis which faced physicists at the beginning of this century. Some forty years earlier the great British physicist James Clerk Maxwell (1831-1879) had shown that light consists of waves of electric and magnetic fields. These spread out at a velocity which can be calculated from the electrical properties of a vacuum, and this velocity agrees well with the experimentally measured speed of light (300,000 km per second). Nineteenth century physicists assumed that these waves must travel in some 'medium', the *ether*, just as sound waves require air in order to propagate. The ether, however, must fill the entire Universe, both matter and vacuum, because light traverses both transparent bodies (like glass or water), and the vacuum of space.

The ether was thus thought to be a universal background, and all movement could be measured *absolutely* with respect to it. Since the Earth orbits the Sun at a speed of over 29 km per second, its motion through the ether should have been detectable by optical methods. A precision instrument to achieve this was built by Albert Michelson (1852-1931) and Edward Morley (1838-1923) in 1887 at the Case School of Applied Science in Cleveland, Ohio. In their *interferometer*, a light beam was split into two beams at right angles to one another by a half-silvered mirror. Each beam was reflected back by a mirror at the end of a ten-metre arm, and recombined in an eyepiece.

The light beam which moved out and back *across* the Earth's direction of motion should have taken slightly less time, according to the ether theory, than that which moved with the motion, and then been reflected back against it. This small difference should have shown as a change in the pattern of bright and dark stripes (interference pattern) seen when the beams recombined. Michelson and Morley rotated their apparatus back and forth through 90°, so that the two interferometer arms would reverse roles, and expected to see a corresponding change in the interference pattern. Not the slightest change was observed. The simple ether theory was incorrect, and modifications to explain the negative result of the Michelson-Morley experiment were not very satisfactory.

Einstein, however, realized that the problem lay in a misunderstanding of Maxwell's results—even by Maxwell

Above: 'Relativity', a lithograph by M. C. Escher, illustrates the way in which circumstances appear to change when viewed from different positions. Each element of the picture appears to be geometrically correct only when viewed from the right angle and considered in isolation from the others. The relativistic concepts of the space-time continuum pose similar intellectual problems; space and time, considered locally, appear quite straightforward, but viewed on a universal scale they become much more complex and confusing, and may even appear to be in direct contradiction to everyday common sense.

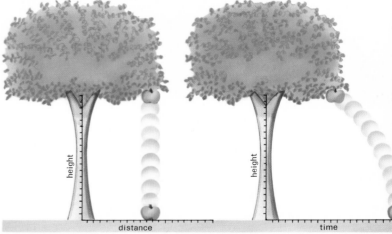

himself. As a simple example, imagine two laboratories, one fixed on the Earth, and another in a moving train. As long as the train moves at a *constant speed* (relative to the Earth), the occupants cannot tell that they are moving, unless they look out of the windows. Indeed, they could claim that they are stationary and that the Earth is moving backwards.

Einstein generalized this idea in his *Principle of Relativity*. It states that the results of any experiment will be the same regardless of how the laboratory is moving, so long as there is no force acting on the laboratory to accelerate it. As a consequence, we cannot in any way distinguish a particular *frame of reference* (the laboratory, for example) as being absolutely at rest.

This being so, then in the case of

Above: These two diagrams, based on the graphs that would be obtained by plotting the height of a falling apple against horizontal distance and against time, represent the idea of the curvature of space-time. The apple's path is straight in (local) space, but *curved* in space-time.

Below: One of the predictions of the General Theory was that light is deflected by gravity, and so starlight passing near the Sun on its way to Earth would be deflected by the Sun's gravity and appear to be coming from a different angle. This was confirmed during a solar eclipse in 1919.

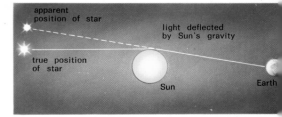

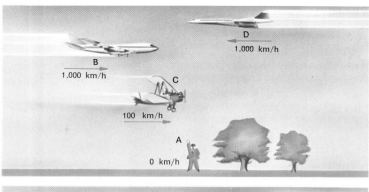

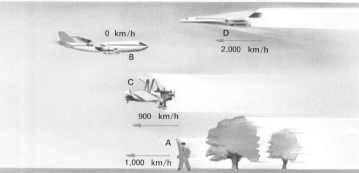

British Transport

Above: If two trains stand side by side in a station, and one begins to move, passengers in the stationary train often think that it is *their* train which is moving. In fact, the two trains can *both* be considered as moving relative to each other, although only one is moving relative to the Earth.

Right: These two diagrams illustrate how observed motion is relative to the motion of the observer. In the upper diagram, the observer is stationary on the ground. Ground features are stationary, and the aircraft are moving at the speeds and in the directions shown. In the lower diagram,

however, the observer is moving along with aircraft B. From this viewpoint, aircraft B could be considered to be stationary, with the ground and aircraft C and D moving from right to left at the speeds shown. Nothing can be *absolutely* at rest or in motion, only at rest or in motion *relative* to something else.

CEGB

CEGB

Left and above: One aspect of the Special Theory was the equation $E = mc^2$: the total energy in a piece of matter equals its mass multiplied by the square of the speed of light. A nuclear power station, such as the one above, operates by converting some of its fuel's mass into energy. This yields much more

energy from a given mass of fuel than would be obtained by burning it. The heap of coal on the left is capable of producing about 2.2 million MWh of electricity when burnt in the power station; if all its mass could be converted to energy, about 34.3 million million MWh could be produced.

electromagnetism the electrical properties of a vacuum must be the same in all laboratories. Since the speed of light is related to these properties, it too must also be the same in all reference frames. This is where the difference with the ether theory arises. The older theory had light moving at a constant speed in a medium at rest, and hence one could measure the *absolute* velocity of one's laboratory. In Einstein's theory, light travels at a constant speed *relative to whoever is observing it*. For example, if two spaceships were travelling at 200,000 km per second, one towards the Sun, and the other away from it, they would *both* measure the velocity of sunlight to be 300,000 km per second (and *not* 500,000 and 100,000 km per second, respectively).

The result of the Michelson-Morley

experiment follows quite naturally from the Principle of Relativity, because the two light beams actually travelled at the same speed relative to the apparatus, and hence returned at the same instant.

To understand the other results of Relativity we can consider two rockets passing each other at high speed. Each flashes a light bulb the instant they pass. The light from each bulb travels at the same speed regardless of the speed of the bulb itself (Einstein's second postulate of Relativity). So both flashes expand in all directions as a *single* sphere of light. Now, an observer in rocket A must remain in the centre of the expanding sphere from his own flash bulb, and hence he is also at the centre of the sphere from rocket B's flashbulb. He sees rocket B travelling away from the centre, so to him, B is no

longer centrally placed within the sphere. To an observer in rocket B, on the other hand, he (B) is always at the centre of the spheres, and A is moving away; to him, A is *not* at the centre.

To resolve this apparent contradiction, we must admit that the distance between B and the sphere as measured by A is *not the same* as that measured by B himself. In other words, distances appear to alter when the object under study moves relative to the observer. From this it can be shown mathematically that the physical length of a body always appears to decrease with increase of speed, and becomes zero if the moving object approaches the speed of light. This effect is often known as the *Lorenz-Fitzgerald contraction*, after the two physicists Hendrik Lorentz (1853-1928) and George Fitzgerald (1851-1901) who proposed it as an explanation of the result of the Michelson-Morley experiment.

Similarly, experiments have shown that a moving clock always goes more slowly than one which is fixed relative to the observer, and would appear to stop altogether if it could travel near the speed of light. In addition, it can be shown that the *mass* of a body *increases* with velocity, and becomes infinitely large for

103

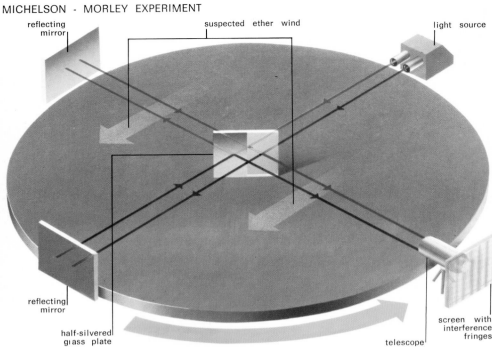

reflecting mirror

suspected ether wind

light source

reflecting mirror

half-silvered glass plate

screen with interference fringes

telescope

rotation of experiment

20.00 hrs January 2

movement of Sun and solar system

20 km/sec

1,728,000 km

20.00 hrs January 1

20.00 hrs January 2

Earth's movement with Sun

20 km/sec

Earth's orbit around Sun

29.79 km/sec

20.00 hrs January 1

Above left: One of the atomic clocks used in experiments which have tested Einstein's theories concerning the effects of speed, acceleration and gravity on time. This one went on a 2-hour rocket flight, during which its timekeeping was compared with that of similar clocks on Earth.

Above: The Michelson-Morley experiment of 1887 set out to detect the 'ether wind' which was supposed to be passing over the Earth as it moved through space. It hoped to show that the speed of light was affected by the ether wind; its failure resulted in the rejection of the ether theory, and led Einstein to his ideas about relativity.

Left: If you stay at home for 24 hours you will not normally feel that you have travelled anywhere. Taking the Earth as your frame of reference, this is quite true, but taking a larger area of space as your reference frame you find that you have, in fact, travelled millions of kilometres during that 24 hours.

---

speeds near that of light. Since more force is required to speed up a more massive body, it is never possible to accelerate a particle until it actually moves at the velocity of light. The latter thus constitutes a natural 'speed limit' for the Universe.

This slowing of time and increase in mass have both been verified for sub-atomic particles, the only objects that can be made to reach speeds approaching that of light. At these speeds, fairly appreciable relativistic changes can be observed.

Another way of looking at the increase of mass with speed is to say that when a body is given energy of motion (*kinetic energy*), this energy is converted into extra mass. In 1907, Einstein realized that the converse must also be true: the

normal 'at rest' mass of a stationary body must be convertible to energy. The exact amount of energy (E) is calculated by multiplying the mass (m) by the speed of light (c) squared: in symbols, $E = mc^2$. This prediction was not verified for another 25 years, but it led eventually to the atomic bomb, a development which Einstein himself opposed strenuously.

The General Theory

After the Special Theory, Einstein started work on a General Theory of Relativity which would hold for accelerating laboratories as well as for those moving at constant speed. The Principle of Relativity does not hold here: we all know that acceleration can be felt by the human body, and an experiment does not give the same result on an accelerating train as it

does on a constant-speed train. Einstein realized, however, that (in a small laboratory where the force of gravity is constant) it is impossible to tell the difference between the effects of acceleration and those of gravity. The inmates of an enclosed rocket, for example, cannot tell whether it is at rest on Earth, or in free space and accelerating at a rate of 9.81m per second. In either case they are pressed against the floor with the same force.

With this *Principle of Equivalence*, and the requirement that Special Relativity shall hold good when no accelerations or gravitational effects are present, Einstein built up the mathematical structure of the General Theory. It is too complex to describe accurately without complex mathematical formulae, but roughly speaking it combines time and the three dimensions of space into a four-dimensional 'space-time continuum'. This is impossible to visualize, but its geometry can be described mathematically just as the geometrical theorems of Euclid can.

The Principle of Equivalence shows that matter changes this geometry in a subtle way (somewhat analogous to curvature in ordinary geometry). Objects passing through this 'curved space-time' have their motion affected by it—they are *gravitationally deflected*. Einstein changed the concept of gravity from a force to being an alteration of the basic background of space-time.

This mathematical formulation of space and time also allows the properties of accelerating systems to be predicted. Acceleration is found to slow time, for example, so a space traveller who experiences accelerations as he leaves Earth, changes course at his destination and eventually lands again on Earth will find that he has aged less than his twin who has remained on Earth. This 'twins paradox' has now been confirmed experimentally by flying extremely accurate atomic clocks around the world. They ran more slowly, by an infinitesimal amount, than identical clocks kept on the ground.

Astronomy and Astrophysics

About 18,000,000,000 years ago, all the matter in the universe seems to have been contained in a small region. Just how small, and precisely how long ago, are debatable points; neither can we say what happened before that. Ever since then, however, the material has been expanding outwards, possibly as a result of an enormous explosion which has been nicknamed the 'Big Bang'.

The main component of the material which expanded out of this Big Bang was hydrogen, each atom consisting of a nucleus with a single proton, and a single electron. About 10 per cent of the atoms, however, were formed by the Big Bang into helium atoms consisting of two protons, two neutrons and two electrons. Since that makes them four times as heavy as hydrogen, some 28% of the *mass* of the early universe was helium. From this hydrogen and helium, all the other elements that we know today were formed.

How do we know all this? As we look at the universe, we can see distant objects such as galaxies. The fainter these objects are, the more their light appears to be shifted to the red end of the visible spectrum. This is not quite the same thing as saying that they are reddened: that would mean that something is filtering out the blue light, as happens to sunlight at sunset. What is actually happening is that their spectral lines—the wavelengths in the spectrum caused by, say, hydrogen, calcium or other elements—are further to the red than they ought to be.

What interpretation is put on this finding is crucial to our whole understanding of the universe. The most familiar way in which spectral lines can be shifted is by the *Doppler effect*, the change in wavelength due to a source's motion. On this interpretation, which is generally accepted, all objects are moving away from all others, and the universe is expanding. The rate at which this Doppler shift takes place is the same wherever we look.

By searching for objects of known brightness or size, a value can be put on the expansion rate, and the most recent figure is 55 kilometres per second for every *megaparsec* (Mpc) of distance. (A parsec is an astronomical unit of distance, and is equal to 30.857×10^{12}km). This rate is called the *Hubble Constant*, H, after the American astronomer Edwin Hubble (1889-1953) who first investigated the subject. So if an object has a redshift of 1100 km/sec, it is about 20 Mpc away (although random motions also have to be taken into account). The value of 1/H now gives a figure for the time elapsed since the Big Bang—that is, the age of the universe in seconds. It works out to be some 18,000,000,000 years.

As we search to greater distances, so we are in effect looking back in time. Light and radio waves travel at nearly 300,000 km/sec, but the most distant objects are so far away that the radiation now reaching *us* left *them* several thousand million years ago—when the

Left: The observatory built in the eighteenth century at Jaipur, India, by Sawai Jai Singh. Much early astronomy was devoted to studying the motion and measuring the positions of the Sun, stars, Moon and planets. In the West, including the Arabic countries, one of the main uses of astronomy was to produce tables of astronomical data for use in navigation. Serious studies of the actual nature of the universe did not begin properly until telescopes came into general use.

Below: Stars emit electromagnetic radiation covering a very wide spectrum. Ordinary telescopes are used for observing the visible light emitted by stars, but radio telescopes, such as this one in the US, detect the longer-wavelength radio emissions from stellar objects.

Below: The radio source Cassiopeia A is the remnant of a supernova, a star which exploded in about 1700. Its radio intensity has been measured by the 5 km radio telescope at Cambridge, England, and has been converted into this 'radio photograph'.

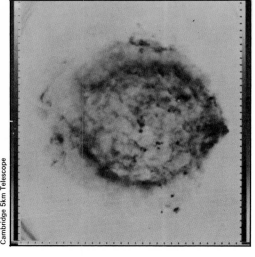

universe was very much younger. Much interest centres on looking as far as possible, to try to discover whether the universe looked any different then. The signs are that it did. Objects seem to have been closer together, as one would expect with an expanding universe.

Another piece of evidence in favour of the Big Bang hypothesis is the discovery that wherever we look in the universe, there is a background glow, a sort of very dull warmth. This is at a temperature of only 2.76 K—just above the absolute zero of temperature—but even so it represents a challenge to astronomical theory. It seems to be the residual heat of the later stages of the Big Bang itself, spread out in every direction equally. Its temperature agrees with what we should now expect from an original fireball temperature of over a million degrees, which in turn would create the observed ratio of hydrogen to helium.

Quasars

The objects with the greatest redshifts, and which are therefore assumed to be

105

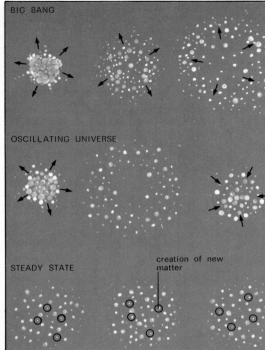

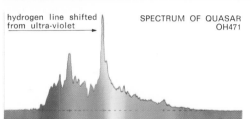

hydrogen line shifted from ultra-violet →

SPECTRUM OF QUASAR OH471

Left: The spectrum of one of the most distant observable objects —the quasar OH471. This object is about 10 billion light years away, which means that what we see of it now is in fact that way it looked 10 billion years ago. The graph shows the intensity of its light at each wavelength. The tallest spike represents the emission due to its hydrogen; this spike would normally be in the far ultraviolet region to the left of the spectrum, but the Doppler effect due to the quasar moving rapidly away from us has shifted the spike towards the 'red' end, so it appears in the visible region.

Above left: The 'Milky Way'. The brightest part is obscured by gas clouds which are in the spiral arms of the galaxy, and the glowing red areas are clouds of hydrogen from which stars are formed. The white streak is the track of an Earth satellite crossing the sky when the picture was taken.

Above: Three theories of the origin of the universe. The 'Big Bang' theory, top, says the universe expanded out from a condensed mass of matter. A second theory, centre, says that the universe is continually expanding and contracting, while a third, bottom, says that matter is being created continuously.

the most distant, are the *quasars*. The name comes from 'quasi-stellar radio sources', and they were first identified in 1963 as sources of radio waves which looked like stars. Their properties include a very high redshift, measured from strong bright lines in their spectrum; they generally look bluer than ordinary stars, and they flicker in brightness slightly on a time scale as short as a few months. Nowadays, any star-like object with these properties is classed as a quasar, though many of them are not radio sources. Observations indicate that quasars are fairly small, and so they must be exceedingly bright to be visible at these enormous distances.

Galaxies

Closer at hand, and more familiar, are the galaxies. These are giant star systems, each containing as many as a million million stars and which come in a variety of types—spiral, elliptical, irregular and so on. Our own Milky Way is one fairly typical spiral galaxy. As we look to greater distances, we find curious things happening in the centres of some galaxies. These may have bright centres or nuclei; in some cases there are signs that explosive events have taken place.

The nuclei of such galaxies behave in many ways like mini-quasars—they are bright and blue, they flicker, they have the same bright lines, and they may be radio sources. In recent years, new detection techniques have revealed that some comparatively nearby objects once thought to be quasars are actually *N-galaxies*, consisting of a bright nucleus with a surrounding 'fuzz'; the underlying fuzzy area, previously hidden in the glare,

Above: The galaxy M82, in the constellation of Ursa Major. Signs of explosive events can be seen in the nucleus of the galaxy, and it appears reddish in the central region because the stars there are old. The blue colour of the outer regions is due to the stars there being newer ones.

Right: A planetary or ring nebula within our own galaxy, number M57 in the constellation of Lyra. Planetary nebulae may be glowing shells of material thrown off by dying stars. In this picture, the material appears to be spreading outwards from the bright star at the centre of the ring. Alternatively, a dying star may flare up and become a nova.

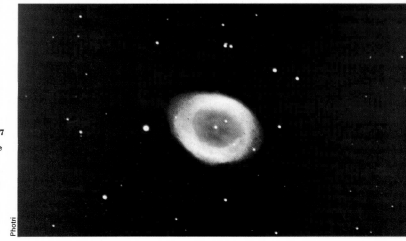

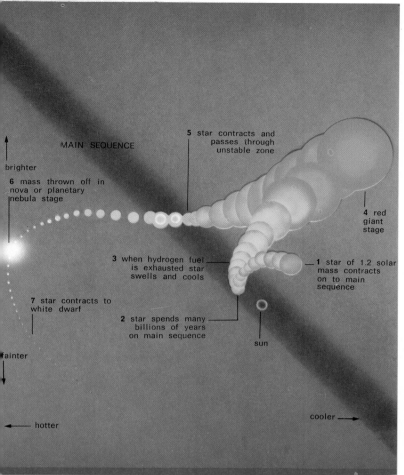

MAIN SEQUENCE

brighter

5 star contracts and passes through unstable zone

6 mass thrown off in nova or planetary nebula stage

4 red giant stage

3 when hydrogen fuel is exhausted star swells and cools

1 star of 1.2 solar mass contracts on to main sequence

7 star contracts to white dwarf

2 star spends many billions of years on main sequence

sun

fainter

← hotter

cooler →

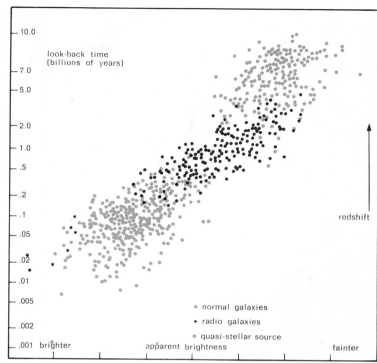

look-back time (billions of years)

— 10.0
— 7.0
— 5.0

— 2.0
— 1.0

— .5

— .2
— .1
— .05

— .02
— .01

— .005

— .002

— .001 brighter

redshift →

• normal galaxies
• radio galaxies
• quasi-stellar source

apparent brightness

fainter

Left: The Hertzsprung-Russell diagram represents the relationship between the temperature and brightness of a star at different stages in its life cycle. Stars usually spend most of their lives at some point along the main sequence, which is where our own Sun is at present.

Above: The Hubble diagram is produced by plotting the red shifts of objects (vertical axis) against their apparent brightnesses (horizontal axis). The faintest objects have the greatest redshifts; they are also the oldest, the furthest away and the fastest-moving. The 'look-back time' scale represents how far back into the history of the universe we are looking when we observe an object, and the diagram suggests an evolutionary pattern of quasar into radio galaxy, and then radio galaxy into normal galaxy. Normal galaxies appear brighter in the sky than do quasars, but only because they are nearer.

Mount Wilson/Palomar Observatory/Alphabet & Image

Alphabet & Image

Sky & Telescope

Left: A nearby spiral galaxy, number NGC2841, in the constellation of Ursa Major. The round objects in the picture are stars in our own galaxy, which itself is similar in shape to this one although its spiral arms are not so tightly wound. This picture was taken with a 200 inch telescope.

Above: The upper object is Comet West, which appeared in March 1976, and the lower is the track of a meteor—a tiny piece of rock which entered the Earth's atmosphere and burned up while the picture was being taken. Comets are members of the solar system, travelling in orbits around the Sun.

has now been seen. Efforts are being made to study more distant quasars, in the hope of proving that they, too, are really the very bright cores of galaxies.

Most galaxies occur in clusters, ranging in size from a couple of dozen to thousands of members. Our Milky Way is in a small cluster which contains about 24 members, called the Local Group. The largest galaxy in the Local Group is not our own but the Andromeda Galaxy, also called M31, which can be seen as a misty patch with the naked eye on a clear night. This is perhaps twice as large again as our own Galaxy, which ranks second. A galaxy called M33 is third, while fourth and fifth are the Magellanic Clouds, two fairly large misty patches visible from the Earth's southern hemisphere. These appear to be satellites of our own Galaxy.

Our own Galaxy is a fairly typical one. There is an important difference between the spiral arms or disc and the central hub, a difference found in other galaxies too. If you could take the disc away, the hub would look like a small elliptical galaxy—a flattened globe of stars, with almost no gas or dust mingled in. All the stars have the appearance of being old.

Around the outside of the hub, like moths round a street light, are a couple of hundred *globular clusters*. These too are globes of stars, but are much smaller than galaxies—each contains up to a million stars only. These globular clusters contain very old stars, distinguished by their red colour. Again, there is an almost complete absence of dust and gas.

The spiral arms, however, are quite different. They contain a large number of blue, white and yellow stars, as well as copious amounts of dust and gas. In the 107

ZEFA

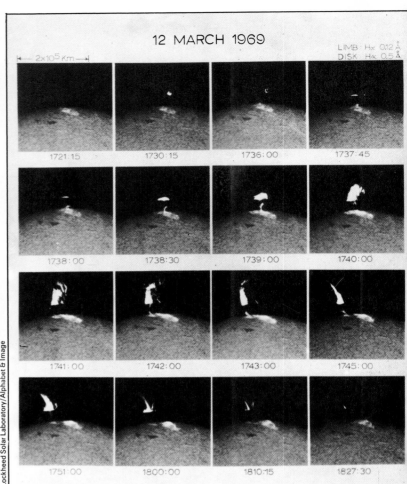

LIMB Hα 0.12 Å
DISK Hα 0.5 Å

|←— 2×10⁵ Km —→|

1721:15 1730:15 1736:00 1737:45

1738:00 1738:30 1739:00 1740:00

1741:00 1742:00 1743:00 1745:00

1751:00 1800:00 1810:15 1827:30

Lockheed Solar Laboratory/Alphabet & Image

Above: A solar eclipse occurs when the Moon moves directly between the Earth and the Sun, and briefly obscures the view of the Sun from the Earth. The bright flash is caused by more of the Sun being visible at that point because of a large lunar valley at the rim of the Moon's disc.

Below: A diagram, not to scale, of the principal members of our solar system. The asteroids are small lumps of rock which circle the Sun in a large range of orbits, but most of them are concentrated in a belt of orbits between Mars and Jupiter. The largest is Ceres, 955 km in diameter.

Right: A sequence of photographs showing the eruption of a flare of gas from the surface of the Sun. Particles and radiation thrown off by these solar flares interact with the charged layer in the Earth's atmosphere known as the *ionosphere*, and this can often be a source of radio interference.

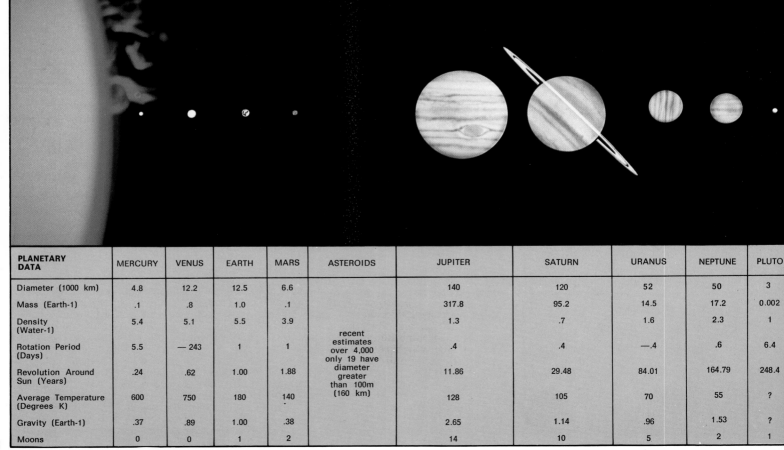

PLANETARY DATA	MERCURY	VENUS	EARTH	MARS	ASTEROIDS	JUPITER	SATURN	URANUS	NEPTUNE	PLUTO
Diameter (1000 km)	4.8	12.2	12.5	6.6		140	120	52	50	3
Mass (Earth-1)	.1	.8	1.0	.1		317.8	95.2	14.5	17.2	0.002
Density (Water-1)	5.4	5.1	5.5	3.9	recent estimates over 4,000 only 19 have diameter greater than 100m (160 km)	1.3	.7	1.6	2.3	1
Rotation Period (Days)	5.5	— 243	1	1		.4	.4	—.4	.6	6.4
Revolution Around Sun (Years)	.24	.62	1.00	1.88		11.86	29.48	84.01	164.79	248.4
Average Temperature (Degrees K)	600	750	180	140		128	105	70	55	?
Gravity (Earth-1)	.37	.89	1.00	.38		2.65	1.14	.96	1.53	?
Moons	0	0	1	2		14	10	5	2	1

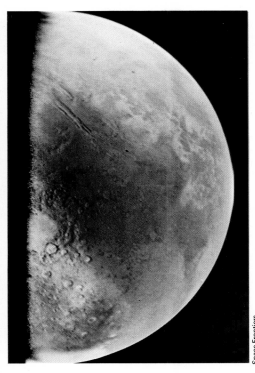

Left: A star track picture taken with a time exposure of about four hours. The tracks show the motion of the stars around the sky during the exposure period, and this kind of picture can be taken with almost any camera. The thick track near the centre of the tracks is that of the Pole Star.

Above: A picture of Mars taken from the Viking I spacecraft. Just above the centre, at the top of the darker region, are the Valles Marineris—an enormous system of valleys and ravines that might have been caused by water flowing on the surface or by a fracturing of the surface.

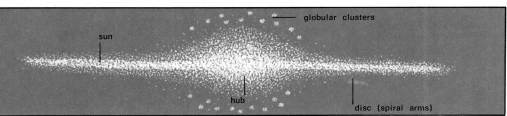

globular clusters

sun

hub

disc (spiral arms)

Above: This diagram represents an edge-on view of our own galaxy, which has a thick central hub and spiral arms. The Sun is situated about two thirds of the way out from the central hub. The total diameter of the galaxy is about 30,000 parsecs, which is about 100,000 light years.

Below: Saturn is unique in being circled by a series of rings consisting of billions of ice-covered rock particles. The rings are only a few kilometres thick, and the particles range in size from about 1 metre down to a few centimetres. Saturn also has 10 known satellites.

disc, stars seem to be forming and dying all the time. All around us we can see clouds of dust and gas, some of it obscuring the stars behind and producing dark lanes in the sky, where no stars appear. In other cases, the material is illuminated by nearby stars to produce glowing clouds in the sky, such as the Orion Nebula.

Stars

It is from such clouds that stars are born. Some of the material will begin to collapse on itself, just as on a larger scale the Galaxy itself once formed. As it does so, it attracts nearby material and after a while enough mass has formed to generate heat in the densest regions of this *protostar*, simply by virtue of the gravitational contraction. Eventually the central regions become sufficiently hot and dense for the atoms, already stripped of their electrons, to combine and release energy in a process which results in the formation of helium, and the star begins to shine.

If the original material has been rotating rapidly, it will probably form a disc around itself as it contracts. This disc in turn gathers into small bodies, which then accumulate to form the solid bodies called planets, all orbiting the

star in the same plane and in the same direction.

A star which happens to be particularly massive—say 20 times the mass of the Sun —will become very hot in its interior, where the nuclear reactions go on, and will squander its hydrogen fuel at a great rate. Such stars shine brilliant blue-white, and can be many thousands of times as bright as the Sun. They go through their life cycle much more rapidly and within a few million years they have used up all their fuel. By contrast, yellow, orange and red stars are normally much less massive and longer lived.

In their later stages, massive stars use up first their hydrogen, then their helium, then progressively heavier elements, each one formed in turn by the previous nuclear reactions. Eventually, however, these stars are no longer able to support the pressure of the overlying material by the outward flow of energy produced. After undergoing further collapse, they may undergo a cataclysmic explosion, throwing off much of the material. This is the rare event known as a *supernova*—rare because only three have been observed in the Galaxy in the last thousand years.

The heavy elements produced in the star are now scattered throughout the surrounding regions of space, where they will become fixed with the interstellar gas and may eventually become part of new stars and planetary systems. All the elements on Earth, other than hydrogen and helium, are thought to have been formed long ago within massive stars.

The remains of the star itself are probably what radioastronomers observe as a *pulsar*—a pulsating radio source. These strange objects send out a stream of radio pulses, rather like the ticking of clocks, every second or so with great regularity. They are best explained as being rotating *neutron stars*—objects so dense that all the electrons and protons are forced together to form neutrons, all very densely packed.

The whole thing is so compact that material with the mass of the Sun may be squeezed into a globe no more than a few kilometres across. Such an object is able to rotate very rapidly, and as it does so it sends out the stream of pulses, rather like the flashes from a lighthouse as its machinery rotates.

Black holes

Some objects may be so massive that they form *black holes*. The existence of such objects has not been proven, but they seem theoretically quite likely and their existence was suggested as long ago as the eighteenth century by the French mathematician Pierre Laplace (1749-1827). What happens, astronomers ask, when an object has so great a mass that nothing, not even light, can escape from it? Since Einstein's theory of relativity states that nothing can exceed the velocity of light, once material enters a black hole it can never be accelerated fast enough to escape. There are a few candidates for black holes in the heavens—the signs are that in some systems there are objects of comparatively small size with considerable mass but which are quite invisible.

Most stars, however, are never likely to become black holes, and may end their lives by simply shedding mass, as *planetary nebulae*, *novae* or *white dwarfs*. White dwarfs are fairly numerous, and are about the same size as the Earth.

Paranormal Phenomena

Along with the recent upsurge of interest in the occult there has been a corresponding rise in scepticism about the validity of *paranormal* events, that is events that defy normal scientific explanation. Some of the scepticism is as irrational as is the level of belief on the other side of the fence. The belief in some paranormal phenomena does give cause for concern, however; cases have been reported where people have committed murder or suicide out of fear of spirits supposedly controlling them or communicating to them.

There is also the possibility of the abuse of psychic powers, if they exist, for military purposes. The US Department of Defense, for example, is believed to spend at least five-figure sums annually on research into various aspects of the paranormal, and Soviet interest appears to be at least as high. If psychic abilities are real then indeed they could be misused in both times of war and peace. Telepathy and clairvoyance could both be used for surveillance purposes as well as for long distance communications, such as communication with nuclear-armed submarines.

The basic question still at issue in the paranormal is the validity of the phenomena. This problem has to be investigated with great care to avoid bias on the part of subjects and observers involved leading to distorted reporting of cases. There is also the problem of fraud, conscious or unconscious, practised by the subject ('medium' or 'psychic') or even by the investigator. Cases of the exposure of conscious fraud abound in the history of the subject since its beginnings around the middle of the last century.

The ideal evidence for a psychic event would involve a phenomenon which could be made to occur again and again, and under a variety of conditions. This criterion of repeatability is a prerequisite of scientific respectability. Without it there would seem to be little hope of authenticating a phenomenon or, as importantly, of understanding it. The level of repeatability seems to have improved somewhat for psychic phenomena in the last few decades, but there is still a great deal to be desired. No truly repeatable psychic phenomenon is presently known.

Scientifically impossible phenomena

Into this category fall life after death, precognition and materialization. The first of these would require the persistence of a high level of information after the death of a highly organized brain. Such persistence would require energy, and therefore matter, and would be impossible to organize under earthly conditions without a structure like a brain. Precognition would contradict the notion of *causality*, that cause must come before effect. Materialization, along 'Star Trek' lines, would require millions of times more energy than is naturally available to the human body. And such a feat has never been demonstrated scientifically, even at the microscopic level involving atoms and molecules.

The evidence for life after death in-

Below: A sequence of photographs showing the supposed materialization of an Indian girl during a seance. Materialization was once a popular spiritualist trick, but is now so discredited that it is rarely performed today.

Below right: A pair of witches demonstrating some of their rituals. The circle laid out on the floor is to protect the witches from the demons that they claim they can summon by constant incantation of their names. There are a number of varieties of witchcraft practised today, and the main attraction of many of them is probably the sexual and sado-masochistic nature of their rituals.

Psychic News

TABLE OF PARANORMAL PHENOMENA		
PHENOMENON	ENERGY REQUIRED	FEASIBILITY (from 1 = feasible to 4 = impossible)
life after death	?	4
precognition	?	4
materialization	megajoules	3
spoon bending	joules	2
levitation	joules	2
poltergeists	joules	2
Bermuda Triangle	kilojoules	2
UFOs	kilojoules	2
ball lightning	megajoules	1
faith healing	millijoules	1
dowsing	millijoules	1
ghosts	millijoules	1
astrology	millijoules	1
ley lines	millijoules	1
meditation	millijoules	1

Left: A table showing the energy levels that would be required to activate some well-known paranormal phenomena, and their scientific feasibility. The feasibility of each phenomenon is determined by the amount of energy that it would require; the classification of a phenomenon as 'feasible' does not imply that the phenomenon actually exists, only that its existence would not be beyond the limits of the laws of nature as we know them. It has been suggested that the increasing interest in the paranormal is symptomatic of a psychological need formerly catered for by traditional religions, now in decline.

Syndication International

Below: One dowsing method involves the use of a forked rod, which supposedly twists downwards when the dowser walks over an underground water source.

Right: In the 1920s Alfred Watkins suggested that ancient sites such as prehistoric earthworks, stone circles, and early churches, were sited so as to form a network of straight lines, which he called *ley lines*, that possibly marked out travel routes. Since then some people have claimed that ley lines possess some mysterious psychic energy detectable by sensitive individuals such as dowsers.

John Goldblatt

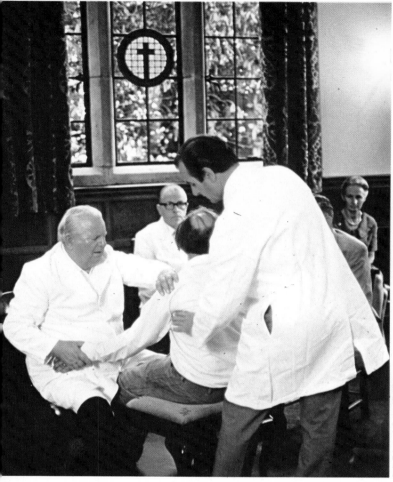

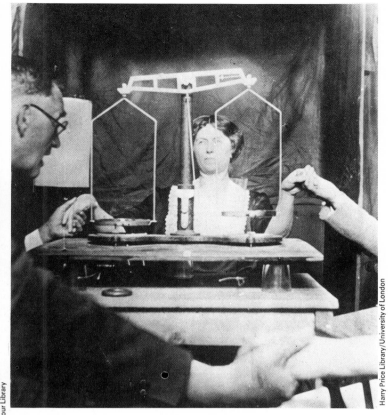

Left: Faith healer Harry Edwards, right, treating a patient at a healing session. Faith healing undoubtedly works for many patients if they have absolute faith in the healer; the healing process may be initiated by the mind of the patient, just as psychosomatic illnesses are caused by emotional disturbances.

Above: A medium apparently tilting a balance by means of psychokinesis; this may be possible, but it is not necessarily a psychic effect.

Daily Telegraph Colour Library

Harry Price Library/University of London

cludes messages from the dead or claims of the knowledge of earlier lives by those presently living. The information coming from the dead is mainly very naive, though there are a few items told which appear unlikely to have been learnt by normal means by the medium who is transmitting the message. Information on earlier lives is quite extensive in certain cases, but very few of these bear up under more careful examination. Thus a man who claimed to have lived an earlier life, being killed at the Battle of Sedgemoor in 1685, gave a great deal of seemingly authentic historical data relating to that period, but it was subsequently found that the eight dates of births, marriages and deaths associated with his supposed former family were not recorded in the local parish church register.

Materialization, involving either the appearance of solid objects inside boxes or completely closed rooms, or its converse of dematerialization, has been reported as an adjunct to poltergeist ('noisy ghost') phenomena. It was also very popular at seances in the last century, though is not currently demonstrated. The complete appearance or disappearance trick involves so much energy as to be physically impossible, as was noted earlier, but a more tenuous form is feasible. This might even be explained in terms of the well-documented but poorly understood natural electrical phenomenon of ball lightning. However, very strong electric fields would be required to produce such an effect in psychic events, and since they have not been noted in materialization seances of the past such a possibility is not likely to be correct.

Faintly possible events

This category includes spoon bending, poltergeists, levitation and more general *psychokinesis* (the willed moving of objects). All of these involve energies which are naturally available to the human body. There are many people who claim to be able to cause various items of cutlery to bend or break by gently stroking them, and some have claimed the ability to cause such items to bend without actually touching them.

The validation of spoon bending by direct contact has proved very difficult. Many anecdotal reports support the authenticity of the phenomenon, but no subject able to perform the feat repeatably and under perfect conditions has come forward. The criteria for scientific validation require at least that the mechanical pressure being used by the subject be monitored all the time the test occurs, and that videotape records be taken simultaneously to ensure that fraud be demonstrably absent. No evidence has been produced at this level. Validation of indirect bending has been attempted by setting 'impossible' tasks, such as the distortion of pieces of metal in sealed glass tubes or globes. Some progress has been made in this, but again without the desired level of validation.

Poltergeist cases are, by their nature, far less repeatable than other psychic events, and also less accessible to scientific investigation. Many cases have been reported, some of which appear to have been carefully witnessed by respectable members of the community, although they are not completely fraud-proof.

Levitation has been witnessed numerous times in the past, the most famous

111

medium to demonstrate it being D. D. Home, who supposedly floated out of a second floor window to return through another one. There have not been any detailed tests of such an ability, and the evidence is too imprecise to support the authenticity of the phenomenon at any real level. It is just feasible on scientific grounds, the most reasonable suggestion being that it is achieved by means of some electric field effect. If the medium had electrically charged himself then he might be repelled upwards by the electric field near the Earth's surface. However, there should be various clues that such electricity was involved, such as the medium's hair standing on end; photographs of levitators never show this.

The willed movement of objects has been performed by many subjects, notably two Russian women, Kulagina and Vinogradova. Some of these have used trickery such as 'invisible' threads, though others, very likely including the Russians, are clearly authentic. Indeed, there are various cases of intensive investigation of willed object movement where fraud can be completely ruled out. Thus various cases are known of subjects moving a small item, such as a needle, hung by a thread inside a plastic or glass container, or rotating straws on a disc floating on water in a beaker inside a glass jar. Yet all these instances can be explained either in the known terms of electrostatics or heating effects; none of them can be regarded as paranormal, though at first sight they look as if they are so. Such explanations may also be relevant to the powers of the two Russian women mentioned earlier.

Just possible events

Such phenomena as faith healing, dowsing, telepathy, clairvoyance, ghosts, astrology, plant intelligence and UFOs (unidentified flying objects) are classified under this heading. If they occur at all they would be expected to be activated either by energies naturally accessible to the human body (for the first seven phenomena in the above list) or, in the case of UFOs, by natural phenomena. Ghosts and hauntings have only anecdotal evidence to support them, and so will not be considered further here.

Faith healing has a venerable tradition; for example, it was mentioned in the Bible as one of the powers of Jesus Christ. Many cases of miraculous cures of diseases, from arthritis to cancer, have been reported, some of them extremely well documented. Fraud may well be practised in 'psychic surgery', where the healer's hands are supposed to enter the patient's body and remove diseased tissue without the use of any surgical instruments, the hole in the patient's body closing up without a scar immediately the healer's hands are removed. But the cases remarked on above, and associated with the 'laying-on of hands' are undoubtedly authentic. Yet there are hundreds of cases of spontaneous regression of cancer, so that it is difficult to disentangle the psychological effect the healer has on the patient from anything deeper.

Dowsing has also been practised for a long time, a forked twig or a pendulum being the usual tool used to detect water or buried objects. In spite of many anecdotes of successful dowsing, careful tests have not uncovered any ability to

Above: An example of the early 1970s spoon bending craze. In November 1973 the Israeli entertainer Uri Geller, during a British radio broadcast, invited listeners to concentrate on metal objects such as keys or spoons to see if they could bend them. This lady, Dora Portman of Harrow, near London, reported the bending of a ladle that she was using at the time, and many other listeners phoned in to report the bending of cutlery, keys, nails and jewellery, and the stopping or starting of watches and clocks. No cases of metal bending have yet been scientifically verified.

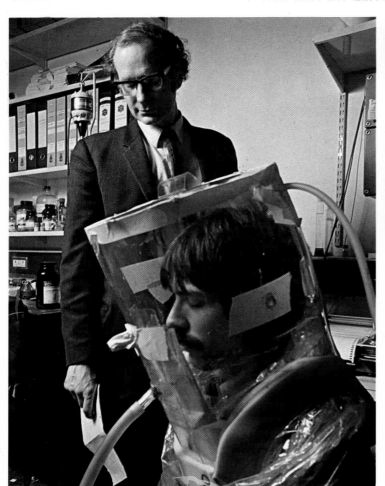

Left: The study of the brain and body functions of people in altered states of consciousness, for example during meditation, may prove of great value to the study of many psychic phenomena such as faith healing and telepathy.

Above and right: A Soviet *Vostok* rocket, and (right) a picture of a cylindrical object bearing the name 'Vostok'. The picture on the right is one of many claimed to have been produced by the American Ted Serios, who can apparently project images psychically on to photographic film. Most of Serios's pictures have been produced on Polaroid film in a Model 95 camera.

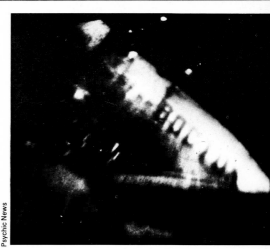

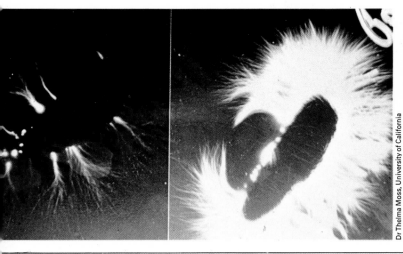

Dr Thelma Moss, University of California

Left: Kirlian photographs of the 'aura' around the fingertip of a patient before (left) and after treatment by a faith healer. Kirlian photography, which involves the use of a high voltage, high frequency electric field, is claimed to show the supposed aura of the subject. The size and shape of the aura is said to be indicative of the health of the subject, but variations in the aura (probably just the electrical phenomenon known as a *corona discharge*) are due to variations in the moistness of the finger and other unmysterious factors.

Below: The principles of Kirlian apparatus.

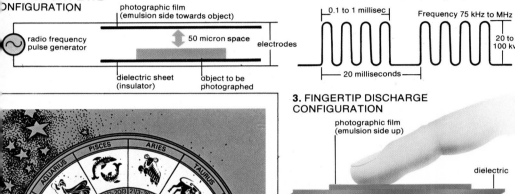

1. CAPACITOR PLATE CONFIGURATION

radio frequency pulse generator

photographic film (emulsion side towards object)

50 micron space — electrodes

dielectric sheet (insulator)

object to be photographed

2. TYPICAL APPLIED WAVEFORM

0.1 to 1 millisec

Frequency 75 kHz to MHz

20 to 100 kv

20 milliseconds

3. FINGERTIP DISCHARGE CONFIGURATION

photographic film (emulsion side up)

dielectric

high voltage rf pulses   metal electrode

detect hidden objects, and many of the successes are now ascribed to the fact that a dowser gives the confidence to go ahead and dig in otherwise unpromising locations.

Telepathy also has its stores of anecdotal cases supporting its authenticity, and also has a considerable wealth of more carefully controlled tests. Most of these have involved various types of card guessing in which a long series of cards would be transmitted from a 'sender' to a 'receiver'. The test is successful if the receiver guesses the cards significantly more than would be expected on pure chance alone. Some tests of this type have been remarkably good, such as that of Dr. B. F. Riess and a young woman with a distance of a quarter of a mile between them.

Of the 1,850 guesses 73 per cent were successful, whereas the chance level of success should have been 20 per cent; the odds against this being pure chance are astronomical. However, this and other similar tests have been strongly criticized, and have not been accepted by many. There have also been attempts to see if telepathy is greater in young children than adults, or enhanced during dreaming or in altered states of consciousness. There have been encouraging results on these problems, but telepathy has still failed to prove as repeatable as hoped.

Clairvoyance testing has had a similar history, with some remarkable successes obtained by Dr J. B. Rhine and his colleagues during the 1930s and 1940s. These have all been strongly criticized by certain sceptics, as have the apparently highly successful tests at the Stanford

Starcast

your personal computerised horoscope

Above: Astrology has become one of the most popular aspects of the paranormal, but studies claiming to have verified its effectiveness by statistical means have been disputed by other researchers. Many serious astrologers feel that the subject has been trivialized by the generalized horoscopes published in the popular press, which make vague predictions about the whole population of the world; horoscopes, they claim, can only work on an individual basis.

Right: The unidentified flying object (UFO) controversy began in June 1947, when Kenneth Arnold, piloting a private plane from Chehalis to Yakima in Washington, US, saw nine saucer-shaped objects flying in formation near Mount Rainier. Since then there have been thousands of reports of UFO sightings and hundreds of photographs of them. Many of the photos are fakes; this one is of a model, made of a pair of car hubcaps, thrown into the air.

John Cutten

Top: The summer of 1952 was a peak period for UFO sightings in the United States and elsewhere. This picture was taken at a coastguard station at Salem, US, on 16 July 1952, and shows what seems to be four objects flying in formation. Visual sightings by military personnel are often reported, and there are many instances of strange objects being detected by radar. The great majority of UFO sightings have been explainable in terms of known natural phenomena such as optical illusions created by temperature inversions, or as mistaken identification of objects such as aircraft, meteors and weather balloons. Some sightings remain inexplicable, however, but there is no evidence at all that UFOs are alien spacecraft. The ideal evidence for this would be a well-observed landing of such a craft and contact with its occupants. Contacts have been claimed, but never proven.

Above: Some of the main areas of UFO sightings in England and Wales. One of the most intriguing periods of UFO activity in England was in the mid-1960s, around the town of Warminster. Phenomena reported included UFOs, strange noises and vibrations, and birds falling dead from the the sky.

Below: The so called 'Bermuda Triangle', an area in the western Atlantic in which it has been claimed an alarming number of ships and planes have disappeared in mysterious and terrible circumstances. The books and articles which have been written by advocates of the phenomenon consist of ludicrous but very entertaining (and lucrative) combinations of fiction, supposition and distortions of known facts. For example, their accounts of the disappearance in 1945 of a flight of Avenger aircraft, plus a Mariner aircraft sent to look for them are completely at odds with the known facts.

Research Institute by Drs Puthoff and Targ with several subjects. These results have been published in the British journal *Nature*, though with an accompanying editorial strongly criticizing the experimental procedure.

A certain amount of statistical investigation has been carried out to test the validity of astrology. Recent work by two French psychologists has claimed to show a relationship between the date and time of birth of a person and their later career, though since there are apparently more births in late summer such analysis has to be done with great care.

Many UFO cases have been reported, but since there is no unequivocal evidence such as a piece of an alien spacecraft or being, the 'alien' interpretation of such events is less likely than one of the many normal ones, such as planets, noctilucent (luminous) clouds, or ball lightning. Plant intelligence is unlikely, but response of plants to external human body fields is possible. There is not yet enough evidence to show whether this occurs or not.

Finally, it must be pointed out that the only *scientific* explanation of paranormal events can be in terms of electromagnetism, since the other three forces of nature (nuclear, radioactive, gravitational) can be excluded as being impossible for humans to activate at the required levels. A radiowave hypothesis had been proposed for telepathy in the 1920s by the Italian Cazzamali, but doubt was cast on it by experiments with subjects in shielded rooms.

More recently, a series of tests performed by Professor J. G. Taylor and E. Balanowski failed to discover *any* radiowave emission associated with psychic phenomena over the whole range of possible wavelengths, other than that naturally emitted by humans. Since at least a millionfold higher level of such waves would have been needed to achieve the various phenomena it is very doubtful that electromagnetism can explain the paranormal (excluding ball lightning and perhaps UFOs).

What can only be described as a UFO showed up in a photograph taken in 1972 at the Plymouth Zoo in Devon, England. The photographer, Wilfred Power, was unaware of it until the film was developed.

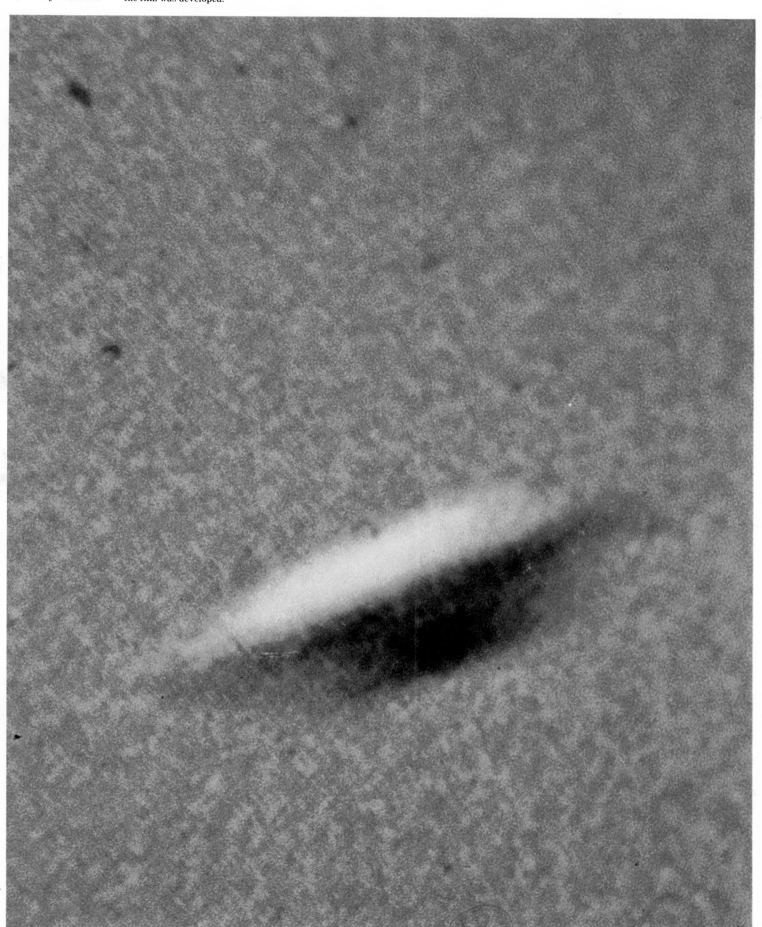

Optics

As you look at this page, you are actually observing a certain type of reflection. Almost everything we can see, except for actual sources of light such as the Sun or a light bulb, is visible only because of reflection. We normally think of reflection as being a property of mirrors or shiny objects, but the kind of reflections which produce images, such as those in a mirror, are really just one type, known as *specular* reflection.

Far more common is *diffuse* reflection, which causes this page to be visible. A beam of light striking the paper is reflected by it in all directions. Whichever angle you look at it from, it appears equally as bright. The printer's ink does not reflect as much light as the white paper—it absorbs some of it—so it appears darker by comparison. The coloured ink in the pictures absorbs some colours more than others, so only these others are reflected.

If you experiment by holding the page so as to catch the light from a table lamp in an otherwise dark room, you will find that at a certain angle it reflects slightly more light, as if it were behaving a little like a mirror. That is, the paper is not giving completely diffuse reflections—there is, in effect, also a slight specular component.

A mirror, however, gives purely specular reflections—the beam of light is reflected in one direction only, so that only when you are looking at the correct angle to the mirror will you see a particular object reflected in it. This, and the fact that light always travels in straight lines, accounts for the way a flat mirror produces reflections.

What makes some materials give diffuse, and some specular, reflections? The answer lies in the roughness of the material. If a light beam strikes a surface which is rough on a scale comparable with the wavelength of light (about 0.5 thousandths of a millimetre), then it may be reflected in any direction. But if the surface is within a few wavelengths of being flat, the beam will be reflected at a definite angle. The situation is comparable with throwing a tennis ball at a wall—if the wall is very rough, the ball may come off at any direction, but if it is smooth the ball will be 'reflected' at a predictable angle as long as it has no spin.

To make a mirror, therefore, one has to produce a very smooth surface. For normally rough surfaces, this can be done by applying a coating, such as the layer of varnish or wax on wood, or by including china clay in glossy paper. If the surface itself can be polished, as can glass or metal, so much the better. Glass can be made smooth fairly easily; to produce a mirror a sheet of glass is coated on the back with a thin layer of metal such as aluminium or silver, which reflects all colours equally well and therefore does not give a noticeable tint.

Specular reflection always obeys certain laws. In particular, the angle at which the beam strikes a surface (the *angle of incidence*) is always equal to the angle at which it is reflected (the *angle of reflection*). These two angles are measured from a line perpendicular to the surface, called the *normal*. The angles of incidence and reflection and the normal are always in the same plane. Using these laws, we can easily predict how a ray will be reflected, just as a billiards or pool player can predict how a ball will bounce off the cushion at the side of the table.

Refraction

Although light normally travels in straight lines, it sometimes appears to bend. This occurs when it passes from one medium, such as air or water, into another, such as glass or clear plastic, which has different optical properties. The obvious example of this is when a stick is put into water at an angle—it appears bent where it enters the water.

This phenomenon is called *refraction*, and the optical property which causes it is called the *refractive* index. We can see its effects if we watch a beam of light passing into a glass block from air. Instead of carrying on in a straight line, it deflects towards the normal as it enters the block. The refractive index is a measure of the light-bending ability of a medium, usually compared with that of air, and is expressed as a number.

When light enters a parallel-sided glass block, the refraction at the first surface deviates the beam. As it emerges from the

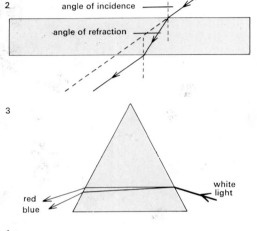

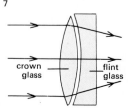

Left: These drawings show several aspects of the reflection and refraction of light.
1. When light strikes a smooth surface, such as a mirror, it is all reflected in the same direction, producing a reflected image of the object from which it is coming. This is known as *specular* reflection. If the surface is rough, the light is scattered in all directions. This *diffuse* reflection does not create a reflected image.

2. Light passing from one medium to another of different density is deflected or *refracted* slightly. Light passing through a piece of glass with parallel sides is refracted twice, by equal amounts but in opposite directions. Its direction of travel remains the same, but it is shifted slightly to one side.

3. Light passing through a prism is refracted twice in the same direction. The different wavelengths of light are refracted by different amounts, long wavelength (red) light being refracted the least and shorter wavelengths, such as blue, the most. White light passing through a prism is split into its component colours.

4. A mirage like this, an apparent reflection of actual objects, is caused by some of the light from them being refracted as it passes from cool air into hot air of lower density.

Radio Times Hulton Picture Library

Below: 5. and 6. A convex lens is, in effect, a series of prisms, each deviating light by a different amount, arranged so that light passing through them is all deviated to the same spot. As there is a different focus for each colour of light, the image formed has coloured fringes around it.

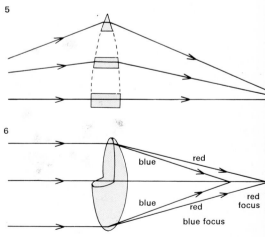

Left: 7. The *achromatic* lens produces an image with no colour fringing. The lens has two elements, made of two types of glass, and the colour dispersion caused by the first is corrected by the second. This eliminates the fringing effect or *chromatic aberration* which occurs with simple convex lenses.

other side, the beam is refracted back by an equal amount so there is no overall change in direction. But if the block does not have parallel sides, the result is an overall deviation in the light's direction. A triangular block of glass, usually called a *prism*, does this—but with one other important effect.

Unlike the law of reflection, which applies to all colours of light equally, the refractive index changes with the colour —blue light is refracted more than red when it enters a medium with a higher refractive index. For the parallel block, this *dispersion* into colours is cancelled out, just as the deviation was. But in the case of a prism, the dispersion is also increased with the result that white light is split up into all its colours, forming a *spectrum* of the colours of the rainbow.

(White is simply the visual appearance of all the rainbow colours seen together). This property is exploited in *spectroscopes*, which are used to analyze the colours in a source of light.

Diffraction

There is another way in which light can be bent and split into colours—by *diffraction*, which occurs on such a small scale that we rarely observe it in everyday life. It happens more obviously with sound waves. Imagine a band marching, hidden by buildings. To start with, you hear only the bass notes. When the band emerges into full view, you can hear the high notes as well. Long waves (deep notes) can bend round corners, while short waves (higher pitched) can do so less easily.

Left: Spectacles, pairs of lenses for correcting sight defects, have been in use for over 700 years. This picture shows a 17th-century Dutch spectacle shop.

Right: A selection of high quality prisms.

Below left: The way a pair of contact lenses fit onto the eyes can be checked by dropping a special fluid into the eyes and shining ultraviolet light onto them. The fluid glows brightly and any irregularities in the fit of the lenses can easily be seen.

Below: Photo-elastic stress analysis is a method of determining the stresses within a structure subjected to a load. A model of the structure is made from clear plastic, and loads are applied to it. When viewed under *polarized* light, light in which all the waves are vibrating in the same direction, patterns are produced which correspond to the area of stress. The brightest areas of the pattern are those where the stress within the model is at a maximum.

Rank/Taylor /Hobson

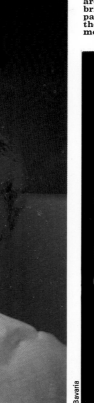

Bavaria

UKAEA

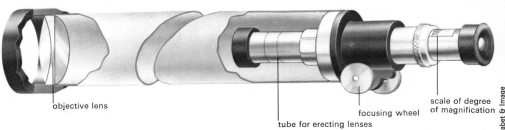

objective lens

scale of degree of magnification

focusing wheel

tube for erecting lenses

ERECTING THE IMAGE IN A TERRESTRIAL TELESCOPE

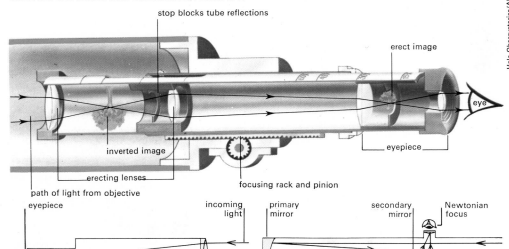

stop blocks tube reflections

erect image

eye

eyepiece

inverted image

erecting lenses

focusing rack and pinion

path of light from objective

eyepiece

incoming light

primary mirror

secondary mirror

Newtonian focus

primary

Cassegrain secondary

objective

prime focus

Cassegrain focus

REFRACTING

NEWTONIAN

CASSEGRA

Hale Observatories/Alphabet & Image

Left and below: The large diagrams show the basic design of a terrestrial telescope and the way in which an upright image is obtained. The smaller drawings show the principles of the optical systems of four types of astronomical telescope: the refracting, Newtonian, Cassegrain and coudé.

Above: An observer sitting in the prime focus cage within the 200 inch (508 cm) telescope at the Hale Observatory on Mount Palomar, USA. The prime focus is the point where light reflected from the primary mirror first comes to a focus, and the largest telescopes have cages at this point.

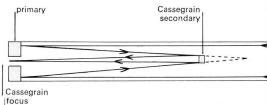

Coudé focus

primary mirror

COUDÉ

Coudé secondary

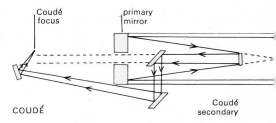

Below: A Questar *catadioptric* **telescope. Catadioptric telescopes use a combination of refraction and reflection to form an image. Light enters through a large concave lens, and a concave mirror at the rear reflects it on to a small reflective spot on the rear of the lens. From here, it is**

reflected down a central tube to a 45° prism, which directs it up to the eyepiece on top of the rear of the instrument.

Right: A pair of prismatic binoculars, which use pairs of Porro prisms to 'fold' the light path and make the system more compact.

William MacQuitty

A similar thing happens with light waves. They will bend—very slightly—round obstacles, the long waves (red light) more so than the shorter ones (blue). If a regular series of obstacles is used, the effect can be seen by eye. This accounts for the colours seen in the grooves of an LP record. Lights seen through finely woven fabric also show spikes caused by this diffraction effect. A spectroscope may use a surface with finely ruled grooves, called a *diffraction grating*, in place of the prism.

Lenses
Imagine a series of prisms one on top of the other, each deviating light to a different extent and arranged so that the top one deviates the light most, while the bottom one does not deviate the light at all—that is, it is parallel-sided. Clearly it is possible to arrange the prisms in such a way that all the light coming from any particular source is deviated to the same spot.

This, in effect, is what an ordinary *convex* lens is—a series of piles of prisms, arranged in a disc so that light entering it from any direction can be deviated to one spot. This is why lenses form images. If an object is very distant—effectively 'at infinity'—its light will be refracted to form an image at a *focal point* a certain distance from the lens. This distance is called the *focal length*. A fat lens, with steeply curved sides, has a short focal length compared with its diameter while a thin one, whose sides are almost parallel, has a long focal length.

The image-forming properties of a simple convex lens allow it to be used as a magnifying glass. A short focal length

lens will always magnify more than a long focal length one, whatever their diameters. In a telescope of the simplest type, one lens of long focal length (the *objective*) is used to form an image. This image can then be looked at with a shorter focal length lens which acts as a magnifying glass, called the *eyepiece*. The magnification is simply given by dividing the focal length of the objective by that of the eyepiece. Eyepieces of different focal lengths give a range of magnifications.

Astronomical telescopes
Telescopes with just two convex lenses are simple astronomical telescopes: they give upside down images, which is no great drawback in astronomy. But they have one more serious disadvantage. Just as a single prism gives colour dispersion, so a single lens has a different focal length for each colour. This results in images with coloured fringes. The longer the focal length of the lens, the less obtrusive this false colour is for a given magnification. Consequently, early astronomical telescopes had to be made impractically long to give good results.

Isaac Newton applied himself to this problem in 1668, and decided that the best solution would be to form the image not with a lens but with a mirror. A concave mirror behaves just like a lens in that it focuses light to a point—but with the advantage that since all colours are reflected equally, there is no false colour. The only drawback is that the image is formed in the path of the incoming light. To overcome this Newton placed a small flat mirror to intercept the light just before the focus and reflect it through 90° so that the image was formed outside the

Left: Using an optical alignment telescope to check the alignment of the bores for the main drive shafts of a light armoured tracked vehicle. The shafts pass through four bore holes in the hull, and the alignment telescope is fitted to one of the outer bores. An illuminated target is fitted into the outer bore on the other side of the vehicle, and a crossline mark on the telescope is lined up with the centre of the target by means of adjusting knobs on the telescope. The target and telescope are at the centres of their respective bores, and the adjusting knobs are calibrated to show by how much these two centres are out of alignment.

Left: A modern compact microscope designed for use by students. This one has five sets of objective lenses mounted on a revolving turret or nosepiece.

Right: This is an enlarged photograph, taken through a microscope, of a section of a porpoise's tooth. The tooth was illuminated with light polarized in one direction, and viewed through a filter polarized in another. Normally this would mean that no light could pass through the filter, but the material of the tooth has rotated the direction of polarization of the light falling on it so that some of it can pass through the filter.

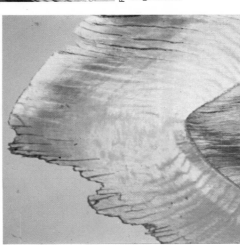

Above: The structure of the tooth is such that different wavelengths or colours of light are rotated more than others, so the original white light is split up to give a coloured image, which shows the structural detail more clearly than if it were viewed under non-polarized white light.

adjustable eyepiece

hinge

fixed eyepiece

2 + 0 - 2

Porro prisms

focusing barrel

objective

light path

tube. There it can be viewed with an eyepiece, just as in a refractor except that the observer looks at right angles to the tube. These *Newtonian* telescopes, as they are called, are fairly easy to make and are popular with amateur astronomers.

Meanwhile, others studied the same problem and came up with the *achromatic lens*—a combination of two lenses of differing refractive index which are able to *deviate* light without *dispersing* it into colours. Achromatic lenses are now used in all high quality optical instruments.

The larger the diameter—or *aperture*—of a telescope, the more light is focused to an image and the brighter the view. For this reason, telescopes are described by their aperture rather than by their magnification (which is variable anyway). The largest telescope in the world, in the USSR, has a mirror with an aperture of 6 m (19.7 ft).

Terrestrial telescopes and binoculars

The upside down images given by astronomical telescopes are awkward when the telescope is to be used for everyday purposes. *Terrestrial telescopes*, the ordinary type used for viewing distant objects on land or sea, get over this by means of additional lenses which erect the image. Alternatively, the image can be reflected upright by a pair of *Porro prisms*, using the phenomenon of *total internal reflection*.

Because light 'bends' as it goes from a more dense medium into a less dense one, it is possible for the emergent light to be bent so much that none of it escapes from the prism at all. In this case, all the light is reflected from the surface inside the glass. In Porro prisms the light enters at right angles to one face, is totally internally reflected twice through 90° by the other two sides of the prism, and emerges at right angles to the original face, thus not suffering dispersion but turned through 180°. These prisms are used in *prismatic binoculars* to erect the image: they have the advantage over mirrors of never being able to tarnish, while their use shortens the tube length required by 'folding' the light path. Prismatic binoculars are thus two achromatic telescopes side by side, using Porro prisms to erect the image.

Simple binoculars, such as opera glasses and field glasses, are basically two-lens telescopes mounted side-by-side. These telescopes are known as *Galilean* telescopes, being based on the design invented by Galileo Galilei (1564-1642). The Galilean telescope uses a convex objective lens, but the eyepiece is *concave*. Concave lenses have one or both faces curving inwards, instead of outwards as they do on convex lenses.

Microscopes

While a simple magnifying glass can be used to give an enlarged image, it has the drawback that a high magnification would require a lens with an extremely short focal length. This would have to be so fat that it would be spherical; furthermore, it would have to be very small and it would be difficult to use. So in *compound* microscopes, the same ploy is used as in the telescope—one lens forms an image, which is then magnified by a second lens. The lenses have the same names of objective and eyepiece, but this time the objective has a short focal length and the eyepiece a longer focal length.

119

Radar

Radio waves, like light waves, are reflected by obstacles in their path. The detection of these reflections enables such objects to be located. This is the basis of *radar*, a word coined from Radio Detection and Ranging. The phenomenon of reflection was known from the earliest days of radio communications, but was often only regarded as a nuisance.

The development of radar in Britain arose from a suggestion by Sir Robert Watson-Watt who had been carrying out research on the ionized layers in the earth's upper atmosphere. This work involved using pulses of radio waves to measure the height of these layers and Watson-Watt saw that the same principles could be applied to the detection of distant aircraft. The outcome was the rapid development of a chain of early warning radar stations round the coasts of the British Isles. They were in operation in time for the start of World War II and contributed greatly to winning the Battle of Britain.

Having started under the impetus of a defence need, radar has developed enormously and its uses now extend to a wide range of both civil and military applications.

Basic principles

Acoustic echoes are a familiar phenomenon. Knowing the speed of sound through air one can measure the distance of a remote cliff or high building by

aircraft B

aircraft A

transmitted signal

echo

Below: A diagram showing the basic principles of radar. A stream of transmitted pulses are reflected by any object they encounter. The reflected pulses are picked up by the antenna when it is in the receive mode (controlled by the transmit/receive cell), amplified and displayed. Two displays are shown.

plan position radar (ppl)

range radar display

milemarks

range

transmit/receive cell

receiver

transmitter

Royal Signals and Radar Establishment Malvern

Left: CH (Chain Home) towers near Dover, England. These were part of a long range, early warning system developed prior to the Second World War. By the beginning of the war the whole of the east coast of Great Britain was covered by this system. It could detect aircraft taking off in Germany.

Bottom left: An air defence station used during the Second World War. The plan position indicator on the left gave the range of approaching aircraft. Aircraft altitude was determined using the right hand display by adjusting the angle of the aerial until a maximum return signal was received.

Below: A radar controlled searchlight. This one was an experimental model with four Yagi receiving aerials around the searchlight and a folded dipole transmitter aerial mounted further back. This apparatus was extremely advanced for its time because it could automatically lock on to, and track, a moving target.

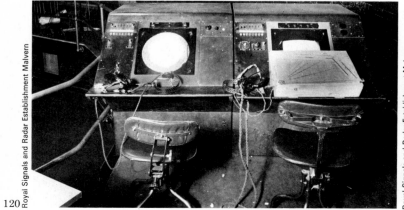

Royal Signals and Radar Establishment Malvern

Royal Signals and Radar Establishment Malvern

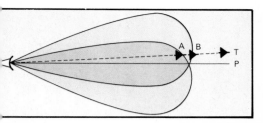

Above: Direction can be accurately determined in radar by using two partially overlapping beams. A target lying on the line of beam intersection (OP) produces an echo containing the two signals at equal strength. For a target at T, the ratio of signal strengths provides an accurate measure of the angle TOP.

Below: The Plessey ACR 430 airfield control radar system. This employs microwaves in the X-band frequency range (8,200 to 12,400 MHz). It uses a two-beam aerial system—each beam derived from a separate transmitter and fed via a waveguide to a separate horn. One of the beams is pencil-shaped for accurate surveillance.

ZEFA

Above: A radar tower with primary and secondary radar facilities. Secondary surveillance radar (SSR) allows extra information (such as flight data) to be returned to the flight controller along with ordinary data obtained from the primary radar system. Special apparatus is needed in each aircraft to obtain this information.

Right: A US tactical air control system with primary and secondary surveillance radar facilities. This control centre provides commanders with computerized tactical air control capability. Radar and other information can be rapidly exchanged between this and other command centres.

Hughes Aircraft Co.

Plessey

Below: A resonant cavity magnetron. The development of this device revolutionized radar, permitting the use of high frequency (short wavelength) radio waves at high powers. A waveguide is attached to the rectangular section on the front to channel the radio waves to the aerial. The fins cool the device.

Right: The Plessey WF-3 primary windfinding radar system. This operates in the X-band microwave frequency range. The antenna has automatic tracking facilities and a digital readout device for displaying range, azimuth and elevation. This particular version is of a portable design and is simple to instal.

Plessey

EMI

observing the time that an echo takes to return. This is how radar works but using radio waves which travel at a speed of 300,000 km/sec rather than sound which only travels at about 340 m/sec. If both the total time of travel of the transmitted/reflected beam and its direction are measured the position of the distant reflecting object is obtained.

Either *continuous* waves, such as are used in broadcasting, or interrupted (*pulsed*) signals can be used, but the principles of radar are easier to understand in the case of the latter. Imagine a radio transmitter sending out a train of short pulses of radio energy. Each pulse may be a few millionths of a second long; the time interval between successive pulses is arranged to be longer than it would take for radio waves to travel out to any distant object of interest and back.

If these pulses meet an object (the *target*) they are reflected and some of this reflected energy is picked up by a receiver alongside the transmitter. The train of received pulses will be slightly retarded relative to the transmitted pulses by an interval corresponding to the out and return time of the waves. If directional aerials are used for transmitting and receiving then both the distance (range)

and direction of the target are obtained.

Usually the same aerial is used for transmitting and receiving. The receiver is protected against damage from the powerful transmitted pulses by being *suppressed* during the brief periods when they are emitted but *re-activated* in time to detect any reflected pulses. The rapid acting switch used for this protection of the receiver is known as *Transmit-Receive* (or *TR*) *Cell*.

The aerial directional pattern used depends on the purpose of the radar. For general surveillance as in Air Traffic Control a common pattern is the 'fan beam'. This is typically 1° or 2° wide in azimuth and 15° or 20° wide in elevation. With such a pattern, range and bearing can be measured quite accurately but no elevation information is available. This is adequate for many purposes.

It is possible to obtain full three dimensional information by using a 'stack' of beams each of which is narrow in both azimuth and elevation. The stack is arranged so that all beams lie in one vertical plane but pointing at different elevations. An alternative arrangement is to scan a narrow beam very rapidly in elevation while it scans much more slowly in azimuth. The rapid elevation scan is sometimes done by varying the frequency, the aerial having been designed so that its elevation angle is dependent upon the radio frequency.

Normally, direction is obtained as the angle at which maximum signal is received. This occurs when the peak of the aerial beam points at the target. If more accurate directional information is required the principle of overlapping beams is employed. In this arrangement the receiving aerial has two partially overlapping narrow beams. The exact direction of the target relative to the centre line of the system is obtained from the ratio of the signals in the two beams. Along the central cross-over line of the beams the signals are equal. The principle can be extended to measure two ortho-gonal angular co-ordinates, for example, elevation and azimuth.

ZEFA

Lockheed

A close relative of this form of aerial is the *conical scan* aerial in which a narrow pencil beam is caused to rotate at high speed about a line slightly displaced from the axis of the beam maximum. When a target lies exactly on the axis of spin, the echo has constant amplitude, but if it lies slightly off this axis the amplitude of the echo varies in sympathy with the rotation of the beam. Missile fire control radars use these principles.

Radar waves are essentially confined to line of sight although the atmosphere does produce a small amount of downwards bending. Thus radars do see marginally beyond the horizon. For practical purposes, however, the range of a radar is determined ultimately by geometrical considerations. High-flying aircraft can be seen at considerable range but to detect distant low targets the radar must be raised to extend the horizon.

Subject to these considerations it is possible to see aircraft up to 300 km (approx 200 miles) away. A typical modern long range air traffic control radar uses a wavelength of about 25 cm, a peak power of 2 MW and an aerial some 12 m wide by 5 m high scanning at a rate of 10 rpm.

Generation
At the heart of a radar equipment is a powerful radio-frequency generator. While radar is possible over a wide range of wavelengths, the most common lie in the range from about 25 cm to 3 cm (corresponding to frequencies of 1,200 MHz to 10,000 MHz). The most common radars are of the pulsed variety in which the transmitted signal consists of short pulses of radio-frequency energy, about 1 to 5 microseconds long, emitted in a stream at intervals of between 1 to 4 milliseconds. The peak power in the pulse may lie typically in the range of a few kW to a few MW, depending on the purpose of the radar. But the mean (average) power is less since the transmitter operates only during the short pulses. The ratio of mean to peak power is the *duty cycle* and for the figures quoted is about 1/1000.

Above: The deck of the warship HMS Charybdis (a Leander Class general purpose frigate) with various radar installations for defence and attack systems.

Above right: The US Navy's newest ships are being fitted with these electronic gunfire control system consoles, shown here on the USS California nuclear guided missile frigate.

Right: The Fylingdales early warning radar system in Yorkshire, England. Vast resources have been spent on developing military applications of radar (both defence and attack systems) but there are many ways in which radar can be put to peaceful purposes.

Syndication International

Two types of microwave transmitting tubes are particularly important. In one, the *cavity magnetron*, a beam of electrons circulates under the influence of a powerful transverse magnetic field inside a metal structure which has cavities of a particular size. Radio energy is generated at a frequency determined by the dimensions of the cavities. The pulses are created by switching the electron beam on and off by a suitable high speed switch known as the 'modulator'. This is the commonest generator in current use.

The other important transmitting tube is the *klystron*, in which a beam of electrons passes through a series of metallic cavities 'tuned' to the required frequency. The velocity of the beam varies in sympathy with the radio frequency voltages within the cavities. The interaction between kinetic energy of the electrons and radio frequency energy in the cavities is used either to generate oscillations or to amplify oscillations already present. The tube is normally used as an amplifier, the short pulses being generated initially at quite low power.

Detection and display
The detection of the pulses returned from

targets is carried out in a receiver similar to the vision receiver of a television set. Nowadays this is almost always a *solid-state* receiver. The output of the receiver is a stream of video pulses which have to be displayed suitably.

The most important display device is the *cathode-ray tube* (CRT), similar to the tube in a TV set. In the earliest radars the display tube was arranged to indicate directly the delay time of the echo pulses as follows. The cathode-ray beam is deflected across the screen of the tube at a steady rate commencing at the moment a pulse is transmitted. This produces a bright line across the tube face. Any returned pulse is arranged to cause a momentary upwards deflection of the beam thus producing a characteristic mark or 'pip'. If the speed at which the beam moves across the CRT is known, the distance of this mark from the commencement of the trace provides a direct measure of the time delay of the echo pulse and hence of the distance of the target.

In an alternative arrangement the cathode-ray beam, initially of reduced intensity so as to produce very little fluorescence on the tube face, traverses a line starting from the centre of the screen.

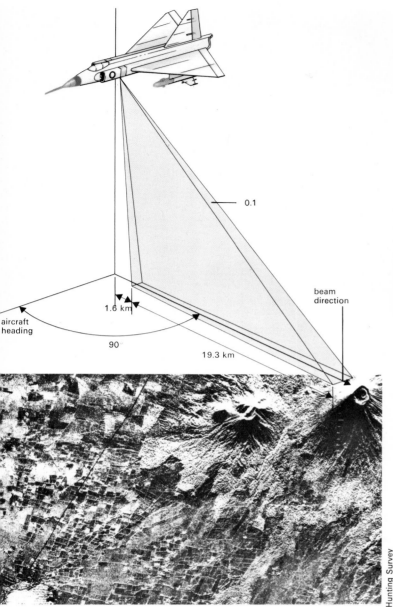

0.1

beam direction

aircraft heading

1.6 km

90

19.3 km

Above: An airborne radar system. Because radio waves travel in straight lines, ground radar systems are limited in range to the horizon (except for small bending effects caused by the atmosphere). To increase the range of a radar system it is necessary to use airborne radar.

Above left: A side-looking radar system for mapping ground features. This uses a sharp and highly directional beam from a fixed antenna on the aircraft. The motion of the aircraft itself provides the scan across the earth's surface.

Left: A reconstructed image of Chinandega and the San Cristobal volcano area of western Nicaragua taken by side-looking radar (SLR). This system has the advantage that it can be used at night, in fog or cloud and any adverse conditions that prevent normal photography.

Returned pulses are made to momentarily intensify the beam and so produce a bright spot on the tube face at a distance from the centre corresponding to the distance of the target. If the line across the tube face is made to rotate about the centre in sympathy with the rotation of the aerial beam a map-like picture is produced on the tube face showing the position of reflecting targets around the radar. This is the well-known *Plan Position Indicator* or PPI.

Doppler radar

When a source of sound is approaching or receding, its apparent pitch is raised or lowered. This is the *Doppler Effect*. Similarly, radio waves reflected from a moving target have their frequency raised or lowered according to whether they are moving towards or away from the observer. One important use of this is to distinguish moving from stationary objects. In air traffic control, for example, reflections from buildings, trees or high ground may obscure the returns from moving aircraft. However, the latter reflections exhibit a Doppler shift in frequency.

In *Moving Target Indication* or MTI this shift is detected, causing only moving targets to be displayed. Another important use of Doppler is in airborne navigational radar, enabling an aircraft to measure its speed relative to the ground by the Doppler shift of the waves reflected by the ground.

Applications

From its birth as an early warning device against air attack, radar has expanded to a very wide range of applications both civil and military. It is the basis of air traffic control in all areas of dense traffic and is indeed essential for safety in air transport. It is used in aircraft to detect high ground and storms and to measure relative speed over the ground. At sea, the majority of merchant ships of any size carry a navigational radar enabling them to navigate in bad visibility, while land-based radar is used in busy ports to supervise and control movements in the shipping lanes. Radar also has many meteorological uses, such as detecting and tracking storms and hurricanes.

Below: This is the Ferranti mobile X-band (that is, microwaves in the frequency range 8,200 to 12,400 MHz) target illuminating radar. This is used with surface-to-air missiles, such as the Thunderbird, in a guided weapon system. Various microwave aerials are attached to the antenna tower.

Right: The Ferranti Seaspray radar is in production for the naval version of the Westland Lynx helicopter. Small and lightweight, it is able to detect small targets, such as fast patrol boats, even in very rough sea conditions. The antenna waveguide, which channels the microwaves, can be clearly seen.

123

Lasers

Lasers are devices which encourage atoms to emit visible light in a regular manner, rather than the sporadic and random emission which normally occurs in nature. Masers operate on the same principles as lasers but produce microwaves rather than light. The unique properties of lasers and masers have already been applied in many fields, including industry, communications, and medicine, and new applications are continually being developed.

Light and microwaves are both forms of *electromagnetic radiation*. The only difference between them is the frequency (and hence also wavelength) of the radiation—light is of a much higher frequency (shorter wavelength) than microwaves.

Electromagnetic radiation is produced when electrons, which move in orbits or 'levels' around the nucleus of an atom, give up some of their energy. But to understand how this happens, and how lasers harness this energy into a regular, ordered form, it is necessary to explain the mechanisms of the atom.

Electrons in orbit

Whether in molecules or atoms, electrons are not free to move as they please but are confined to relatively few distinct orbits, which are always the same for any two atoms of the same element but can vary widely between elements. Electrons in each orbit have a fixed energy, those closest to the nucleus having low energies and those further out have higher. Only one electron can occupy any orbit at a time.

Electrons can move from their orbit to any empty orbit, but in so doing they must also obey the law of *conservation of energy*. So electrons wanting to move outwards from the nucleus must somehow gain enough energy to make the jump and those moving inwards must lose energy. They can do this by emitting or absorbing light in the form of small 'packets' known as *photons*. Photons are the smallest possible packets of light that can exist and the light we see consists simply of vast numbers of individual photons whose abundance gives the impression of a continuous stream of light.

Each photon has a fixed energy and a wavelength which is inversely proportional to this energy. When an electron moves from an outer to an inner orbit it emits a photon whose energy equals the energy difference between the two orbits. The reverse process, in which an electron jumps from the lower to the higher level (from the inner to the outer orbit), requires that the electron gain the same amount of energy. One way of achieving this is for the electron to absorb a passing photon of exactly the right energy and wavelength.

Spontaneous emission

The lowest energy state of an electron is called the *ground state* and all others are known as *excited states*. Electrons may be excited to higher states by several methods other than the photon absorption process just described. Heating a substance will excite the electrons of its atoms or molecules as will subjecting it to an

Above: A photograph of Washington monument illuminated by lasers.

Right: The important difference between a laser and, say, an electric torch is that the laser produces *coherent* light. Ordinary light contains a jumble of light waves with different frequencies (between red and blue). These are randomly generated and scattered in all directions: it is the torch reflector that organizes these waves roughly into a beam. Such light is termed *incoherent*. With coherent light, the waves have exactly the same frequency and are in step with each other. That is, the 'crests' of the waves line up to form a *wavefront*. Laser beams are also nearly perfectly parallel.

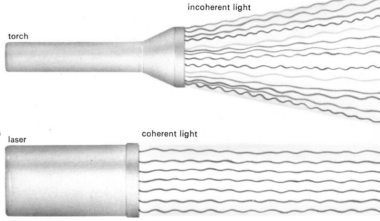

incoherent light

torch

coherent light

laser

Left and below: A diagram showing the mechanism of a ruby laser. The electrons in the chromium atoms are excited into higher energy levels by the light from a powerful spiral flashtube. As these electrons drop back to their ground state (lowest energy level) they each emit a photon of light of the characteristic ruby red colour. This is spontaneous emission. To produce laser action, the crystal is cut to a special shape to enhance stimulated emission along the ruby crystal axis.

RUBY LASER
ruby rod

xenon tube
metal case (cutaway)

flashtube pumps energy (photons) into ruby rod

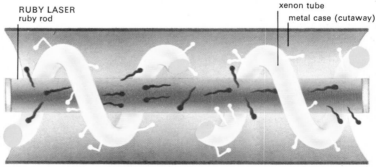

totally reflecting mirror

photons from flashtube

photons align in a pulse of laser light

partially reflecting mirror

photons in ruby rod

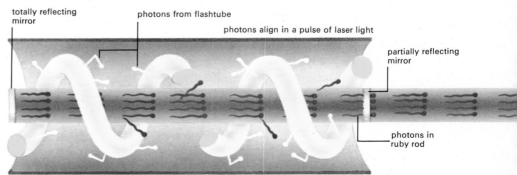

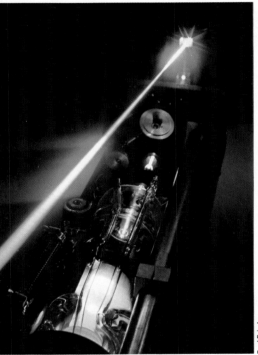

Left: This green beam of
laser light is produced
by an argon laser. The
specific colour of a
laser depends on the
electron configuration
of the element employed
to initiate stimulated
emission. The larger
the energy difference
between the ground state
and excited state of
these electrons, the
higher the frequency of
emitted radiation (and
smaller wavelength).

Right: This was the
first gas laser to
produce a continuous
beam of visible light.
Present day lasers
produce a vast range of
frequencies from
microwaves (masers)
through infra-red and
the visible spectrum to
ultra-violet.
Theoretically, even
higher frequency laser
radiation is possible.
Scientists are
considering the
possibility of using it for
X-rays and even gamma
radiation.

Below left: The inventor
of the ruby laser,
Theodore Maiman, with
one of his instruments.
The spiral flashtube
can be clearly seen and
inside this is the
cylindrical ruby crystal
with machined
and silvered ends.

intense electric field or bombarding it
with free electrons.

Electrons which have been excited to
higher states by any method are, however,
not stable. They spontaneously drop back
to any empty lower level, emitting the
appropriate photon as they do so. This
spontaneous emission is quite random and
there is no way of telling when the photon
will be emitted or what direction it will
move in, although for a large number of
excited atoms it is possible to predict
quite accurately how many photons will
be emitted in a given time.

Spontaneous emission by excited electrons produces all the light that we
normally see—the various light sources
differ only in the method used to excite
the electrons, for example nuclear heating
in the sun, electric heating in a light bulb
and electron bombardment in a neon tube.
Because of the random nature of spontaneous emission these sources all emit
light in all directions and the component
photons are out of step with one another.
Such light is *incoherent*.

Stimulated emission

We have seen that an electron can be
excited to a higher state by the impact of
a photon of the right energy. But what

happens if the electron is already in the
excited state when it is struck by the
photon? Common sense suggests that it
will be unaffected but common sense is no
guide in atomic physics. In fact what
happens is that the excited electron drops
back to the lower state emitting a photon
as it goes. This process, called *stimulated
emission*, was first predicted on theoretical
grounds by Einstein in 1917.

Even more interesting, the photon
emitted in this process moves in the same
direction and exactly in step with the
stimulating photon (that is, they are
coherent). The two identical photons are
now free to stimulate further emission of
photons from any other excited electrons
they encounter and these photons too will
match the original. Thus, if conditions are
right, the original photon will be amplified
again and again by each successive stimu-
lation of an excited electron. The word
laser was coined to describe this process
by its initial letters which stand for Light
Amplification by Stimulated Emission of
Radiation.

One factor prevents laser action under
normal circumstances, namely the possibility that photons, instead of stimulating
emission from electrons in the higher
state, will encounter electrons in the 125

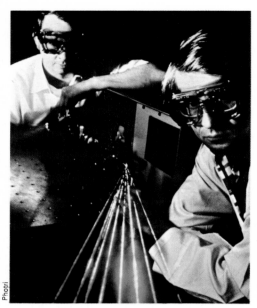

Left: This *dye laser*, produces a range of colours from ultra-violet to yellow. One device of special interest is the argon/krypton gas laser whose output of mixed radiation gives the appearance of white light.

Right: A portable laser microwelder. Because the beam from a laser is almost perfectly parallel, the focal point of the beam when focused by a lens is extremely small and distinct. Therefore the intensity of light at the focus is very high—high enough to be used in welding applications. Theoretically, a perfectly parallel beam aimed at a perfect lens will produce a *point* of light (of zero area and infinite intensity). A conventional source of light produces a large and hazy spot. More powerful types of laser, such as the carbon dioxide version, can cut through sheet metal. Such welding devices are gas jet assisted.

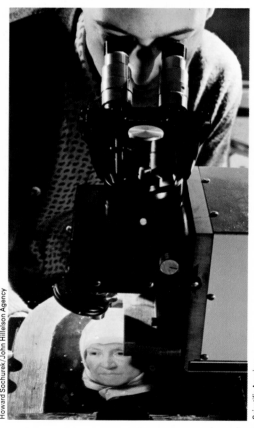

LASER-FUSION REACTOR

high-intensity laser light

hot expanding surface of disintegrating pellet

laser beams focused onto fuel pellet

containment vessel (cutaway)

heat given off by fusion reaction is removed by heat exchangers, and used to raise steam which powers turbogenerators

'hot' electrons
alpha particles
neutrons

Above: Detecting an art forgery using laser techniques. One way to achieve this is by detecting the undulations of the paint surface, by which means the number and thickness of paint layers underneath can be determined. The technique employed is similar to that used in holography where the depth nature of a scene (in this case the paint undulations) modifies the laser beam reflected from the surface.

Right: Using laser light to illuminate a scene for television. The principle is not to flood the whole scene with laser light, but to scan across the scene in a manner similar to that used in a television camera and receiver.

Above: How lasers could be used to create the energy source of the future—nuclear fusion. If a very short but intense burst of laser light could be focused from all sides onto a frozen pellet of deuterium and tritium (isotopes of hydrogen), the nuclei would fuse together to form helium with a large release of energy. As the light strikes the pellet, the surface temperature rises and becomes ionized. 'Hot' electrons move inwards, carrying energy with them and heat the interior. As this happens, neutrons and alpha particles explode outwards causing an equal and opposite implosion of the interior which creates sufficiently high temperatures and pressures to cause fusion.

Above, right and below: Even if laser 'death rays' are at present confined to the realm of fiction, the uses of lasers in military applications have not been slow in developing. The apparatus above can aim a laser beam precisely at a target. The light scattered from this is registered by apparatus in the nose of the strike aircraft (right) and used to 'home in' on the target. Similar devices can also be fitted to missiles. Below the diagram shows how the apparatus is used. The aircraft receptor filters out all light except that from the laser and so this system can be used in daylight although this is much brighter than the laser light. The equipment can also be used for rangefinding. Systems such as this were used by the Americans in Vietnam. Even such sophisticated technology marks only the beginning of its military uses.

lower state and be absorbed by them. Since there are normally more electrons in lower states than higher, this means that emitted photons are annihilated more rapidly than they can breed. For amplification it is necessary to ensure artificially that the majority of electrons are in the excited state, which will tip the balance in favour of creation rather than destruction of photons. Such a situation is called an *inversion*.

The ammonium maser

The first ever maser used a very simple method of obtaining an inversion in molecules of ammonium gas. These molecules have many different energy states but the ammonium maser uses only two of these, which differ in energy such that when an electron drops from the upper to the lower it emits a photon of wavelength 1.2 cm. If ammonium gas is passed through an electric field the molecules in the upper of these two states will be deflected in one direction and those in the lower state in another, giving two beams of molecules, one predominantly upper state and the other lower. The beam of excited molecules in the upper state is then a suitable medium for laser action, until spontaneous emission degrades it once again to the lower state.

The excited beam is directed into a metal box or cavity where it is exposed to a weak microwave signal of 1.2 cm wavelength. This stimulates emission of 1.2 cm photons from some of the molecules, which quickly avalanches to full maser action. Provided a continuous supply of excited molecules is fed to the cavity, the ammonium maser will emit a continuous coherent microwave beam from a small hole in the cavity. The power is not great, being less than 1 microwatt (10^{-6} watt), but the frequency of the radiation is so stable that it is used as a standard for measuring time.

In most cases it is not so simple a matter to create an inversion as it is with the ammonium maser. The energy levels of interest cannot usually be separated by electric fields and in any case this method is obviously useless if the atoms form part of a solid. Several other methods have been developed for obtaining an inversion, each of which is appropriate for a different lasing medium.

Types of laser

The first laser (producing visible as opposed to microwave light) used a crystal of ruby as the medium and employed a process known as *optical pumping* to excite the electrons to an inverted condition. Ruby is a regular crystal form of aluminium oxide in which are embedded some chromium atoms. The chromium atoms are really only impurities in the crystal but they are responsible for the characteristic red colour light which is produced naturally by spontaneous emission from their electrons. The ruby laser produces the same colour light in coherent form by stimulated emission. To do this it makes use of *three* of the energy levels of the chromium atoms.

The middle and lower levels are those used in the laser action. The upper level really consists of a large number of levels so closely spaced that they are effectively a broad band of energy which many chromium electrons can occupy. The principle of optical pumping is to flood the crystal with light from a xenon flash lamp. 127

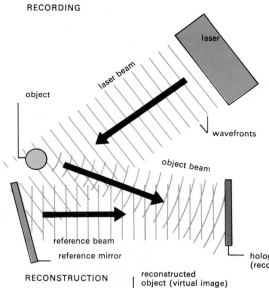

laser

laser beam

object

wavefronts

object beam

reference beam

reference mirror

holographic plate
(recording pate)

reconstructed
object (real image)

screen

RECONSTRUCTION

reconstructed
object (virtual image)

reconstructed
object (real image)

laser

the laser beam travels to the hologram
and is split into two beams

eye sees
virtual image

Above: How lasers are used in *holography* to record and reconstruct a 3D image. A normal photograph only records the intensity of a scene, but a holographic record or *hologram* also records phase information of the impinging light waves. This is possible because laser light is coherent. For this, a standard is necessary—achieved by directing part of the laser light directly on to the hologram (this is the reference beam). To reconstruct the image, the hologram is viewed in laser light— the image appears beyond it.

Right: A typical layout for holographic recording. On the right is the laser which floods both the scene to be recorded (bottom left) and a mirror (top left) which directs the reference beam on to the hologram.

Below: Here, the laser beam is split into two. One is aimed at the mirror, the other at the object to be recorded. The shape of an item can be checked against a standard by replacing the mirror with the standard. The hologram records the *differences* between them.

Howard Sochurek/John Hillelson Agency

Photri

Electrons in the lower level absorb photons of this light and jump directly to the upper band. Once in this band they soon lose energy to the atoms of the crystal and decay to the middle state.

If more than half the chromium electrons can be pumped like this to the upper levels, then an inversion exists with more in the middle than in the lower level. The middle level electrons will start to spontaneously emit, in all directions, photons of wavelength 0.6943 micrometres (which is 0.6943 millionths of a metre or 6943 A and corresponds to light in the red region of the spectrum).

The crystal is specially shaped to ensure that some of these cause the system to lase. It is cut in the form of a long rod and the ends polished and silvered. When a spontaneous photon is emitted along the axis of the rod it is reflected back along its path whenever it reaches one of the ends, ensuring that it travels a very long path which gives it a high probability of encountering a chromium electron in the middle state. As soon as this happens the laser avalanche is initiated. One of the ends is made less than 100% reflective so that part of the laser light can escape.

There are now many similar lasers which use a variety of crystals. One, which relies on neodymium impurities in a crystal of yttrium aluminium garnet, is of interest because its energy levels are so spaced that it can be pumped by sunlight.

Another large class of lasers uses gases as the lasing medium. Perhaps best known of these is the helium-neon laser which emits coherent neon light. The initial excitation is produced by passing an electric current through a mixture of helium and neon gas. This raises the energies of the helium electrons and as these collide with neon atoms the neon electrons are in turn raised to excited states. The gases are contained in a long tube with mirrors mounted at either end so that an initial spontaneous emission from an excited neon along the axis causes the whole system to lase back to a lower state.

Gas lasers give the most coherent light, but they are generally quite inefficient, requiring about a thousand times as much energy to be fed in as is extracted in the form of laser light. An exception is the carbon dioxide (CO_2) laser which emits up to 15% of its energy input as light. Another interesting gas laser contains a mixture of argon and krypton and is capable of lasing at several different wavelengths at the same time so that its mixed output appears as white laser light.

Applications

Because stimulated emission creates new photons which move in exactly the same direction, the beam of light from a laser is almost perfectly parallel. This means that it can be focused by a lens into an extremely small area. In this area the intensity of the light is so high (even if the unfocused beam is weak) that it can easily vaporize metals and even diamond. This has made the laser a useful tool for all sorts of cutting, drilling and welding operations, especially for small scale work where accuracy is very important. Perhaps the most spectacular application in this field is the use of a laser by surgeons to weld back a detached retina. The laser beam can be precisely aimed at the spot where the retina is detached and the eyeball itself is used to focus the beam.

The unvarying wavelength and frequency of lasers means that for the first time visible light can be manipulated in a similar way to radio waves and much research is now going on to develop a communications system based on laser light. The main advantage of using visible light is that its very high frequencies enable millions more telephone or television channels to be carried on the same beam than on a single radio wave. Also the highly directional beam means that less power is required to communicate between two points as energy is not wasted in other directions. This also means that a laser is useless for general broadcasting, which requires an aerial that will radiate in all directions. And laser light cannot penetrate cloud any better than normal light can usually.

Laser beams in Oxford St., London. A laser — the word stands for Light Amplification by Stimulated Emission of Radiation — is a powerful flash tube device to encourage atoms to emit light in a regular, coherent way and not randomly as they do when left to themselves.

Medical Technology

Doctors have always sought to use physical and engineering principles to help their patients. By their own ingenuity, or with the help of craftsmen or engineers, they have devised mechanisms like splints or 'peg-legs' which would help in times of injury or allow the patient to cope with handicap. The enormous progress made in the last few decades is, however, largely due to the emergence of a new profession, the bio-engineer or medical physicist, working in close conjunction with medical personnel to use the potential of modern technology in the fields of health care. This has led to a whole range of developments, from the most complex achievements to such simple innovations as the plastic disposable syringe—which have had a major impact on practical medicine.

X-rays and nuclear radiations

X-rays, also called Roentgen rays after their discoverer, are a type of penetrating electromagnetic radiation which is created when electrons, accelerated in a vacuum by very high voltages (20,000 to 1,000,000 volts), are suddenly arrested by impact into a target. Their extraordinary usefulness in diagnosis is due to the fact that their absorption varies from tissue to tissue, being least in air-containing structures and greatest in bone. Thus the

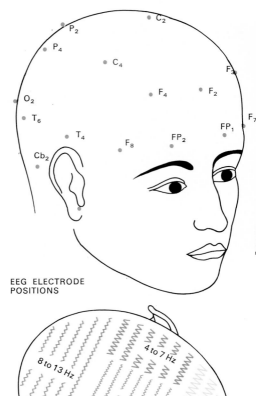

EEG ELECTRODE POSITIONS

EEG WAVES

8 to 13 Hz
4 to 7 Hz
over 13 Hz
LESS THAN 4 Hz
4 to 7 Hz

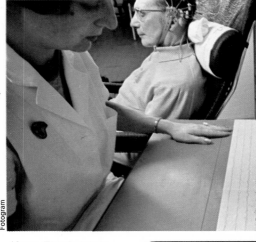

Fotogram

Above: The electrical activity of the brain can be examined by an electroencephalograph (eeg). The minute electrical impulses produced in the brain are picked up by electrodes attached to the scalp, and the eeg produces a chart which shows the waveforms detected from various parts of the brain.

Left: The upper diagram shows points on the scalp at which the electrodes are placed, and the lower shows the typical frequencies of brain waves detected at various areas around the scalp. If a patient's waves differ significantly from those expected, then some form of brain malfunction or damage is indicated.

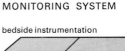

bedside instrumentation
ECG pulse rate blood pressure temperature etc)

PATIENT MONITORING SYSTEM

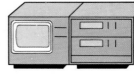

bedside instrumentation

STARPAHC HEALTH SYSTE

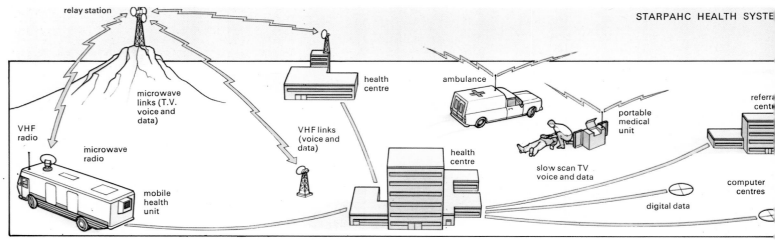

relay station

microwave links (T.V. voice and data)

VHF radio

microwave radio

VHF links (voice and data)

mobile health unit

health centre

health centre

ambulance

slow scan TV voice and data

portable medical unit

digital data

referra cent

computer centres

Lockheed

Above: The STARPAHC (Space Technology Applied to Rural Papago Advanced Health Care) system provides medical services to the Papago Indian reservation in Arizona, US. Mobile medical teams visit villages on the reservation. They are linked by VHF radio to health centres and computer centres which provide them with specialist information and advice. STARPAHC was developed initially by NASA and Lockheed in order to evaluate health care systems for use by astronauts during long missions.

Left: A STARPAHC Mobile Health Unit.

Right: A physician's console at one of the Health Centres.

Lockheed

Right: A patient monitoring system in use in an intensive care unit. Patient monitoring systems contain several types of equipment, such as ecg and eeg machines, a blood gas analyzer and a blood pressure monitor, which provide continuous information about the condition of the patient's body systems.

Below: The layout of a large patient-monitoring system. This type of system, designed for monitoring five or more patients, consists of a set of instruments next to each bed, which are connected to a central station from which the condition of each patient can be supervized.

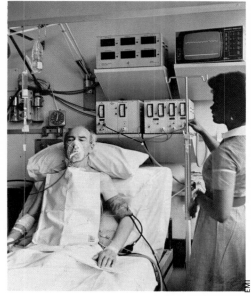

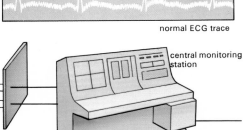

normal ECG trace

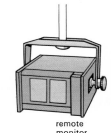

central monitoring station

connecting cables

remote monitor

ECG of heart beating very fast (120 beats per minute)

Below: An EMI-Scanner CT1010, a computer-assisted tomography unit which produces X-ray images of cross-sections of the brain and scull. The X-ray tube and detectors are mounted within the scanning gantry surrounding the patient's head, and the gantry is rotated 3° at a time. The machine produces images of two cross-sections during each scan, which takes 60 seconds. Three scans are needed to image the whole brain, which takes a total of about ten minutes.

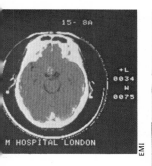

15- 8A

+L
0034
W
0075

M HOSPITAL LONDON

EMI

Above: A scan taken by an EMI-Scanner at the Atkinson Morley's Hospital, London.

Below: The scanning pattern and basic system of an EMI-Scanner CT1010.

─SCANNER CT1010

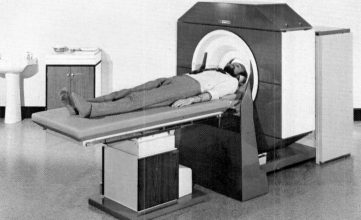

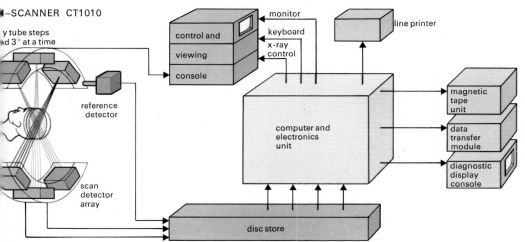

y tube steps
d 3° at a time

reference detector

scan detector array

control and viewing console

monitor
keyboard
x-ray control

line printer

computer and electronics unit

magnetic tape unit

data transfer module

diagnostic display console

disc store

shadowgraph picture, produced by interposing part of the body between the X-ray tube and a photographic film (which is darkened by X-rays), will show fractures in bones, wear in joints or abnormalities in the lungs.

A different application of X-rays, and of the even more penetrating gamma-radiation given off by radium or artificial radioactive isotopes, is in the treatment of cancer. The destructive effect of these rays in high dosage is much greater for some tumours than for the surrounding healthy tissues. Careful adjustment of dose and concentration of the radiation in the tumour area, by the use of different but overlapping approach routes, will arrest the growth of a tumour, or destroy it altogether with minimal effect on surrounding tissue.

The equipment for generating X-rays consists of a high-voltage generator connected to the X-ray tube by heavily insulated cables. In this vacuum tube, the electrons given off by a heated filament are accelerated towards a spot on a target, where some of their energy is converted into X-radiation when they strike it. The tube is heavily shielded by lead cladding to confine the emission of X-rays to the wanted direction. Much of the bulk of modern machines is made up of equipment for adjusting the patient's position so that the beam is correctly directed and by provision for holding the photographic plates or direct-viewing devices.

To produce the most penetrating radiation, the electrons must be accelerated to energy levels greater than those which can be conveniently provided by a transformer power supply. When this type of radiation is required, the electrons are accelerated in particle accelerators such as betatrons or travelling-wave linear electron accelerators, devices in which a relatively low voltage is used over and over again in accelerating the electrons.

Computer-assisted tomography is a special X-ray technique capable of imaging cross-sections of the head or body with good contrast between tissues which cannot be visualized by conventional techniques. The X-ray source and a radiation detector, which measures the intensity of a narrow beam of X-rays as it emerges after passage through the tissues, are moved in a compound pattern so that each part of the section is traversed by the beam in several directions.

Measurements of the absorption experienced by the ray in its various directions of transit are fed into a computer which forms part of the machine. This calculates with great accuracy how much of the beam was absorbed in each minute region. The local brightness of a cathode ray tube display is then modulated so as to map the pattern of absorption in the cross-section. Organs having slightly different X-ray absorptions can be visualized and abnormalities of, say, the blood content of the different tissues noted. This powerful technique has greatly extended the range of conditions in which X-rays can give diagnostic information.

Isotope scanning is another technique used for similar purposes. Diseased tissue will often take up disproportionate amounts of compounds containing radioactive isotopes, which are introduced into the patient's circulation. As these emit X-rays or gamma-rays to the outside, regions where concentration has taken

131

place can be detected by passing Geiger counters or other radiation-sensitive devices over the patient and noting where increased activity is present.

Ultrasonics

Ultrasound or ultrasonics, sound vibrations at frequencies beyond the upper limit of human hearing, is used in medicine in three different ways: as a therapeutic (healing) medium, for soft tissue imaging and for observing the motion of the heart or blood. Quartz or other piezoelectric materials are used to turn a high-frequency electrical oscillation (1-10 MHz) into a mechanical vibration at the same frequency. Devices such as these which convert one form of energy into another, in this case electrical into mechanical, are known as *transducers*. The beam of ultrasonic vibration is then transmitted into the body via a thin film of oil or aqueous (water-based) jelly.

In therapeutic applications, power levels of the order of a watt per square centimetre are used to produce accelerated healing of injuries, but just how this happens is still not fully understood. In the other two applications, the power levels are too low to have any effect on the tissues. The transmitting transducer, or a separate receiving transducer, translates some of the energy which is reflected by the tissues in the path of the beam into electrical waveforms.

For soft tissue visualization, the transmitting transducer is energized periodically and emits brief bursts of waves. Reflections from interfaces at increasing depths will be received with increasing delays from the time of their transmission. A map of the interfaces encountered in a section of the body is produced as follows. A spot on the cathode ray tube is deflected from a starting position, representing the position of the transducer, in the direction of the beam at a speed which corresponds to the speed of the ultrasound in tissue. The spot is brightened up whenever reflections are received. As the clinician moves the transducer so as to sweep the beam through the section, the pattern of brightness on the oscilloscope tube shows the position of organ boundaries and changes in tissue density. A common application of this technique is to follow the development of the foetus in the mother's womb.

If the reflecting interface is moving, the frequency of the reflected ultrasound will differ slightly from that of the transmitted beam. This phenomenon, the *Doppler effect*, permits the detection of moving interfaces within the body and also under favourable circumstances allows the speed of motion to be measured. The beating of the foetal heart can thus be detected by ultrasonic Doppler instruments from the tenth week of pregnancy.

An expanding use of this principle is in the measurement of the speed of blood flow in various vessels, the red blood cells acting as ultrasonic reflectors. Abnormalities of the pulsating pattern of flow in limb arteries points to the presence of obstructions. Cardiac function may also be monitored by Doppler measurements of blood velocity in the aorta, the main artery leading from the heart.

Electrophysiological instruments

Much useful information can be obtained about function in certain parts of the body

132

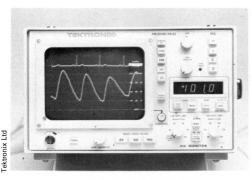

Tektronix Ltd

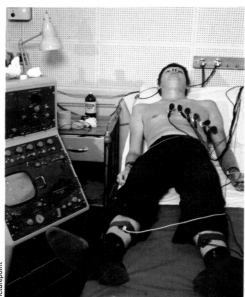

Picturepoint

Above: A patient connected to an electrocardiograph machine. The electrodes on the chest pick up the signals from the heart, and those on the arms and legs provide reference voltages that enable the heart signals to be correctly interpreted. The lead on the right leg is an earth connection.

Below: A diagram of a heart-lung machine, with an exploded view of the oxygenator on the left. The heart-lung machine takes over the functions of the heart and lungs during major heart surgery. The oxygenator removes carbon dioxide gas from the blood and adds oxygen to it before it returns to the patient.

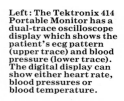

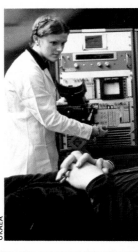

Left: The Tektronix 414 Portable Monitor has a dual-trace oscilloscope display which shows the patient's ecg pattern (upper trace) and blood pressure (lower trace). The digital display can show either heart rate, blood pressures or blood temperature.

Below: An MEL SL75-20 linear accelerator which produces high-intensity radiation for the treatment of cancer tumours. Many forms of tumour tissue are much more susceptible to high doses of radiation than are the healthy tissues surrounding them, and so they can often be destroyed by radiation therapy. This machine operates at an energy level of 20 million electron-volts (20 MeV).

UKAEA

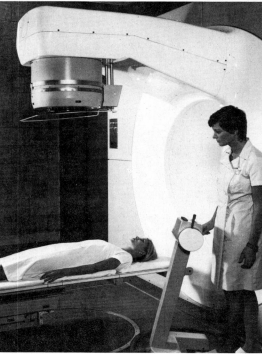

M.E.L. Equipment Ltd

HEART-LUNG MACHINE

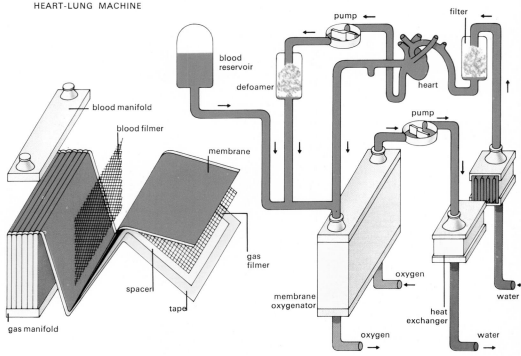

blood reservoir · defoamer · blood manifold · blood filmer · membrane · gas filmer · spacer · tape · gas manifold · membrane oxygenator · oxygen · heat exchanger · oxygen · water · pump · filter · heart · pump · oxygen · water · water

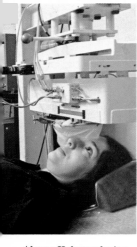

Above: Holography is a three-dimensional photographic technique originally based on interference patterns between two laser beams. This machine uses ultrasonic waves in place of lasers to produce holographic pictures of the eye for diagnostic purposes.

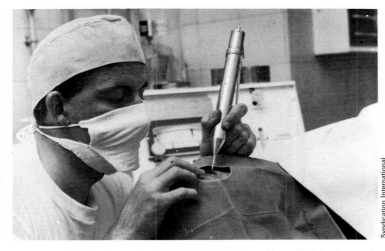

Above: This instrument developed for eye operations has a metal probe which is cooled by liquid helium to —120°C. Used like a scalpel, it can remove cataracts and 'weld' back detached retinas, operations which can also be performed by using heat created by laser beams.

Left: A heart pacemaker powered by a nuclear battery, which is implanted into the patient and maintains regular heart operation by stimulating it electrically.

Below: The Diapulse machine speeds the healing of damaged tissue by means of the energy contained in high frequency electromagnetic pulses.

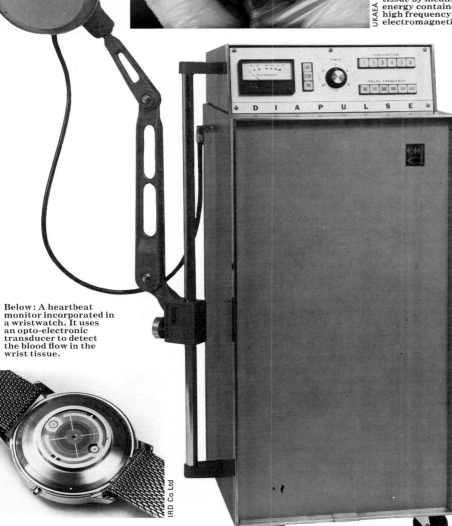

Below: A heartbeat monitor incorporated in a wristwatch. It uses an opto-electronic transducer to detect the blood flow in the wrist tissue.

by observing the minute voltages which accompany muscle contractions and the passage of nerve impulses. *Action voltages* of about 1/20 volt can be picked up in their immediate vicinity, but it is also possible to sense the much smaller voltages which are transmitted to the body surface by using electrodes applied to the skin to determine the activity of underlying nerves and muscles. Specially constructed amplifiers are used to display the observed waveform by deflection of the spot on a cathode-ray tube or of the pen in a paper recorder.

A widely used electrophysiological instrument is the *electrocardiograph* (ECG) which gives information about activity of the heart from voltages picked up on the chest wall or even from the extremities. A comparison of the waveforms recorded from various electrode positions is useful in determining the location and extent of damage which may have occurred in, for example, the muscular wall of the heart. It is also possible to observe whether the muscle mass of the heart contracts in regular sequence, so that defects in the nervous pathways which co-ordinate the atrial and ventricular contractions may be detected.

Another application of electrocardiography is to the detection of rhythm disturbances (*arrythmias*). Occasional irregularities occur in normal health—'when I saw it happen, my heart missed a beat'—but potentially life-threatening ones may develop during a heart attack. Electrocardiographs are therefore widely used in coronary care units for patient-monitoring. Treatment of arrythmias in the early stages often prevents them from progressing to *asystole* (total stoppage of heart action) or a condition known as *ventricular fibrillation* in which the co-ordination of different parts of the ventricular muscle is totally lost and effective pumping stops.

A *defibrillator* can be used to restore co-ordinated contractions in the latter case. As Galvani showed when he applied a battery to a frog's leg—or anyone who has experienced an electric shock will remember—powerful muscular contractions are produced by currents which pass through the body. A defibrillator applies an electric shock of controlled magnitude, from a capacitor which has been charged to a high voltage, to the patient's heart via large electrodes placed on the chest. If the current is sufficient to cause the whole of the cardiac musculature to contract strongly at the same instant, synchronous contractions will often continue, so that co-ordinated heart action is restored.

The instrument which is used to record electrical activity from the brain is called an *electroencephalograph* (ecg). This differs from the electrocardiograph in that a number of recording channels are used simultaneously to display the electrical activity picked up by electrodes applied to various regions of the scalp, and that more sensitive amplifiers are required to amplify the weaker signals which reflect neuronal activity in a broad region underneath the electrodes. The waveform shape and frequency content of the recordings gives information on the nature of brain activity in alert, sleeping or unconscious subjects and allows regions of abnormal activity to be identified.

133

Computers

Throughout history, man has attempted to produce mechanical aids to assist in the organisation and processing of information. The requirements have been for the storage of information, the processing of it in the form of sorting and arithmetic, and rapid retrieval of selected information.

Where the information to be processed is numeric, it can be represented either by a physical quantity, such as length or voltage, or by a combination of digits. In the first of these two methods, the physical feature used is said to be an *analogue* of the number. Possibly the best known example of this is the slide rule, in which a number is represented by a length proportional to its logarithm. This choice of representation enables the multiplication of two numbers to be performed by the addition of two lengths.

The modern analogue computer generally uses variable voltages to represent quantities, and it is particularly suited to performing computations on quantities which vary with time, and require the solution of differential equations.

In *digital* device, numbers are represented by positions on wheels, the fingers of the hands, or by a row of lights which represent the number in binary arithmetic. In the latter case, a light switched on would represent a binary '1' and a light switched off would represent a binary '0'.

Most examples of information processing do not require the particular aptitudes of analogue machines. They do, on the other hand, require an extensive storage capability and an ability to handle literal information, and for these requirements digital representation is appropriate. For this reason, the word 'computer' generally refers to the digital computer.

Personal computers.

Many people are now more familiar with computers than they ever thought they would be. In recent years, costs have fallen so dramatically and technology increased so rapidly that computers are now no longer room-filling monsters requiring numerous skilled staff to operate them. Instead, the *personal* or *home* computer is now a reality. Personal computers are widely used for playing sophisticated electronic games, but they are also capable of being useful round the house — helping with the homework, keeping the family budgets, maintaining names and address records for clubs and so on. And their use is widespread in business, too, for accounting, stock control, data management and word processing (producing letters and reports in electronic form so that they can be easily corrected and amended before being finally printed). It is not only small businesses that use personal computers — many large businesses use fleets of the machines for individual tasks, as well.

Personal computers form the *micro* end of the market. Slightly larger systems are referred to as *mini* computers, and for the largest tasks giant conventional computers — known as *mainframes* are still needed.

For any process to take place, with or without a computer, there must be some

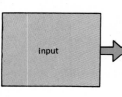

Left: The operator's console of an IBM System/370 computer.

Right: A schematic diagram of a computer system: the arrows indicate the directions in which data flows around the system. Input/output devices, not shown here, perform both input and output functions.

backing stores

working store

input

control unit

arithmetic logic unit

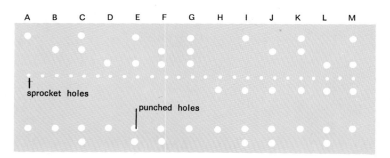

Above: A general view of a computer system. The cpu is behind the operator's station in the centre background, with the magnetic tape units along the left hand side and the magnetic disk units on the far right. To the left of centre are two card machines and a display unit, and opposite these are two line printers. This system is an IBM 370/168.

Right: Some of the patterns of holes used to represent letters in 8-hole punched paper tape. 5, 6 and 7-hole tapes are also used.

A	B	C	D	E	F	G	H	I	J	K	L	M

sprocket holes

punched holes

Below: 96-column punched cards have three rows of holes containing 32 columns each.

Right: The ferrite cores and wiring assembly of a magnetic core store.

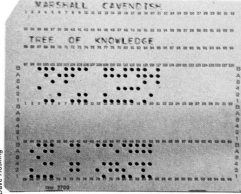

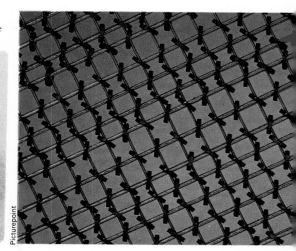

Right: A row of magnetic tape units. The tape itself is similar to that used by domestic tape recorders, but it is 13 mm (0.5 in) wide and normally wound in 732 m (2,400 ft) lengths on to 25.4 cm (10 in) diameter spools. Tape speeds as high as 508 cm/sec (200 in/sec) are used.

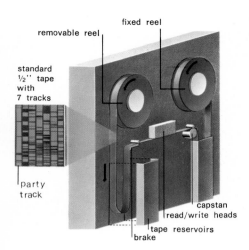

Above: A simplified diagram of a magnetic tape drive. The bits of data are written in rows across the tape, with one bit per track; one of the edge tracks is used for recording the *parity bits* which are part of an in-built error checking system. The capstan and brake shown are those used for forward tape motion.

Right: Digital information can be stored in the form of patterns in a laser-activated holographic plate. Holographic memories are just one of the many forms of storage under investigation by computer manufacturers; others include thin films of magnetizable alloy deposited on to non-magnetic base materials, and patterns of magnetic 'bubbles' in specially developed alloys. Most of the latest equipment, however, uses integrated circuit memory devices for the main storage. Integrated circuit memories operate at about ten times the speed of core storage.

Below: Magnetic disks are usually used in packs, mounted on a central hub with spaces between them to allow the read/write heads to scan the disk surfaces. The method used to move the heads across the disks varies from one manufacturer to another. Typical operating speed is 2,400 rpm.

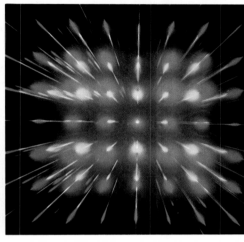

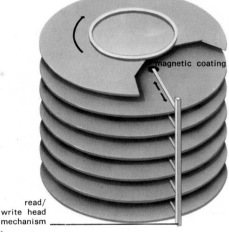

inputs			out put
A	B	C	
0	0	0	0
0	0	1	0
0	1	0	0
0	1	1	0
1	0	0	0
1	0	1	0
1	1	0	0
1	1	1	1

output			inputs	
A	B	C	or	ex or
0	0	0	0	0
0	0	1	1	1
0	1	0	1	1
0	1	1	1	0
1	0	0	1	1
1	0	1	1	0
1	1	0	1	0
1	1	1	1	0

input	output
0	1
1	0

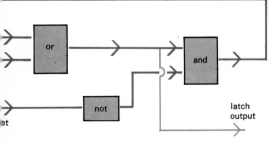

Above: Schematic representations of four types of *logic circuit* used in computers. These circuits are some of the basic elements of a computer, and are built up into complex combinations which enable the computer to perform its calculations. The *truth tables* next to the AND, OR and NOT circuits show what their outputs would be for any possible combination of inputs; for example the AND circuit only gives an output of '1' if A *and* B *and* C are '1'. The latch circuit is the basic element of an integrated circuit memory. Once it has been *set* 'on', it remains on until it is *reset*.

form of *input* to the process, the processing itself, and some result or *output*. The computer — whether micro, mini or mainframe — will always follow this essential pattern.

Input
The commonest form of input these days, whatever the size of computer, is the *vdu* (visual display unit) or *terminal*. Operators type in their information at typewriter-style keyboards and see their commands, and the feedback from the computer, displayed on a television-like screen. Changes and corrections to the information being fed in can be easily made, before the data are assimilated by the computer.

Processing
The input signals, which may represent data or instructions, pass as a pattern of pulses to the heart of the computer, the *central processing unit* (cpu). Here, the patterns are stored in an *immediate access* or *working store* which employs a two-state system — a pattern of 'ons' and 'offs' — to represent the data and instructions.

The main form of working store, or *memory*, is based on solid-state electronic circuits. Hundreds of thousands of these logic circuits form the storage in each computer — a density of electronics made possible only by the use of integrated circuits, popularly known as 'chips'.

Despite the great reductions in price, storage on chips is still very expensive. It is also usually *volatile* — the computer 'loses' its memory when the power is switched off. So cheaper, permanent, backing storage is also needed — see

Output.

In addition to the working store, the cpu has two other main components: the *control unit* and the *arithmetic logic unit* (alu). The control unit takes procedural instructions from the store, and sets up circuits to enable each instruction to be carried out, for example the transfer of data from an input device to the store, or from the store to the alu. A complete set of instructions is called a *program*, and the control unit will action each instruction of a program until an instruction indicates that it is a final one.

The arithmetic logic unit is the part of the cpu where the actual computation takes place. Words from store are passed to the alu so that, for example, they may be added or subtracted, multiplied or divided, compared or modified, according to the program instructions from the control unit. Comparison is one of the most important features of the alu; one simple example is to determine which of two names is alphabetically earlier so that sorting can take place.

Output
The output from the cpu can be obtained in various forms, such as the printed output from a *line printer*, as the display

135

Nixdorf Computers

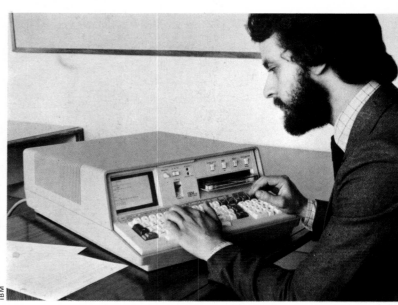

fuser roller

preheat platen

form stacker

form supply

transfer station

toner supply

rotating mirror

modulator

laser

photoconductive surface

charge

cleaner

forms overlay

Right: Programs are the computer's operating instructions. This simplified flow chart shows some of the steps of a payroll calculation program.

Right: The IBM 3800 printer uses a laser to 'write' characters on a photoconductive drum, which picks up toner 'ink' and transfers it to the paper.

Above: Following the development of large computer systems, a wide variety of smaller systems were developed for use either as small-scale individual computers or as satellite units linked to a larger system. The machine shown here is a Nixdorf 8870, which includes a printer and a display.

Below: 'Viewdata' is a public computer system being developed by the British Post Office. Subscribers are linked to a central computer system by telephone line, and the data they request can be displayed via an ordinary tv set, or on a purpose-built terminal such as this one shown here.

Right: The IBM System 360 Model 30 computer, introduced in 1964, weighed about 2,545 kg (5,600 lb). This machine, the IBM 5100 portable computer, was introduced twelve years later; its processing functions are roughly the same as those of the 360/30, but it weighs only about 23 kg (50 lb).

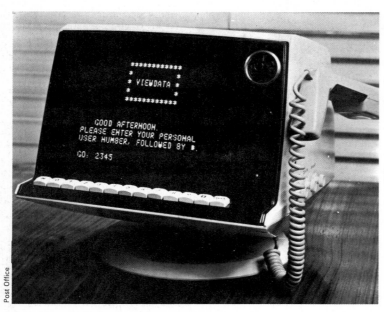

```
*************
*           *
*  VIEWDATA *
*           *
*************

GOOD AFTERNOON.
PLEASE ENTER YOUR PERSONAL
USER NUMBER, FOLLOWED BY #.

GO: 2345
```

Post Office

IBM

Federal Screwworks

Right: Two forms of voice synthesizer. The upper one is the phonetic keyboard of a Votrax system, which is used to enable computer systems to talk to their users. The lower one is a Marconi Marvox unit which can encode speech into digital information, and decode it again to reproduce the original speech.

MARVOX

on a *visual display unit*, or recorded onto a magnetic storage medium such as *magnetic tape* or magnetic disk.

Vdus are (for human beings) a particularly useful output device. They enable an operator to call up the results of calculations, or the analysis of data, or some sub-section of information as often as necessary, but without cluttering the office with printed paper. Totally up to date information can therefore be viewed, as well as stored, electronically.

Both tape and disk units are used on everything from micros to mainframes — but the appearance and working method varies depending on the size of computer.

Micros often use normal audio cassettes (and players) for tape storage. The system is slow, and often recording and playback has to be started and stopped manually.

But it is very inexpensive. Mainframe computers use large, highly-automated reel-to-reel tape systems.

A common form of disk storage on micros is the *floppy* disk, about 5 inches in diameter. Information is written on (and read off) the disk by a magnetic head, like that in a tape recorder, fixed to the end of a moving arm, somewhat like that in a record player. Storage and retrieval is fully automatic, with the user not even knowing where on the surface of the disk the information is held. Mainframe computers use *hard* disks — usually a stack of large-diameter disks on a central hub. The basic operation is the same as for the floppy disk, but speeds are quicker, and the information stored is greater.

Whatever the type of machine, tape storage usually appears very much slower.

Right: The computer of the Skylab 3 orbital laboratory. Computers have been essential to the development of spaceflight, not only by making it possible to perform all the necessary navigational calculations, but also by their ability to supervise functions such as spacecraft life-support systems.

```
┌─────────┐
│  start  │
└────┬────┘
     │
┌────┴────┐
│ read a  │
│  card   │
└────┬────┘
     │
    ╱ ╲         yes   ┌────────┐
   ╱ is ╲──────────────│  stop  │
  ╱ it the ╲           └────────┘
  ╲last card?╱
   ╲        ╱
    ╲  no  ╱
     │
┌────┴─────┐
│calculate │
│rate x    │
│number    │
│of hours  │
└────┬─────┘
     │
┌────┴────┐
│  print  │
│  gross  │
│  pay    │
└─────────┘
```

Burroughs

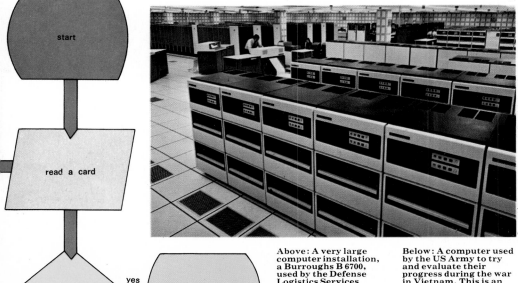

Above: A very large computer installation, a Burroughs B 6700, used by the Defense Logistics Services Center in Battle Creek, Michigan, USA. The system incorporates a disk storage *data base* or file of data which contains 13 billion bytes of information. This picture shows some of the disk units.

Below: A computer used by the US Army to try and evaluate their progress during the war in Vietnam. This is an example of the use of a computer 'model' of a situation such as war; the machine analyzes changes in various aspects of the situation, and predicts their probable consequences.

John Hillelson Agency

Aspect

This is because, to reach any particular piece of information on a tape, the whole length of the tape has to be wound through. This is known as *serial access*. With a disk, the read/write head can move almost instantaneously to any part of the surface where information that is needed is stored: *random access*. Not all applications need random access — making out payslips to a standard list of employees, for example — and in this case tape can appear much faster.

Programs

The program instructions are stored and handled within the machine in the same way as the other data, in the form of words of bit patterns. In the early days of computers, the program writers had to know the bit patterns for every instruction, and also the storage location for every item of data.

It was soon realised that programming could be made easier by getting the machine itself to do some of the work. The programs themselves are now written in *symbolic* programming languages, in which the instructions are written in abbreviated forms such as 'ADD' or 'MLT' (multiply) known as mnemonics. A program held within the computer then translates these mnemonics into the bit patterns or *machine codes*.

Such translator programs are said to 'assemble' other programs and so are known as *assemblers*. Assemblers, however, are only the first level of sophistication in translator programs. Computer languages have been designed which require programs to translate one instruction into several machine instructions, and for which addresses may be designated by letters or words.

These translators, which also detect some programming errors, may be *compilers*, which translate a whole program before it is executed, or *interpreters* which translate and execute each instruction in turn. Languages which are far removed from the fundamental machine codes are said to be *high level*, in contrast to the *low level* machine code and assembly languages.

There are now a large number of high level languages, each designed for certain types of application. Thus FORTRAN (FORmula TRANslation language) is used for scientific and mathematical programs, and COBOL (COmmon Business Oriented Language) is used for business programs in which files of data, such as invoicing details, are to be processed. Personal computers use BASIC (Beginners' All-purpose Symbolic Instruction Code).

The main advantage of a high-level language is that it uses near-English words and phrases in its commands and instructions. This makes it much easier to write the programs in the first place, and later to trace and correct errors in them—*debugging*. For example, one command that is often necessary in programs is the *conditional branch*, which directs the computer to carry out different instructions depending, perhaps, on the results of earlier calculations. This is handled in BASIC by the *IF* command, which is written in the general form IF (the result has one value) THEN GOTO (a certain part of the program and carry out, or *execute*, the instructions listed there). If the result had a different value, then the instructions immediately following the IF command would be executed.

137

Pollution Control

Action to reduce pollution to acceptable limits is now known to be essential if man is to survive. Such action can be taken only by governments, who are notoriously reluctant to take appropriate measures unless forced to by a major catastrophe, and even then only if little economic sacrifice is involved. Pollution may conveniently be discussed in terms of its effect on the rivers and seas, the atmosphere and the land.

Water pollution

When man was a nomadic creature and his numbers were small, water pollution problems were negligible as the rivers into which his waste passed were largely self-cleansing. As communities grew and became more or less static, they tended to settle near large sources of clean water which could accept the polluting load without serious detrimental effect. The River Thames at London, for example, was reasonably clean up to the early nineteenth century as it received only surface water drainage, domestic soil going into cesspits. With the introduction of the water closet, which coincided with a significant increase in population, cesspits overflowed and it was found necessary to connect them to the street drains discharging to the river. Not surprisingly, a rapid deterioration of the river ensued with, as a consequence, several massive cholera epidemics.

The public alarm which followed eventually resulted in a metropolitan sewage system with somewhat rudimentary sewage works at the end of the line. This improved matters for a time, but the growth of population and industry in the London area produced so much pollution in the tidal part of the Thames that as recently as 1950 the river frequently

Above: The ecological balance of many lakes and river systems, such as the Norfolk Broads in eastern England, is being disturbed by increasing nitrate levels in the water. These nitrates enter the water from nearby farmland where nitrate fertilizers are widely used, and lead to *eutrophication*—an overabundance of aquatic plants such as algae.

Right: Examining fish caught in the River Thames.

Below: Some of the fish now found in the tidal section of the River Thames. Over 90 species have now been found there; in 1957, because of pollution, there were virtually none.

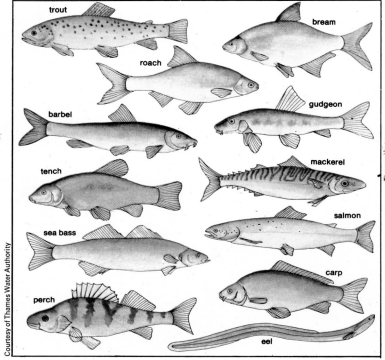

trout
bream
roach
gudgeon
barbel
mackerel
tench
salmon
sea bass
carp
perch
eel

Right: In the notorious smog of December 5-8 1952, anticyclonic weather conditions, combined with temperature inversions, resulted in an almost total lack of air movement, horizontal or vertical, in the London area. This resulted in a dense accumulation of smoke and sulphur dioxide in the air; smoke levels were 16 times higher than normal, sulphur dioxide levels were 12 times higher, and over 4,000 people died.

Courtesy of Thames Water Authority

Picturepoint Ltd

CEGB

Thames Water

Radio Times Hulton Picture Library

POLLUTANT SPECIES	MAJOR SOURCES
sulphur dioxide	electricity generation, oil refineries, iron and steel works
smoke, dust, grit	iron and steel works, power stations, foundries, gas works, cement works
carbon monoxide	combustion of fossil fuels
carbon dioxide	combustion of fossil fuels
oxides of nitrogen	nitric acid works, electricity generation, iron and steel works, fertilizer plant
ammonia	ammonia works
sulphur trioxide	sulphuric acid works, brick works
sulphides and sulphur	generating stations, metal smelting, rubber vulcanizing, coke ovens
chlorine and hydrogen chloride	chlorine works, secondary aluminium works, chromium works
chlorinated hydrocarbons	dry cleaning works, aerosol sprays
mercaptans	oil refineries, coke ovens
zinc oxide	copper works

Above: Coal- or oil-fired power stations have tall, multi-flue chimneys and separation equipment that removes most of the smoke and sulphur dioxide from the flue gases. Any pollutants that are not removed are carried high into the air by the chimneys so that they are dispersed well above the ground (the white plumes issuing from the cooling towers are steam, not smoke). Tall chimneys are used by many industrial plants to disperse the smoke away from ground level, but if the flue gases are not cleaned the pollutants can be carried a long way before returning to the ground; it has been suggested that the 'acid rain' falling in southern Scandinavia is a result of sulphur compounds 'exported' there from British factory chimneys.

Above right: The main sources of common air pollutants.

Right: The Taj Mahal, built by Shah Jahan in the seventeenth century, is beginning to turn brown because of air pollution from factories in the area. Steps are being taken to reduce this pollution and thus protect both the Taj and the health of the local population.

Below: Some major air pollution episodes of the past century.

Spectrum

DATE		PLACE	EXCESS DEATHS
Feb.	1880	London, England	1,000
Dec.	1930	Meuse Valley, Belgium	63
Oct.	1948	Donora, Penn., U.S.	20
Nov.	1950	Poca Rica, Mexico	22
Dec.	1952	London, England	4,000
Nov.	1953	New York, U.S.	250
Jan.	1956	London, England	1,000
Dec.	1957	London, England	700–800
Dec.	1962	London, England	700
Jan./Feb.	1963	New York, U.S.	200–400
Nov.	1966	New York, U.S.	168

stank during the summer months, and fish had long since disappeared. The commissioning of new, larger and much more efficient sewage works has markedly improved the condition of the river, in which over 90 different species of fish have now been identified.

This improvement arose after the passing of various laws, for example the Control of Pollution Act, 1974, which set out to control pollution of water and the atmosphere, noise pollution, and the disposal of solid waste on land. Control of rivers and other sources of water was placed in the care of the newly-formed water authorities, who extended and improved control of the industrial use of water and of industrial discharges. Trade effluent control sections organize the issue to industry of licences which include rigid limits for pollutants in the discharges, and sample and analyze the discharges to ensure conformity with the licence conditions.

These are set at levels which safeguard the receiving sewers and the workers who maintain them, the sewage treatment processes and the quality of the final effluent and the sewage sludge. Industry has for the most part learned to consult trade effluent officers at the planning stage, to ensure the requirements of the water authorities are met, and to contact them immediately for advice when accidental spillages occur.

Several water authorities have installed automatic unmanned control stations which sample rivers at specified intervals, monitoring the samples for such parameters as pH (which indicates the acidity or alkalinity of the water), and the amounts of ammonia, nitrate, and dissolved oxygen present. The results are then transmitted to a central control station.

The World Health Organization and, more recently, the EEC, have drawn up official standards for drinking water to which water supply authorities conform to ensure the purity of their supplies. These standards cover *organoleptic* factors (detectable by the senses) such as colour, turbidity (cloudiness), odour and palatability; *physiochemical* factors which include pH, electrical conductivity, total and individual mineral contents, presence of acid radicals, and the total and ammoniacal nitrogen contents; *biological* factors, such as dissolved oxygen and oxidability; *microbiological* factors including the count of coliform bacteria and other pathogenic organisms; and other undesirable or toxic factors, which include metals, mineral oils, pesticides and similar organochlorine compounds, and selected carcinogens such as polycyclic aromatic hydrocarbons.

Air pollution

The principal pollutants of the atmosphere are smoke and sulphur dioxide (SO_2) from fires and furnaces. As usual it took a massive disaster, the London *smog* (a combination of smoke and fog) of 1952 in which over 4,000 bronchial sufferers died, to produce protective legislation in the form of the Clean Air Acts, of 1956 and 1968. These controlled the amount of smoke which could be emitted from industrial chimneys, and authorized the creation of 'smokeless zones' where only approved smokeless fuels could be burnt in domestic premises.

The importance of data acquisition in 139

the production of control procedures has been emphasized, and large numbers of air pollution monitors have been installed throughout the UK and in many other countries. These monitors measure suspended particulates and sulphur dioxide, (the major pollutants), and also carbon monoxide and oxides of nitrogen and lead, which are emitted from road vehicles. In the presence of strong sunlight, vehicles' exhaust gases can combine by a photochemical reaction to produce unpleasant *lachrymatory* substances (which make the eyes water), characterized by the presence of ozone (O_3) and nitrogen dioxide (NO_2).

This *photochemical smog* first appeared in American cities which have large concentrations of motor vehicles and which also experience the phenomenon of *temperature inversion*, a meteorological condition under which the air temperature increases with height instead of decreasing, and contaminants are concentrated. Similar occurrences in Tokyo in 1970 and, more recently, in Holland, aroused concern in other large cities such as London.

Although the presence of prevailing winds suggest that photochemical smog in London is unlikely, the Greater London Council has commenced systematic monitoring for nitrogen dioxide and ozone. There are no official standards for atmospheric pollutants, but the following guidelines for large urban areas have been suggested. Sulphur dioxide: 60 microgrammes per cubic metre ($\mu g/m^3$); suspended particulates: 40 $\mu g/m^3$; ozone: 160 $\mu g/m^3$; and carbon monoxide: 10 milligrammes per cubic metre (mg/m^3).

Some concern has been expressed over the concentration of lead in the atmosphere. This has been cited as an active contributor to a level of human ingestion which, while below the threshold of potential clinical poisoning, could by its persistence produce subtle but generally adverse effects. Lead has been cited as one factor in the causes of still-birth, diseases such as gout, and of brain disorders (especially in children where high blood levels of lead are associated with behavioural disturbances leading to delinquency).

Its presence in the atmosphere comes from the use of tetraethyl lead as an anti-knock ingredient in petrol, which as a result used to contain up to 600mg of lead per litre. Reductions in lead anti-knock ingredients have been recommended by the EEC and other bodies but, not surprisingly, implementation of the reductions is more dependent on economic considerations than on health requirements. Even so, the maximum permitted lead level in the EEC is now only 400 mg per litre; in the US all new cars have had to run on lead-free petrol since 1975.

Noise pollution

Although noise in the urban environment is not a new problem, it is strange that the systematic investigation of noise pollution is of quite recent origin—the first major noise survey in the world was made in London in 1960. In addition to the technical problems associated with such investigations, which involve extremely sophisticated equipment, the presentation of noise data in an understandable form is complicated. Sound pressure levels can be measured and expressed in decibels (dB). However, a modifying factor must be introduced to take account of the fact

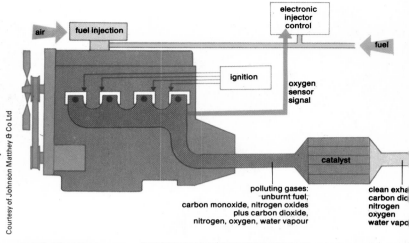

Right: The more dangerous gases contained in the exhaust from vehicle engines can be converted into relatively harmless compounds by means of a suitable catalyst, such as platinum or rhodium, fitted into the exhaust system. In the system represented here, the hydrocarbons (unburnt fuel), carbon monoxide and oxides of nitrogen in the exhaust are converted into carbon dioxide, water vapour and nitrogen gas.

Below: A car exhaust system incorporating a catalytic emission control system. Within the catalytic unit, the catalyst itself (which is usually platinum) is carried on a ceramic or metal alloy support.

Above: In the US the Air Quality Act of 1967 was revised in 1970 by the Clean Air Amendments, which introduced standards governing the level of exhaust emissions permissible from new vehicles. This chart shows how the legislation aims to reduce the emissions (in grams per mile).

	Hydro-carbons	Carbon monoxide	Nitrogen oxide
1957–67 autos, averaged	8.7	87	not know
1970/71 standards	4.1	34	nor
1972/73/74 standards	3.0	28	3.
1975 interim standard			
United States	1.5	15	3
California	0.9	9	2
statutory standard	0.41	3.4	0.

Below: A team from the UK Atomic Energy Authority's Hazardous Materials Service examining a drum of chemicals washed ashore on a Cornish beach. Rapid identification of unknown substances washed ashore in this manner is essential, as they may be extremely poisonous or even explosive.

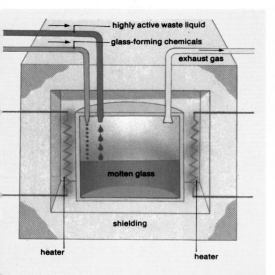

Above: A diagram of a proposed process for turning the highly active, long-lived liquid waste from reprocessed fast breeder reactor fuel into a type of glass so that it can be stored more safely. The vitrified waste would be sealed in stainless steel containers and stored under water.

Above: A section of a cylinder containing simulated vitrified nuclear waste.

Below: Containers of vitrified waste might be stored in special storage 'ponds', or else buried in stable geological formations such as salt domes, or beneath the bed of the ocean.

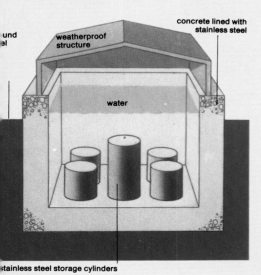

acceptable noise limits for working areas (in dB(A))	
workshops and machinery buildings where communication is necessary	70
workshop offices, plant offices and control rooms, and other areas where easy communication is necessary	60
general offices	50
private offices and small conference rooms	45
offices and conference rooms where a high standard is required	35

estimated community response to noise	
amount in dB(A) by which the corrected measured noise level exceeds the corrected criterion	estimated community response
0	no observed reaction
5	sporadic complaints
10	widespread complaints
15	threats of community action
20	vigorous community action

Left: The generally acceptable noise limits for various types of working areas, and the estimated responses of a community to noise levels exceeding those which normally prevail in its neighbourhood.

Below left: Measuring aircraft noise levels in a street near London's Heathrow Airport.

Below: The noise levels produced by a Concorde airliner on take-off from Heathrow Airport. The Concorde, powered by turbojets, is noisier than the latest subsonic jets because they use turbofan engines.

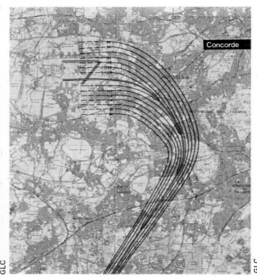

that the response of the human ear to a noise varies according to the frequency of the noise, high frequency noises appearing louder than lower frequencies at the same pressure levels.

To overcome this, it is necessary to 'weight' readings to give emphasis to certain frequencies so as to reproduce the response of an 'average' human ear. Instruments used for measuring sound pressure levels incorporate electronic circuits which automatically compensate for this subjective response. The scale usually used is the 'A' weighted scale, expressed as the dB(A) reading. A further complication is that this scale cannot be treated arithmetically in the same way as can, for instance, measurements of speed.

If the speed of a car increases from 50 kph to 100 kph, its speed has doubled. However, a noise level of 60 dB(A) is doubled by a change to 70 dB(A), an increase of 10 dB(A), not 60 dB(A). The effect of noise sources is not what might intuitively be expected. A single car horn may produce a noise level of 70 dB(A), while the addition of a second, identical horn at the same distance would increase the sound level to only 73 dB(A), a perceptible change but not a doubling of the noise level.

Aircraft noise is a major environmental problem which is being tackled in two ways; reducing the noise at source, and ensuring that no new noise-sensitive developments are permitted at or near a busy airport. The effect of aircraft noise may be reduced by the use of quieter engines, and by the gradual introduction of internationally-agreed improved noise standards for new aircraft. Alternatively, 'minimum noise routes' for flight paths

may be selected, in theory planned to affect the minimum number of people. A third method is the use of noise abatement procedures which plan the rate of climb of an aircraft after take-off so as to cause the minimum of noise to the smallest number of people. Safety considerations for aircraft are very important, and have on many occasions prevented such plans from operating.

Land pollution

Pollution of land is the most difficult form of pollution to measure and control. The land's resources for self-cleansing are fewer and more easily destroyed than are those of the air or water. Land is used for the deposition of domestic and trade wastes and for the construction of special tips to receive poisonous waste. Sludge from sewage works is generally deposited on land either as a suspension in water or in the dry or semi-dried condition.

The sludge contains useful amounts of soil nutrients, such as nitrogen and phosphorus, but it can also contain undesirable amounts of toxic metals, which necessitates not only monitoring of the sludge but also constant control of trade discharges which are the main sources of the sludge metals. Domestic and most ordinary trade wastes can, however, be broken down by contact with soil and their deposition on waste land may make a significant contribution towards its reclamation.

Many countries now carry out general monitoring of levels of hazardous substances on polluted land, and measurement of these substances in plant tissue, in terrestrial animal life, in foodstuffs and in people.

141

Satellites

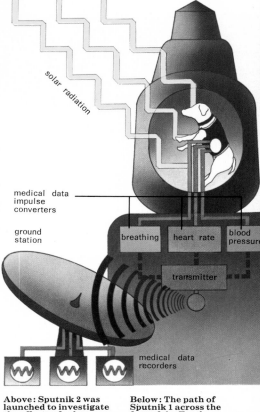

Between 1957 and the end of 1975, approximately 17,500 different payloads were lofted into space from the surface of the Earth. A few made headlines, notably those carrying men to the Moon and back. Others sped quietly off to other worlds, expanding the frontiers of human contact. The majority, all but about 250 of those payloads, were dispatched unobtrusively into Earth *orbit* to serve a considerable variety of purposes.

An orbit is merely a track along which one body travels around another, be it a planet around the Sun, or a moon or artificial satellite around the planet. The primary properties of orbital mechanics were identified as early as the seventeenth century by the German astronomer Johannes Kepler (1571-1630) who formulated them into three laws: 1, the orbit of each planet is an ellipse, with the Sun at one focus; 2, the line joining the planet with the Sun sweeps over equal areas in equal periods of time (so that the planet moves faster when close to the Sun and slower when further away); 3, the square of the time taken for a planet to complete one revolution around the Sun is directly proportioned to the cube of its mean distance from the Sun. In other words, planets farther from the Sun take longer to complete each revolution, and travel at lower speeds.

In his work on gravity, Sir Isaac Newton also formulated a relationship between the orbit speed and its height. These laws are still used as the basis for calculation of the main parameters of a particular orbit.

In concise terms, an orbit is achieved when a satellite body's centripetal (outward) acceleration exactly balances the gravitational (inward) force at a particular height. Up to a certain speed, objects thrown into the sky will fall back to Earth. The harder and more horizontally they are thrown the farther they will travel before falling back. An object thrown horizontally at 7,800 m/sec (25,600 ft/sec) would, in fact, fall back at an angle matching the curvature of the Earth. Without the braking friction of air it would continue 'falling' around the Earth indefinitely. Lifted above the atmosphere it does just that—in orbit. The forces inherent in an 'ideal' or circular orbit compare with those acting on a ball whirled at the end of a piece of string.

Increasing the velocity increases the height of the orbit until, given an initial speed of 11,125 m/sec (36,500 ft/sec) the object will range far enough to take it out of the Earth's sphere of influence and it will break free.

Orbits
As the gravitational force decreases with distance, so the necessary speed decreases. And with increasing height the circumference of the circular track, and therefore the time taken to complete one orbit, also increases. A circular orbit at about 160 km (100 miles) altitude requires a speed of about 7,800 m/sec (26,000 ft/sec) and a revolution time or *period* of about 90 minutes. If the orbit is raised to 386,250 km (240,000 miles) a speed of only about 1,000 m/sec (3,300

Above: One of the first living creatures to orbit the Earth and return alive, the Russian space dog Belka together with its companion Strelka was launched into orbit on 19 August 1960. Another dog, Laika, had made the first spaceflight by a living creature in the Russian satellite Sputnik 2 in 1957.

Below: The first satellite to go into Earth orbit was 'Sputnik 1', launched by the Russians on 4 October 1957 from their launch site at Tyuratam in Kazakhstan. Sputnik 1 carried a radio transmitter which transmitted a series of 'bleeps' so that the satellite could be tracked.

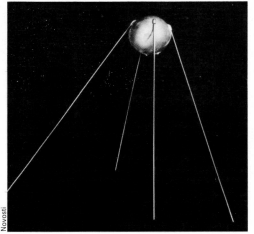

Above: Sputnik 2 was launched to investigate the effects of solar and cosmic radiation and weightlessness on living creatures. Its occupant, the dog Laika, was connected to instruments which monitored its breathing, heartbeat and blood pressure.

Below: The path of Sputnik 1 across the face of the Earth during a 24-hour period. The lines of the path are the result of the rotation of the Earth and the orbital direction of the satellite. Sputnik 1 burned up on 4 January 1958.

ft/sec) will be required, and one orbit will take 28 days. These are, in fact, the parameters of the Moon. At a height of 35,900 km (22,300 miles) the speed is about 3,350 m/sec (11,000 ft/sec), giving a period of 24 hr, the speed of rotation of the Earth at the equator. A satellite at this height, aligned with the equator and travelling in the same direction as the earth's rotation, will parallel the same spot on the Earth's surface, effectively remaining fixed in the sky as seen from Earth. Such an orbit is termed *geostationary* or *synchronous*.

If a satellite has a horizontal attitude at *orbit injection* (engine cut-off point) but is travelling too fast, the injection point will become the *perigee* (or lowest point) of the orbit. Conversely, insufficient speed will make it the *apogee* (highest point). If the attitude is off-horizontal, then the injection point will remain somewhere in between apogee and perigee.

Elliptic orbits, usually termed eccentric orbits, can range from 160 km (100 miles) to tens of thousands of kilometres from the Earth between perigee and apogee. The velocity of the satellite varies according to Kepler's Second Law. Gravity accelerates the craft as it ap-

proaches Earth, then hurls it far out into space again until the speed drops off and, at apogee, it turns back towards the Earth.

The most serious effect on a satellite is, strangely, atmospheric drag. Even at heights of 480 km (300 miles) and more, a perceptible if extremely thin atmosphere can be found. This sparse scattering of air molecules imparts a slow drag on to the spacecraft. Even if the erosion of speed occurs only at the perigee, the momentum of the entire orbit is affected and slowly the apogee is lowered until it too comes under the influence of the peripheral atmosphere. This is known as *orbital decay* and inevitably results in the re-entry and destruction of the satellite. The length of orbital life depends on perigee height and can range from a few months at 130 km (80 miles) to 20 or 30 years at 480 km (300 miles).

Uses of satellites
In the years since Sputnik 1 ushered in the space age in 1957 a huge variety of spacecraft have been dispatched into Earth orbit by several nations. Generally speaking they fall into three main categories—*scientific*, *applications* and *military*.

Spectrum

**Left: A multiple
exposure picture
showing the movement of
a 9.14 m (30 ft)
diameter tracking
antenna at a ground
station.**

**Right: The Russian
satellite tracking ship
Yuri Gagarin. NASA
operate a similar
rocket and satellite
tracking ship, the
SS Vandenberg.**

**Below: The European
Space Agency's GEOS
scientific satellite
undergoing tests at the
BAC Electronic and
Space Systems facility
at Bristol, England.
GEOS carries seven
separate experiments
designed to investigate
the *magnetosphere*, the
area of space
influenced by the
Earth's magnetic field.**

NASA/Alphabet & Image

BAC

**Below: Three types of
orbit. In a *polar
synchronous* orbit the
satellite appears to
follow a figure-of-
eight path over the
Earth and can observe
most of it over a
period of time.
Satellites in
retrograde orbits
travel against the
Earth's spin, those in
direct orbits with it.**

**Right: This picture
shows how
communications
satellites have grown
in size and complexity.
The larger one is
Intelsat IVA (1975),
and the smaller one is
a model of 'Early Bird'
(Intelsat 1, 1965). The
outer surface of each
is covered in solar
cells which produce
its electrical power.**

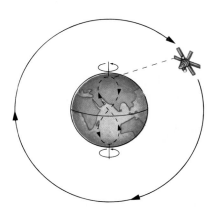

polar-synchronous orbit

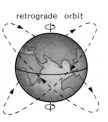

retrograde orbit

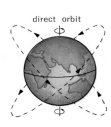

direct orbit

Hughes Aircraft Co

The use of spacecraft has produced a
whole new scientific arena of space
physics. Where the early craft made
revolutionary discoveries, the latest are
developing and refining our knowledge of
these discoveries. Studies of the composition of near-Earth space, and of solar
emissions and their interaction with the
terrestrial environment, involve the use
of numerous low-orbiting and Sun-
orbiting scientific satellites, and satellites with highly eccentric orbits.

Meanwhile, astronomers are reaping
the benefit of looking at the stars free,
for the first time, of the 'dirty window'
of the Earth's atmosphere. Not only are
they provided with optical telescopes in
orbit, but many satellites have been
equipped to examine the sky at radio,
X-ray and gamma-ray wavelengths and,
as the latter two cannot readily penetrate the atmosphere, such satellites
have already contributed as much to
celestial knowledge as all previous ages
together. In this category, too, are technology satellites: spacecraft equipped
purely or partially to test operational and
engineering techniques for application
to other craft.

While scientific satellites look out to
the stars, applications satellites look
inward at the Earth. Applications satellites are considered one of the most
important developments of the century
and concern spacecraft which provide a
direct practical and financial service to
humanity. Improved communications
were the first real benefit to be demonstrated. Networks of satellites chasing
each other around the same orbit or
fixed in geostationary orbit serve as
active repeaters to relay large numbers

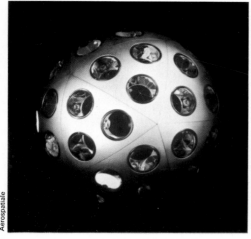

Above: The French 'Starlette', designed for use in *geodetic* (Earth-measuring) experiments, is covered with 60 laser reflectors. By studying the reflections of laser beams transmitted to the satellite from Earth, researchers can make accurate measurements of distances and angles.

Right: A simpler form of geodetic satellite, the Echo II was a 41 m (135 ft) diameter aluminized plastic balloon, carried into orbit by rocket and inflated automatically as it separated from the launch vehicle. It was used for reflecting communications signals as well as for geodetic surveying.

Left: An applications technology satellite in the Space Environment Simulation Laboratory of the Johnson Space Center, Houston, Texas. This part of the laboratory is a huge vacuum chamber in which the performance and structure of space vehicles and satellites can be checked out in space-like conditions.

Below: The European Space Agency's METEOSAT, ready to form part of a system of five geostationary weather satellites spaced around the Earth to provide global weather observations. The other satellites are being provided by the US (2), Japan and the USSR. The satellite's total weight when launched is 697 Kg (1537 lb).

of telephone and television channels around the curvature of the Earth or distribute them economically over wide or remote areas.

The multi-nation Intelsat consortium has been running a global network of geostationary satellites since the mid-1960s. Increasingly, countries are finding such satellites useful for local use, and regional *comsats* (communications satellites) are being operated or planned by developing as well as advanced countries, serving educational as well as entertainment purposes. A new communications application is the maritime or aeronautical satellite which provides vhf radio links for ships and aircraft when far from land.

Weather forecasting has long been a regular satellite activity, using low-orbiting spacecraft which photograph cloud patterns by day and night.

The latest development in applications is the earth resources survey satellite, represented largely by America's Erts or Landsat craft in polar orbit. Continuous infra-red photography of the ground tract has produced unprecedented information on our use and abuse of the Earth. Data on crop disease, pollution, mineral and forestry resources, fish movements and many other subjects can be obtained from these photographs. This programme has been hailed as the most important in the history of spaceflight, and it appears to have enormous potential.

Many military requirements are not applicable to civilian activities, although most provide comparable support roles. America, Russia, Britain and Nato all have their own military comsat networks and the US Defense Department operates its own *metsat* (meteorological satellite) system. In addition, however, it has satellites equipped to detect nuclear tests on Earth or in space, and others to detect missile launches and provide early warning of attack. Satellites are used as navigational aids by submarines, ships and land forces, which calculate their own positions from time and ranging measurements of the satellite's signal.

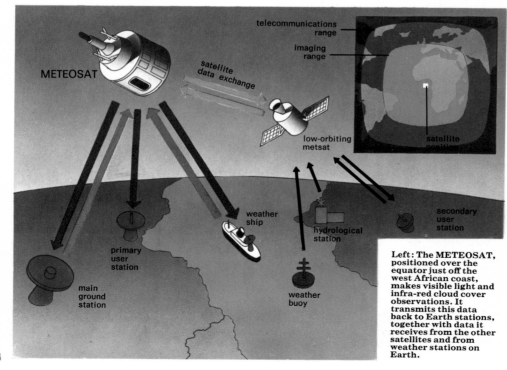

Left: The METEOSAT, positioned over the equator just off the west African coast, makes visible light and infra-red cloud cover observations. It transmits this data back to Earth stations, together with data it receives from the other satellites and from weather stations on Earth.

144

Index